Effective drug regulation

A multicountry study

by

Ms Sauwakon Ratanawijitrasin

Mr Eshetu Wondemagegnehu

World Health Organization
2002

WHO Library Cataloguing-in-Publication Data

Ratanawijitrasin, Sauwakon
    Effective drug regulation: A multicountry study/ by Sauwakon Ratanawijitrasin [and]
    Eshetu Wondemagegnehu.

1.Legislation, Drug 2.Drug and narcotic control 3.Comparative study
I. Wondemagegnehu, Eshetu

ISBN 92 4 156206 4   (NLM Classification: QV 33)

Acronyms

ADEC	Australian Drug Evaluation Committee
ADR	adverse drug reaction
ADRAC	Adverse Drug Reactions Advisory Committee (Australia)
APMA	Australian Pharmaceutical Manufacturers' Association
ASEAN	Association of South-East Asian Nations
CAVEME	Cámera Venezolana del Medicamento [Venezuelan Medicines Chamber]
CENAVIF	Centro Nacional de Vigilancia Farmacológica de Venezuela [Venezuelan National Pharmacovigilance Centre]
DCA	Drug Control Authority (Malaysia)
DCQSS	Drug Control of Quality and Supply Sector (Cyprus)
DDC	Drugs and Cosmetics Directorate (Venezuela)
DIP	Direction de l'Inspection Pharmaceutique [Pharmaceutical Inspection Directorate] (Tunisia)
DIPC	Drug Information and Poisoning Centre (Cyprus)
DPM	Direction de la Pharmacie et du Médicament [Pharmacy and Medicines Directorate] (Tunisia)
DRA	drug regulatory authority
FDA	Food and Drug Administration (United States of America)
GDP	good distribution practice
GMP	good manufacturing practice
GNP	gross national product
HIV	human immunodeficiency virus
ICH	International Conference on Harmonization of Technical Requirements for Registration of Pharmaceuticals for Human Use
INH/ INHRR	Instituto Nacional de Higiene Rafael Rangel [Rafael Rangel National Institute of Health] (Venezuela)
KOAG	Keuringsraad Openlijke Aanprijzzing Geneesmiddlelen [Inspection Board for Public Advertising of Medicines] (Netherlands)
LAREB	Landelijke Registratie Evaluatie Bijwerkingen [National Registration and Evaluation of Adverse Drug Events] (Netherlands)
LAVE	Laboratorios Venezolanos [Venezuelan Laboratories]
LNCM	Laboratoire National de Contrôle des Médicaments [National Medicines Monitoring Laboratory] (Tunisia)
MAB	Medicines Advertisement Board (Malaysia)
MADRAC	Malaysia Adverse Drug Reaction Advisory Committee
MCAZ	Medicines Control Agency of Zimbabwe
MEB	Medicines Evaluation Board (Netherlands)
MOPI	Malaysian Organization of Pharmaceutical Industries
MSDSC	Direccion General Sectorial de Contraloria Sanitaria [Main Sectorial Directorate of Sanitary Comptrollership] (Venezuela)
CECMED	Centro para el control Estatal de la Calidad de los Medicamentos [National Centre for Drug Quality Control (NCDQC)](Cuba)
NDA	National Drug Authority (Uganda)
Nefarma	Netherlands Pharmaceutical Manufacturers Association
NPCB	National Pharmaceutical Control Bureau (Malaysia)
OTC	over-the-counter [medicines]

PhAMA	Pharmaceutical Association of Malaysia
PMAA	Proprietory Medicines Association of Australia
QC	quality control
RBPP	Revisory Board of Pharmaceutical Products (Venezuela)
RIVM	Rijksinstituut voor Volksgezondheid & Milieu [National Institute of Public Health and Environment] (Netherlands)
SAM	State Agency of Medicines (Estonia)
SOP	standard operating procedure
SPC	summary of product characteristics
TGA	Therapeutic Goods Administration (Australia)
TGAL	Therapeutic Goods Administration Laboratory (Australia)
WHO	World Health Organization

Preface

This multi-country study involved only ten countries out of the 191 WHO Member States (5%). In addition, the ten countries included in the study represented different levels of industrial, economic and social development as well as different political (government) systems which made comparison between countries in the development and implementation of drug regulation difficult. Despite these limitations, however, the study has enabled the identification of some of the difficulties that national regulatory authorities, particularly those in the developing world, face in ensuring the safety, quality and efficacy of drugs. It has also provided some examples of strategies that countries in the developed and developing world use to promote effective drug regulation. It is believed that a similar study involving a bigger number of countries representing different levels of development would provide better opportunities to learn more about the strengths and weaknesses of drug regulatory authorities and the different strategies used to improve drug regulation performance. The data collection guide used in this study could therefore also serve as a useful tool for countries and organizations that would like to assess drug regulation performance.

Finally, this synthesis report is based on data collected during 1998-1999 and therefore will not reflect any changes that may have taken place since then.

Contents

Acknowledgements

This report is a synthesis of the results of the multicountry studies carried out by the WHO Essential Drugs and Medicines Policy Unit (EDM) with the cooperation of the following countries: Australia, Cuba, Cyprus, Estonia, Malaysia, Netherlands, Tunisia, Uganda, Venezuela and Zimbabwe. WHO would like to thank the governments of these countries for their cooperation and assistance.

The country studies were conducted by the following national investigators recruited by WHO: Mr George Antoniou (Cyprus), Professor Kamel Boukef (Tunisia), Dr Eibert Rob Heerdink (Netherlands), Dr Susanne Hill (Australia), Dr Charles Maponga (Zimbabwe), Dr Richard Odoi-Adomi (Uganda), Dr Frank Perez Acuna (Venezuela), Dr Julean Perez Pena (Cuba), Professor Dzulkfli Abdul Razak (Malaysia) and Ms Marje Reinans (Sweden).

Dr David Afori-Adjei (Ghana) and Dr Sauwakon Ratanawijitrasin (Thailand) served as advisers, and Mr Eshetu Wondemagegnehu (EDM) coordinated the study.

The guide for collecting data for the multicountry study was developed by Mrs Kari Bremer and Mr Eshetu Wondemagegnehu (EDM) and later refined in a workshop attended by the national investigators, the study advisers, Dr Raffaella Balocco (EDM), Mrs Kari Bremer (EDM) Dr Valerio Reggi (EDM) and Mr Eshetu Wondemagegnehu.

The synthesis paper was prepared by Dr Sauwakon Ratanawijitrasin and Mr Eshetu Wondemagegnehu.

The authors gratefully acknowledge the contribution of the following people, who reviewed and commented on the draft document: Professor Peter Eagles (South Africa), Dr Dennis Ross-Degnon (USA), Dr Kjell Strandberg (Sweden) and Dr Göran Tomson (Sweden).

Thanks also to Dr Jonathan D. Quick (EDM) and Dr Lembit Rägo (EDM) for their invaluable support, Ms Anne Hemsworth (EDM) for the secretarial support and Mr Peter Thorpe, Ms Jacqueline Sawyer and Dr Lalit Dwivedi for editing the paper.

Executive summary

Problems related to the safety and quality of drugs exist in many places around the world today, in developing and developed countries alike. Some incidents have ended in tragedy, often with children as the victims. They are caused by the use of drugs containing toxic substances or impurities, drugs whose claims have not been verified, drugs with unknown and severe adverse reactions, substandard preparations, or outright fake and counterfeit drugs. Effective drug regulation is required to ensure the safety, efficacy and quality of drugs, as well as the accuracy and appropriateness of the drug information available to the public.

This document forms part of the World Health Organization (WHO) project "A multicountry study on effective drug regulation". Its aim was to examine and document the experience of selected countries which have drug regulation in place and identify their strengths and weaknesses and the reasons for them. The 10 countries participating in this study were: Australia, Cuba, Cyprus, Estonia, Malaysia, Netherlands, Tunisia, Uganda, Venezuela and Zimbabwe. Data collection in all the countries was based on a standardized guide developed by WHO and refined by the participating investigators and research advisers.

The objective of this review is to synthesize lessons in drug regulation from the 10 country reports, by comparing and contrasting country experiences. The analyses presented are based on data collected in 1998-1999. The current system of drug regulation in some of the participating countries may be different from that at the time the data were collected. This work does not aim to rank the countries under study against any criteria. Rather, its purpose is to synthesize their experiences and draw generic conclusions from which the participating countries and others may learn. A systematic examination of drug regulation and its environment across countries may shed new light on a country situation, provide a new perspective on the constraints facing it, and provide options for improving the way the system works. The specific aims of this review are to:

- provide simple conceptual frameworks for drug regulation, which policy-makers may use as a basis for designing drug regulatory systems and adapting strategies appropriate to different contexts

- present key features of drug regulatory systems in different countries, compare and contrast them, and highlight and synthesize the generic lessons to be learned

- propose strategies drawn from the experience of countries and from the comparative analyses.

Historical development of drug regulation

The structures of drug regulation that exist today — drug laws, drug regulatory agencies, drug evaluation boards, quality control (QC) laboratories, drug information centres, etc. — have evolved over time. During this process, the scope of legislative and regulatory powers has been gradually expanded, in response both to the ever-increasing complexity of an increasingly sophisticated pharmaceutical sector, and to the perceived needs of society. In some countries, the enactment of comprehensive drug laws was a result of crisis-led change, when public demand led to the adoption of more restrictive legislation to provide stronger safeguards for the public. Drug regulation is therefore a public policy response to the perceived problems or perceived needs of society. Consequently, drug laws need to be updated to keep pace with changes and new challenges in their environment.

Drug laws, norms and standards

Legal structures form the foundation of drug regulation. Some drug laws traditionally omit or exempt certain areas of pharmaceutical activity from their scope of control, thus resulting in a regulatory gap. For instance, some countries do not require registration of herbal and/or homeopathic drugs while, in others, legal mandates are not imposed on the importation of drugs. To protect the public from harmful and dubious drugs and practices, drug laws should be comprehensive enough to cover all areas of pharmaceutical activity in the country.

While drug laws provide the basis for drug regulation, regulatory tools such as standards and guidelines equip drug regulatory authorities with the practical means of implementing those laws. Not all drug regulatory authorities provide documented standard procedures for registration, and even fewer provide documented guidelines and checklists for inspection. The absence of regulatory tools may lead to variations in the implementation of the law, or even lead to questions about the transparency of law enforcement. Standards and guidelines should be established in a written form for all drug regulatory functions. These tools should then be used to guide regulatory practice, as well as being made publicly available to all the parties involved in order to bring transparency to the drug regulatory process.

Structure of drug regulatory authorities

Regulation of drugs encompasses a variety of functions. Key functions include licensing, inspection of manufacturing facilities and distribution channels, product assessment and registration, adverse drug reaction (ADR) monitoring, QC, control of drug promotion and advertising, and control of clinical drug trials. Each of these functions targets a different aspect of pharmaceutical activity. All of these functions must act in concert for effective consumer protection.

In some countries, all functions related to drug regulation come under the jurisdiction of a single agency, which has full authority in the command and control of these functions, as well as bearing the responsibility for their effectiveness. In other countries, drug regulatory functions are assigned to two or more agencies, at either the same or different levels of government. Two phenomena are found in the structural design of drug regulatory authorities which can present problems in regulatory effectiveness — fragmentation and uncoordinated delegation.

When drug laws assign different responsibilities to different regulatory bodies, the exercise of drug regulation is fragmented. Under this type of organizational structure, command and control of drug regulatory functions must be exerted across different government agencies; it is an enormous task to coordinate the multitude of functions to ensure that the overall objectives are achieved. In the absence of effective coordination, there can be no effective drug regulation. In countries with a federal system of government, some drug regulatory activities are delegated to the State. Implementing a public policy through multiple levels of government with autonomous authority requires concerted effort between the agencies at all levels in order to attain the same regulatory objectives for the entire country.

When drug regulatory responsibilities are divided, there is no unity of command over drug regulatory functions. The missing links resulting from fragmentation and delegation can undermine the overall effectiveness of regulation. Drug regulatory structures should be designed in such a way that there is a central coordinating body with overall responsibility and accountability for all aspects of drug regulation for the entire country. An acceptable alternative would be to establish official routes for coordination and information flow to support decision-making in all aspects of drug regulation at the national level, in order to overcome shortcomings in existing organizational structure. In addition, interagency standard operating procedures (SOPs) should be set up. These SOPs should be designed with the ultimate goals of quality, efficacy and safety as the focus, rather than the relative power or existing routines of the agencies involved.

Not all drug regulatory authorities have drug regulation as their sole mission. Drug regulatory agencies in some countries are given non-regulatory functions — such as drug manufacturing, procurement and/or delivery of services. Conflicts of interest in mandates and resource allocation can occur among these multiple functions. Changes in priority among the various functions may be due to political considerations or shortage of resources, and may lead to shifts of personnel and budget resources from one function to another. The consequences of such a change will be to compromise performance in one functional area to the benefit of another. When needed resources are shifted away from drug regulatory functions, overall effectiveness can be undermined.

Resources for drug regulation

The financial sustainability of the drug regulatory authority (DRA) is a critical factor in the continued implementation of the various drug regulatory functions.

Government support in the form of a budget is the method of financing employed in most countries. In only a few countries is the DRA entirely self-financed by fees. The fees charged by drug regulatory authorities financed by a government budget are almost always much lower than the real costs of the regulatory function. In effect, this results in a public subsidy of private interests, by diverting tax revenue to fund functions such as product assessment for registration and assessment of advertisements for the drug industry. Fees should therefore be charged at a level which adequately reflects the real cost of drug regulatory services. However, arrangements should be made so that the financial sustainability of the DRA is not entirely dependent on the fees charged for its services. The government must be fully committed to ensuring the sustainability of drug regulation. Moreover, in order to ensure that fees do not influence regulatory decisions, the salaries of DRA staff and the remuneration of expert committee members who conduct reviews should not be directly linked to specific fees or to the authority's overall earnings.

A shortage of qualified personnel was cited as a major problem facing the drug regulatory authorities. A number of strategies can be considered in order to alleviate the shortage of human resources: better human resource planning; sharing and pooling of international resources on education and training, on information, and on QC; instituting incentives, prioritizing and streamlining work processes, job enlargement and job enrichment.

Implementing drug regulation

Several areas in drug regulation receive relatively little attention in the implementation process. The informal sector, post-marketing surveillance and control of drug information were the most important of these.

Counterfeit products, products of dubious quality and faulty information — especially exaggerated claims of efficacy — are often found to be widespread in the informal sector. Unlicensed manufacturers, importers, wholesalers, retailers and even persons engaged in the pharmaceutical business pose difficult challenges to drug regulation. The DRA should not allow the informal sector to remain a loophole in regulation. Monitoring of pharmaceutical activities should cover the informal as well as the formal sector.

Drug regulatory systems in most countries expend far more time and effort on pre-marketing than on post-marketing activities. No matter how thoroughly pre-marketing assessment is conducted, it is only one of the functions needed if the efficacy and, especially, the safety of drugs are to be assured. Post-marketing surveillance functions, such as ADR monitoring, QC testing and re-evaluation of registered products, should also be priority areas in drug regulation.

Drug information received by both the consumers and the providers of medicines has a significant influence on rational drug use. Drug information is distributed as widely as drug products themselves. Systems of regulating drug information include pre-approval and self-regulation. However, monitoring of the accuracy and appropriateness of information is generally inadequate, and the effectiveness of existing systems of regulation is unknown.

Monitoring and evaluation

The regulatory process should be routinely and systematically monitored in order to identify problems in the process and determine whether the activities actually carried out are consistent with the intended course of action. Several approaches may be employed for assessing the performance of drug regulatory authorities: self-review, supervisory body review and peer review. These approaches can complement one another in appraising the performance of the DRA, as well as assisting it to identify areas for improvement.

Conclusion

This review synthesizes experience with drug regulation in 10 countries in order to draw generic conclusions from the strengths and weaknesses of different systems and identify features affecting the performance of drug regulation.

In drug regulation, the government acts as the guardian of the public by controlling private powers for public purposes. Ensuring the safety, efficacy and quality of drugs available to the public is the main aim of drug regulation. If regulatory goals are to be achieved, appropriate structures must be established and appropriate activities carried out to achieve the desired goals. Comprehensive and up-to-date laws, unified but independent organization, competent human resources, freedom from political and commercial influence, adequate and sustainable financial resources, clear and transparent standards and procedures, outcome-oriented implementation and systematic monitoring and evaluation are critical components contributing to effective drug regulation.

1. Drug regulation: objectives and issues

1.1 Drugs as an instrument of public health

National drug expenditure as a proportion of total health expenditure currently ranges from 7% to 66% worldwide. The proportion is higher in developing countries (24%-66%) than in developed countries (7%-30%). In the former, at the individual and household level, drugs represent a major out-of-pocket health care cost (1).

People and governments willingly spend money on drugs because of the role they can play in saving lives, restoring health, preventing diseases and stopping epidemics. But, in order to do so, drugs must be safe, effective and of good quality, and used appropriately. This means, in turn, that their development, production, importation, exportation and subsequent distribution must be regulated to ensure that they meet prescribed standards.

Since the mid-1930s, many new pharmaceutical products have flourished and trade in the pharmaceutical industry has taken on international dimensions. At the same time, however, the circulation of toxic, substandard and counterfeit drugs on the national and international market has increased. This is mainly due to ineffective regulation of production and trade in pharmaceutical products in both exporting and importing countries. The use of toxic, substandard and counterfeit drugs is not only a waste of money, but may also threaten the health and lives of those who take them. Examples include the sulfanilamide incident that led to the deaths of 107 children in the United States of America in the mid-1930s (2) and the thalidomide disaster of the 1960s which caused birth defects in children (3). More recently, diethylene glycol contamination in drug preparations, such as paracetamol, have led to multiple tragedies in Haiti and India (4,5).

In Niger, fake meningitis vaccines, administered during an epidemic in which more than 26 700 people had contracted the disease, led to the deaths of 2 500 people (6). Substandard and counterfeit products are not only a problem in developing countries, but in developed countries as well (7,8,9,10,11).

Problems relating to drug safety and efficacy are generally due to the use of drugs containing toxic substances or impurities, drugs whose claims have not been verified or which have unknown severe adverse reactions, substandard preparations or counterfeits. All of these problems can be tackled effectively only by establishing an effective drug regulatory system.

1.2 Controlling private behaviour for public purposes

Drug regulation is a public policy that restricts private-sector activities in order to attain social goals set by the State. Drug regulation is the totality of all measures

— legal, administrative and technical — which governments take to ensure the safety, efficacy and quality of drugs, as well as the relevance and accuracy of product information. Public health and safety concerns have obliged governments to intervene in the activities of the pharmaceutical sector.

Although drug regulation is basically a government function, regulatory activities can also be carried out by private organizations, provided that they have been granted authorization by the agency whose own authority is granted by law. Equally, the government may choose to apply the same regulatory requirements to government-owned facilities as to those in the private sector. For instance, the same good manufacturing practice (GMP) standards can be applied to both government and private manufacturers. Self-regulation also occurs, in which members of the group targeted for regulation organize some means of mutual control among themselves.

Guaranteeing the safety, efficacy and quality of drugs available to the public is the main goal of drug regulation, and encompasses a variety of functions. Key functions include licensing of premises, persons and practices; inspection of manufacturing facilities and distribution channels; product assessment and registration (marketing authorization); adverse drug reaction (ADR) monitoring; QC; control of drug promotion and advertising. Each of these functions targets a different aspect of pharmaceutical activities, but all of them must be undertaken simultaneously to ensure effective consumer protection.

Given that drug regulation requires the government to use public resources to impose restrictions on private business, a number of issues related to regulatory actions arise: for example, whether regulation of certain activities is justified; what restrictions should be applied and to what degree; the level of resources used to finance government interventions and their source; how effective regulatory functions are; who is responsible for the impact — both positive and negative — of regulatory actions. These issues have been debated at both philosophical and practical levels (12). This report draws on existing evidence to examine them at a practical level.

Authority and capacity

Regulatory authority is generally founded on laws, which represent policy choices. This authority is assigned to designated organizations, normally part of the bureaucratic apparatus, whose mission is to carry out drug regulation. A host of factors relating to authority and the capacity for exercising such authority affect the operation of drug regulatory activities. These include:

- the scope of regulatory authority, including functions and sanctions

- the structure of regulatory organizations — single or multiple agencies, line of command and control, coordination, communications

- human resources — number, qualifications, remuneration and human resources development

- financing — sources, adequacy and sustainability

- standards, procedures and guidelines used as guidance in performing the authorized functions.

Implementation

As Peters emphasizes: "all laws are meaningless unless they are enforced" (13). Implementation determines the success or failure of regulation. Aspects of the implementation process covered in this report include:

- the type and extent of the actual activities carried out to implement legal provisions, including sanctions for non-compliance
- planning, monitoring and evaluation
- strategies to overcome structural and resource constraints.

Outcomes

The value of all drug regulatory activities depends on whether they produce the intended outcomes. Outcomes can be measured in terms of:

- quality of pharmaceutical products marketed
- proportion of licensed pharmaceutical facilities
- proportion of pharmaceutical facilities meeting certain required standards, e.g. GMP
- number of illegal products
- number of illegal facilities.

Efficiency, transparency and accountability

In addition to effectiveness, policy-makers must also address regulatory efficiency, transparency and accountability when evaluating regulatory policies. Questions are often raised, especially by the pharmaceutical industry and consumers, regarding:

- cost-effectiveness of drug regulation
- the costs for pharmaceutical businesses and consumers of regulatory delay
- political influence over regulatory decisions
- commercial influence over regulatory decisions
- "**regulatory capture**" — whether and to what extent agencies are "captured" by the very interests they are supposed to regulate (14)
- the degree to which regulatory procedures and decision criteria are made public ("**transparency**")
- communication between the regulatory authority, its clients and the consumers
- accountability for the results of regulatory actions.

1.3 Objectives and organization of this report

The aim of this report is to compare, contrast and synthesize country experience in drug regulation on the basis of data collected in 1998-1999 in the 10 countries which participated in the WHO multicountry study on effective drug regulation.

While data collected about drug regulation at a fixed point in time are static, drug regulation itself is highly dynamic. Drug regulatory functions are performed in response to a changing environment. This means that the current drug regulation systems in some participating countries may now differ from the system in operation at the time of data collection.

This work does not aim to rank the countries under study against any criteria. Rather, its purpose is to synthesize their experiences and draw generic conclusions from which other countries may learn.

This work does not intend to prescribe ready-made strategies for drug regulation. Instead, it has broader aims, namely to:

- provide simple conceptual frameworks to enhance understanding of the fundamentals of drug regulation, which policy-makers may use in designing drug regulatory systems

- present key features of drug regulatory systems in different countries

- propose drug regulation strategies on the basis of country experiences and the comparative analyses.

Chapter 2 describes the background of the WHO multicountry study, methods of data collection and comparative analysis. Chapter 3 provides a brief profile of each of the countries under study, and compares a number of background features relevant to drug regulation. Conceptual frameworks to be used in the analysis and synthesis of overall drug regulation in subsequent chapters are presented in Chapter 4. In Chapter 5, the authority, capacity and organization of drug regulatory agencies are discussed. Chapters 6-10 address the main drug regulatory functions. Each of these chapters contains parallel sections covering power, process, personnel, financing, regulatory functions and planning and performance. Chapter 11 sets out concepts, methods and indicators for assessing regulatory performance and discusses the performance of the 10 countries in relation to various aspects of regulation. In Chapter 12, key lessons are presented and strategies for improving drug regulation are proposed.

2. Multicountry study on effective drug regulation

2.1 Project rationale and development

Society's control of the use of medicines, and of those who dispense and prescribe them, dates back several thousand years. Equally, norms, standards, practical guides and guidelines to promote effective regulation have now existed nationally and globally for several hundred years. Both developed and developing countries have practised drug regulation for some time.

WHO and other international agencies, nongovernmental organizations and donor agencies provide support for countries to supplement national efforts. However, despite the efforts made, less than 20% of WHO Member States are thought to have a well developed drug regulation system. Those which do are industrialized countries. Of the remaining Member States, about 50% implement drug regulation at varying levels of development and operational capacity. The remaining 30% either have no DRA in place, or have only a very limited capacity which barely functions at all (15).

Generally, in most developing countries, drug regulation is very weak, and the safety, efficacy and quality of imported or locally manufactured drugs cannot, therefore, be assured. Studies carried out in some countries show that about 20% of tested drug products fail to meet quality standards. Reports have also shown that the prevalence of substandard and counterfeit drugs is higher in countries where drug regulation is ineffective.

WHO has never undertaken a systematic assessment to identify the reasons for ineffective drug regulation and determine why so few Member States have succeeded in establishing effective drug regulation. The aim of this multicountry study is to assess drug regulation performances in selected countries using a standardized study guide, and to document the results so that other countries may learn from them.

2.2 Study objectives

- to map the legal and organizational structures of drug regulation in selected countries

- to determine whether a regulatory function exists, how it is carried out and what financial and human resources are available for its implementation

- to identify the strengths and weaknesses of drug regulation

- to propose strategies that can help policy-makers and implementers to improve drug regulation.

2.3 Method of study

2.3.1 Framework for data collection

The framework for data collection, as depicted in Figure 2.1, lays down the focus and scope of this study. The regulation of human pharmaceuticals, as addressed in this study, has four dimensions: administrative elements, regulatory functions, technical elements and level of regulation. As well as capturing the various dimensions of drug regulation, this framework allows for comparison of drug regulation between countries.

Administrative components are input factors that allow for the functioning of drug regulation, including policy, legislation and regulations, organizational structures, human and financial resources and mechanisms for planning, monitoring and evaluation.

Regulatory functions include licensing of persons, premises and practices, inspection of pharmaceutical establishments, product assessment and registration, QC, control of drug promotion and advertising and monitoring of ADR.

Technical elements concern the existence and the type of standards, norms, guidelines, specifications and procedures.

The **level** of **regulation** indicates the level at which the various regulatory functions are undertaken. The political structures of a country determine the overall **governance** of drug regulation.

Figure 2.1   Study framework showing key components of drug regulation

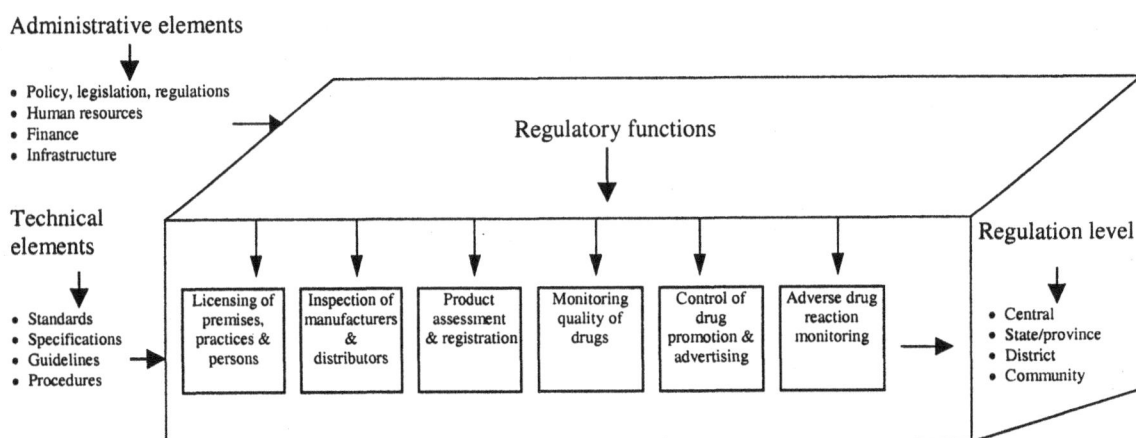

2.3.2 Country selection

Ten countries from the six WHO regions were selected to participate in this study:

- African Region: Uganda and Zimbabwe;
- Region of the Americas: Cuba and Venezuela;
- Eastern Mediterranean Region: Cyprus and Tunisia;
- European Region: Estonia and the Netherlands;
- South-East Asia Region: Malaysia;
- Western Pacific Region: Australia.

The criteria for the selection of countries included:

- existence of a national DRA;
- type of government — federal or unitary;
- developed country/middle-income or low-income developing country/newly independent country;
- willingness of the government to participate in the study.

2.3.3 Data collection methods

Data collection was carried out using a standardized study guide developed by WHO (see Annex 1). This study guide consists of lists of questions developed from the framework in Figure 2.1. The questions are arranged in three sections: Section 1— country background information; Section 2— overview of drug regulation; and Section 3— the various drug regulatory functions shown in the framework. In each of the sections on regulatory functions, there are subsections with questions on legislation/regulations, organization, human resources, financing, activities and monitoring and evaluation. Indicators to measure implementation are found at the end of each section.

The guide was tested before being applied in the 10-country study.

In each country, the study was carried out by independent national investigators recruited from universities and other institutions. Study advisers were also recruited.

Two general methods were used to collect data: archival study and interview of key informants.

Archival study: This involved a review of relevant documents and records, including: drug laws and executive orders; inspection checklists; DRA annual reports; economic, health and other indicators; and reports of other studies available (e.g. opinion surveys, drug use studies).

Key informant interviews: The investigators in each of the participating countries first identified organizations involved in drug regulation, then interviewed key informants in those organizations, using the specific questions listed in the study guide. These organizations included, but were not limited to, drug regulatory agencies, trade groups (e.g. manufacturers' associations, importers, pharmacies), professional societies and associations and consumer groups. Each national investigator then prepared a country report and submitted it to WHO, together with the completed data collection guide. The country reports and study guides served as the basis for this synthesis report.

2.3.4 Methods of data analysis and synthesis

Drug regulation systems in the 10 selected countries were examined using the following methods.

- Data for each question in the study guide, representing a single simple construct, were tabulated by country, and then analysed to identify their similarities and differences. For quantitative data, the range of values was analysed, where meaningful.

- Quantitative data for two or more questions were computed into a ratio to permit further comparison.

- Relationships between certain constructs were identified to find possible explanations for system performance. Quantitative data for some constructs were plotted and correlations computed.

- Each relevant construct, representing an aspect of drug regulation structure, process or outcome, was analysed to show how and why a certain area of drug regulation does — or does not — work.

A number of conceptual frameworks were set up for comparative analysis and synthesis of country data. These included: spheres of regulation, historical development and structure–process–outcome of regulation.

2.4 Drug regulation from a comparative perspective

A comparative approach was used in this study, on the grounds that countries can benefit from learning from one another. A systematic examination of drug regulation and its environment across countries can help shed new light on a country situation, provide a new perspective on the constraints facing it, and suggest options for improvement. There are three basic reasons for conducting systematic comparisons between countries (16).

1. Strategy development: comparing different ways of managing similar problems can suggest both positive and negative lessons, i.e. guidance on what to do and what not to do. Comparing cross-country experiences is a useful way of developing policy instruments for problem-solving in a particular country.

2. Understanding: comparing public policies can help improve understanding of how government institutions operate within their environment, and suggest possibilities for improvement.

3. Interdependence: the interdependence of nations— as reflected in international agreements, regional politicoeconomic groupings, bilateral treaties and collaboration — is constantly increasing. Accordingly, problems that occur in one country can spill over into other countries more easily and rapidly today than at any other time in history. Similarly, policies adopted in one country often have important implications for others. In other words, knowledge about what has occurred in other countries can help a country prepare for new challenges of its own.

However, any comparative study has methodological limitations. The main limitations of this type of study are as follows.

- **Comparability of measurements:** Finding truly comparable measurements can be difficult if, for instance, the terminology used in one country does not have an exact equivalent in another country.

- **Identifying individual attributes:** Certain system attributes— such as the level of development and the influence of public-interest groups— often occur in combination. Disentangling the different factors for the purposes of a study can be problematic. Moreover, each comparative study often involves only a small number of countries. Typically, there are too few cases to permit clear separation of one attribute from another. Consequently, there are not enough national cases available to allow researchers to keep other factors constant while varying only the single factor being tested. Observation under *ceteris* *paribus* ("all other things being equal") conditions is impractical or completely impossible.

- **System uniqueness:** Every system feature is part of a particular, unique combination of contextual factors. However, since every context is different, comparisons cannot easily be made.

- **Causal relationship:** Because of the impossibility of isolating factors within a system and its context, it is difficult to draw a rigorous causal relationship between one factor and another. It is therefore not possible to conclude that a particular factor will always lead to the same result in a different country.

- **Dynamic nature of system:** Systems change over time. However, the comparison is made at a particular point in time. Conclusions about states of development drawn from a comparative analysis of a certain set of countries should not be considered definitive. The value of comparative study lies in the derivation of generic conclusions from the analysis to facilitate learning for system improvement, rather than in any rigid ranking.

3. Profile of the countries

The 10 countries which participated in this study are very different. This chapter presents a snapshot of the participating countries.

3.1 General background

Information on the general background of the 10 countries is presented in Table 3.1. As shown in the table, the geographical size ranges from 7.7 million square kilometres for Australia, to 9 251 square kilometres for Cyprus. In terms of population, Venezuela, with a population of 22.8 million, is the largest in the group, and Cyprus the smallest, with only 0.66 million people. The percentage of urban dwellers ranges from 85% and 86% for Australia and Venezuela, respectively, to only 11% for Uganda. Life expectancy also varies significantly—it is highest in Australia (81 years for females, 75 years for males), and lowest in Uganda (50 years for females, 45.7 years for males).

Malaysia and Australia have a federal system of government. The other countries have a unitary or centralized system of government.

	Area of country in square km	Total pop. in million (year)	Urban pop. As % of total (year)	Life expectancy male (years)	Life expectancy female (years)
Malaysia	329,760	21.7 (1997)	54.10% (1994)	69.5 (1997)	74.3 (1997)
Australia	7,700,000	18.71 (1998)	85%	75.2 (1996)	81 (1996)
Netherlands	41,526	15.65 (1998)	Not available	75.14(1998)	81.03 (1998)
Estonia	45,227	1.45 (1998)	73% (1993)	64.68 (1997)	75.97 (1997)
Cyprus	9,251	0.66 (1997)	68.9% (1996)	75.30 (1996)	79.80 (1996)
Uganda	241,039	20.44 (1997)	11.3% (1991)	45.7 (1995)	50.5 (1995)
Zimbabwe	390,757	11.5 (1998-99)	30% (1996)	58 (1996)	62 (1996)
Tunisia	154,530	9.25 (1997)	61% (1994)	69.9 (1997)	73.9 (1997)
Cuba	110,922	11.12 (1998)	75.1% (1997)	72.9 (1997)	76.6 (1997)
Venezuela	916,445	22.77 (1997)	86.1% (1997)	69.9 (1997)	75.4 (1997)

Values for gross national product (GNP) per capita are shown in Figure 3.1. The GNP is highest in the Netherlands, Australia and Cyprus (US$22 000, US$16 544 and US$13 790, respectively). Estonia and Malaysia rank in the middle with per capita values slightly above US$3 500. Venezuela, Uganda and Zimbabwe have the lowest GNP values of the group, ranging from US$220 for Uganda to US$3 020 for Venezuela.

Figure 3.1   Values of per capita GNP*

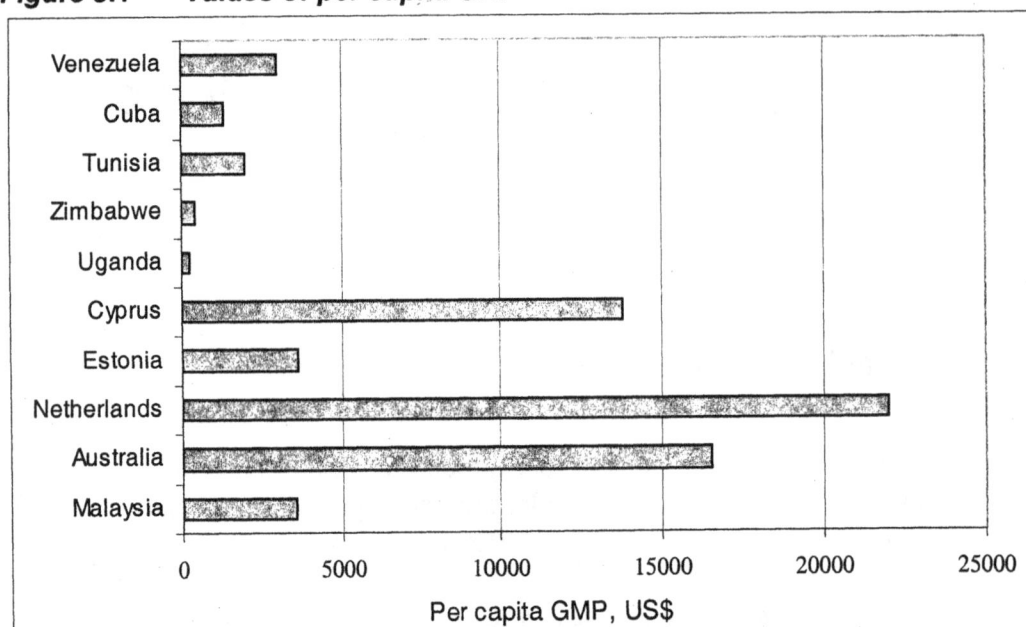

* *Venezuela (1995), Cyprus and Cuba (1996), the rest (1997), the Netherlands (1998)*

Figure 3.2 shows infant mortality rates in the 10 countries. Countries with a low GNP per capita tend to have a high rate of infant mortality, and vice versa, with the exception of Cuba. Life expectancy figures (Table 3.1) show a pattern similar to those for infant mortality, although the ranking among the countries in the middle group, such as Venezuela and Malaysia, may change. The patterns reflected in these three figures—infant mortality rate, life expectancy and GNP per capita—provide a crude measure of how wealth affects health.

Figure 3.2   Infant mortality rates (IMR) per 1 000 live births*

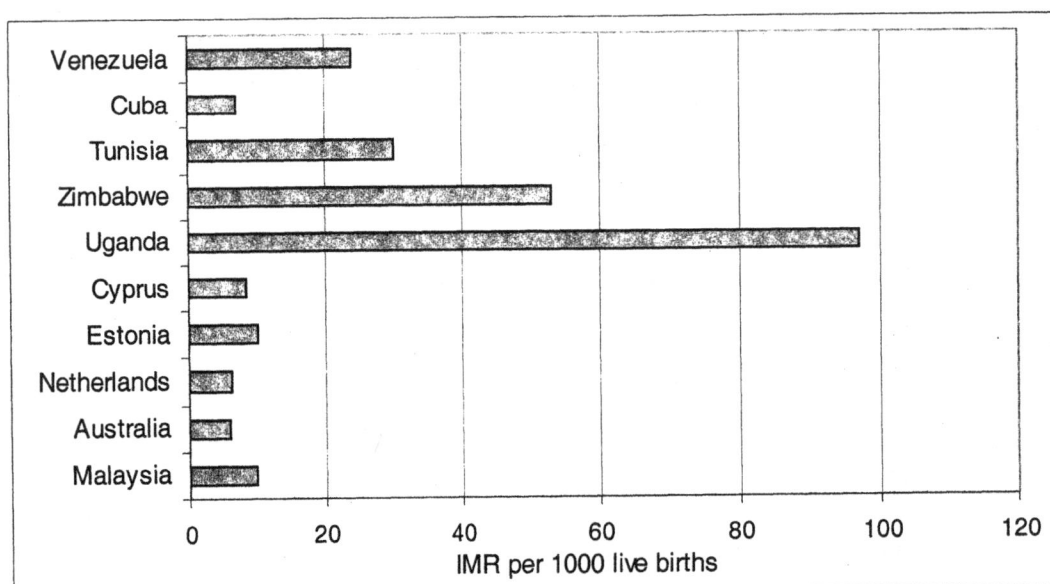

* *Zimbabwe (1994), Uganda (1995), Cyprus, the Netherlands, Venezuela (1996), Australia, Estonia, Malaysia, Tunisia (1997), Cuba (1998)*

It is difficult to determine the implications for drug regulation of these background factors. Nevertheless, it is evident that population size and GNP per capita will influence drug regulatory functions. For example, arranging the inspection of distribution channels in a country where drug outlets are widely distributed across a vast area, may be much more complicated than in a smaller country where drug outlets are concentrated in the main urban areas. Similarly, the wealth of a country is likely to affect the revenue of the government, which in turn will determine the overall budget of the DRA (in those countries where financing for drug regulation is derived solely from the government budget). Similarly, decentralization of regulatory powers or responsibility in a country without effective coordination and communication mechanisms may influence drug regulatory performance.

3.2 Political environment

Key actors within the pharmaceutical sector—government and private and public interest groups—are usually the main influences on drug regulation. The political, social and economic structures of the country generally determine the level of influence of these players.

Among the countries that participated in this study, Cuba is the only country with a single-party socialist system of government. In Cuba, almost all pharmaceutical operations are owned and managed by the Government. The 54 drug manufacturers in the country, which form the national pharmaceutical industry, are part of the National Health System, to which pharmacies also belong. The largest importer, which is the sole importer of pharmaceuticals for the National Health System, belongs to the Ministry of Health. The Government therefore largely determines how drugs are regulated in Cuba.

Although Tunisia has a multiparty system, the Government likewise plays a major role in pharmaceutical activities. Drug importation is centralized, for example. The Government-owned Central Pharmacy imports about 60% of drugs used in the country; the majority of hospitals in the country are also Government-owned. Unlike Cuba, however, most retail pharmacies are private. Professional associations are one of the key interest groups in the pharmaceutical sector. Members of these professional associations can become involved in drug regulation by joining the various advisory committees.

The forces influencing drug regulatory policy in Estonia are changing rapidly as the country's system of government and social structures shift from highly centralized to decentralized. Professional associations continue to exist, but with major changes. Several pharmaceutical trade groups, especially organized pharmacies, have emerged and are engaged in activities related to their own economic interests. At present, the State Agency of Medicines (SAM) still has exclusive power to regulate drugs. Although these trade groups are still in their infancy, do not undertake self-regulation and are not in dialogue with the DRA, they are likely to grow and exert more influence in the future.

In Cyprus and Malaysia, many types of interest groups are found in the pharmaceutical sector. Nonetheless, the DRA appears to be much more dominant, compared with other groups involved in the sector. The Cypriot Pharmaceutical Services Division enjoys significant authority vis-à-vis the industry and pharmacies. Consumer and industrial groups are not well organized. In the past, consumer groups have occasionally made themselves heard and attempted to put pressure on the DRA to accord priority status to certain drugs.

In Malaysia, there are a number of trade and consumer groups, as well as professional associations. Consumer organizations at both federal and State levels keep a check on the regulatory authority's decisions, and raise questions about access to and affordability of drugs. Professional associations focus primarily on price and clinical freedom. It is the Ministry of Health and the Pharmaceutical Services Division which initiate any major changes in drug regulation and other drug policies. The government has also created a forum for discussion and debate on issues related to the pharmaceutical sector.

Many trade and professional groups exist in Uganda, Venezuela and Zimbabwe. Consumer groups have also formed in these countries. However, their influence in relation to drug regulation functions is unclear.

In the Netherlands, associations of the pharmaceutical industry play a role in self-regulation, particularly in relation to drug promotion and advertising. Consumer organizations have a formal presence on the Social Health Insurance Council.

Trade, consumer and professional groups in Australia influence the Therapeutic Goods Administration (TGA) through both official and unofficial channels. Consumer and industry representatives are appointed to the various advisory committees. For instance, the pharmaceutical industry is represented on the Therapeutic Goods Consultative Committee, through which the industry is given an opportunity to provide input into the Therapeutic Goods Administration's strategic planning and budget process. Furthermore, the pharmaceutical industry is engaged with the TGA in co-regulation of drug promotion and advertising. This co-regulation has the primary role in ensuring that advertisements comply with the requirements of the Therapeutic Goods Act 1989 and the industry's code of conduct.

The consumer movement, particularly the Consumers' Health Forum, also has considerable political influence. As a result of political pressure exerted by HIV/AIDS pressure groups and industry, the DRA was reviewed, new legislation introduced and new committees established to ensure that the regulatory authority responded more efficiently to public and political needs. Professional associations, especially the Pharmacy Guild of Australia, have traditionally played an active role in decisions related to pharmaceutical regulation. The Australian Pharmaceutical Advisory Council was established by the Australian Government to advise the Commonwealth Minister for Health on pharmaceutical policy.

In terms of the influence exerted by the public and the private sectors on drug regulation, these 10 countries can be placed along a continuum, as depicted in Figure 3.3 below. Cuba, where the Government has exclusive power over regulatory decisions, is at one extreme, and Australia, where consumers and the pharmaceutical industry have official representation and make recommendations to the TGA, at the other.

To sum up, key players in the pharmaceutical sector in these countries include the government as well as professional, trade and consumer groups. The degree of influence of these groups varies in each country. In a country with a single-party system, such as Cuba, the government controls all regulatory activities. The governments of the other countries also play a dominant role in drug regulation, but public and private interest groups exert varying degrees of influence on drug regulation. Members of professional organizations are usually included on the regulatory authority's advisory committees. Consumer, pharmaceutical industry and pharmacy groups in some countries, e.g. Uganda and Zimbabwe, can influence drug regulation only unofficially, while those in other countries, e.g. Australia, are represented on official bodies related to drug regulation.

Figure 3.3   Relative dominance continuum of the public and private sectors in drug regulation

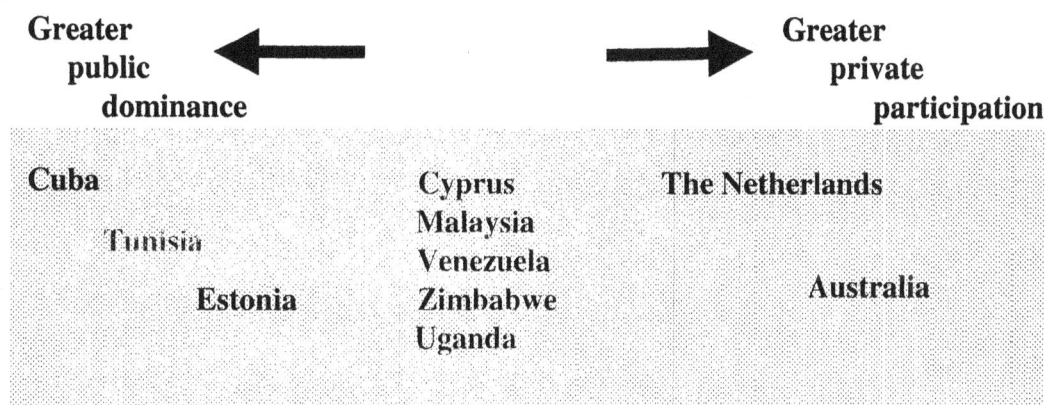

Greater public dominance ← → Greater private participation

Cuba   Cyprus   The Netherlands
   Tunisia   Malaysia
               Venezuela
      Estonia Zimbabwe   Australia
               Uganda

3.3 Pharmaceutical sector environment

The variety and size of pharmaceutical activities in a country determine the type and burden of responsibility which the DRA must bear. Figures 3.4a and 3.4b indicate the size of the pharmaceutical sector in the 10 countries, while Figure 3.5 shows the number of registered products in each country.

From Figure 3.4a it is clear that Australia has a large number of manufacturers to regulate, as do Malaysia and the Netherlands. This means that these countries will require a larger number of GMP inspectors compared with Cyprus, Estonia and Uganda, countries with a relatively smaller domestic manufacturing industry.

Figure 3.4b, on the other hand, shows that the total number of drug suppliers (importers and wholesalers) and retail outlets to be regulated are higher in Malaysia and Venezuela, followed by Australia, than in countries such as Cyprus, Estonia, Uganda and Zimbabwe.

This means that Australia, Malaysia and Venezuela have to invest significant human and financial resources in inspections of the supply channels in their respective countries in order to ensure compliance with the requirements of good distribution practice (GDP) and the provisions of the pharmaceutical laws. Arranging human resources and schedules for inspection is even more arduous when the distribution outlets are widely dispersed through the rural areas.

*Figure 3.4a   Number of pharmaceutical manufacturers**

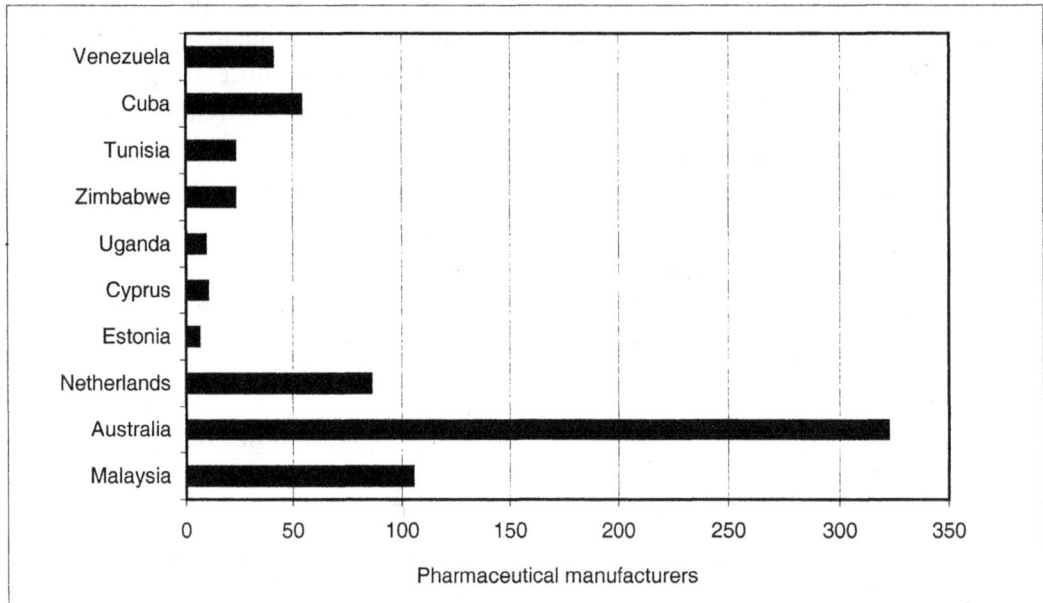

* *Cuba, Cyprus and Tunisia (1997), the rest (1998). Data for Australia include producers of prescription and+OTC products (including complementary medicines and medical devices).*

*Figure 3.4b   Number of pharmaceutical suppliers and retail pharmacies**

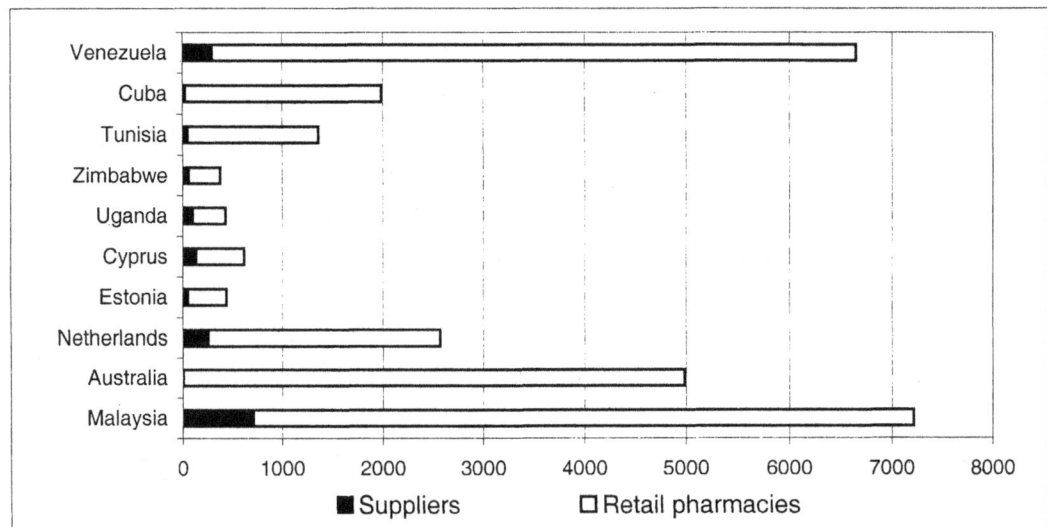

* *Cyprus and the Netherlands (1997), the rest (1998).*

The number of registered drugs, as shown in Figure 3.5, is higher in Australia and Malaysia than in Cuba, Estonia, Uganda and Zimbabwe. The larger the number of drugs on the market, the greater the burden of conducting systematic evaluation and re-evaluation of the safety and efficacy of drugs, carrying out post-marketing quality surveillance and monitoring ADR in drugs available on the market.

Figure 3.5   Number of registered pharmaceutical products for human use*

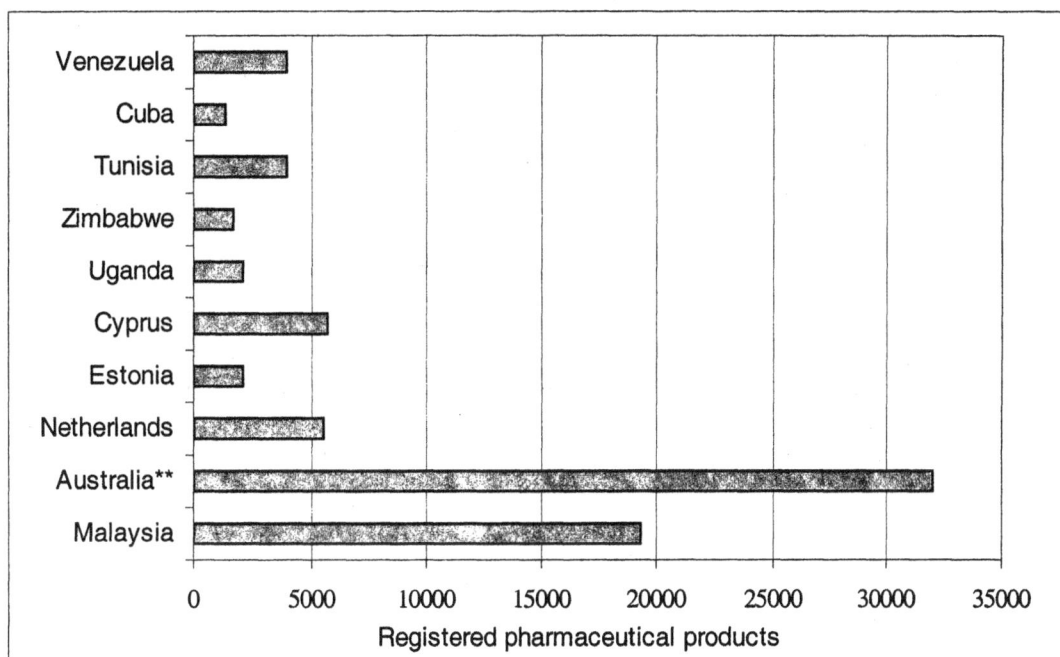

* *Netherlands (1996), Tunisia (1997), others (1998)*
** *The number of products registered with the TGA is approximately 60 000 items (including prescription drugs, OTC medicines, complementary medicines and medical devices). Only approximate data for human pharmaceutical products are shown here.*

4. Regulatory framework

In drug regulation, the government sets legal requirements relating to drugs and specifies what activities must be undertaken before and after a drug is placed on the market.

This chapter examines the missions and goals of drug regulation, maps the present domains of drug regulation and other government pharmaceutical functions, and traces the historical development of drug regulation in the 10 countries in this study.

4.1 Missions and goals of drug regulation

The government's stated missions and goals form the rationale for its decisions to intervene in selected societal activities. It must therefore define the objectives of drug regulation. The majority of the countries under review stated "ensuring the safety, efficacy and quality of drugs available to the population" to be the main goal of government drug regulatory actions. Australia and Malaysia spell out their drug regulatory missions and objectives in terms of the government's role of controlling functions related to medicines. The governments of both countries seek to ensure the safety, efficacy and quality of drugs. Certain countries articulate additional objectives for regulation. Cyprus has an added element related to price. For Zimbabwe, "sustainable cost" is one of the goals of regulation. The mission of the National Drug Authority (NDA) of Uganda is even broader.

Box 1

Missions of drug regulatory authorities of selected countries

Australia

"To develop and implement appropriate national policies and control for medicines, medical devices, chemicals and radiation." TGA Corporate Plan 1997/98-1999/2000

Cyprus

"Safeguarding the public health and interests by requiring the availability of safe, effective, good quality drugs that are rationally priced." Law No. 30 of 1980.

Malaysia

"The National Pharmaceutical Control Bureau shall ensure the quality and safety of pharmaceutical products through the implementation of the relevant legislation by a competent workforce working together in strategic alliance towards improving the health of the people."

Uganda

"To ensure availability at all times of essential, efficacious and cost effective drugs to the entire Ugandan population." National Drug Policy and Authority Statute, 1993.

Zimbabwe

"Ensuring the achievement of quality health services delivery to the public in a safe, accessible and effective manner through the control of the manufacture, distribution, storage, and dispensing of both human and animal medicines throughout Zimbabwe at a sustainable cost." Corporate Strategy and Plan 1999-2001.

4.2 Domains of control

What must governments do to fulfil these multiple goals of regulation? In order to ensure that drugs reaching consumers are effective, safe, of good quality and affordable, governments may exert control in several areas through various means. However, the areas controlled and the agencies responsible for controlling them may differ from country to country. They will therefore require different regulatory functions: licensing and inspection, product assessment and registration, QC, monitoring of promotion and advertising, etc. Some regulatory roles are carried out by most governments, while others are less frequently invoked.

The overall picture of drug regulatory functions undertaken in the 10 countries is presented in Table 4.1. Each regulatory function may cover one or more of the targets indicated above. For example, by requiring licensing of pharmaceutical manufacturing, importation and distribution, the relevant legislation will specify the requisite qualifications (and sometimes also the number) of personnel handling specific tasks, the procedures used to produce, import and distribute pharmaceutical products and the health and safety conditions of the premises in which any of these processes take place. The manufacturing, importation and distribution premises are inspected to ensure compliance with regulatory specifications, as well as to correct and/or prevent mistakes.

Legal requirements for pharmaceutical product assessment and registration specify how pharmaceutical production should be carried out, and lay down requirements concerning packaging, information to be provided by labels and inserts, methods of analysis, etc.

Prohibition of certain categories of pharmaceutical products from public advertising, pre-approval of materials and/or surveillance of advertisements are intended to prevent pharmaceutical businesses from communicating inaccurate, biased and misleading information on drugs to the public and health providers. Governments may also choose to intervene in drug price-setting instead of leaving this to market mechanisms. Drug prices can be controlled in several ways—for example, by imposing a price ceiling or maximum profit margin on general sales, or by setting a fixed price for payment or reimbursement of treatment. Of concern here is either the affordability of drugs for the general public or the cost of public drug programmes. In the same way, generic substitution aims to achieve efficient use of health system resources.

In all 10 countries, licensing of manufacturing, product assessment and registration, GMP inspection, import controls and control of product quality are determined by legislation. Licensing of importation and wholesale trade is not required in Cuba and Cyprus, however. In Zimbabwe, a licence is required for wholesale trade.

Legal provisions for inspection of distribution channels and control of drug promotion and information exist in all the countries, except Cuba. All drug distribution channels in Cuba belong to the National Health System and operate under the Ministry of Health. The National Centre for Drug Quality Control (NCDQC)—the country's DRA—issues guidelines on good storage and distribution practices for distribution channels. Inspections of the distribution channels are carried out by NCDQC, the distribution sub-division of the

Pharmaceutical Industry Union or the pharmacy division of the Ministry of Health. However, these activities are not founded on legislation. Also, Cuba does not have any legislation relating to drug promotion, since the practice does not exist in this country.

Drug prices are regulated by drug regulatory authorities in Cyprus and Tunisia. In Australia, Cuba, Estonia, Netherlands and Venezuela, price controls exist but the responsibility for enforcing them rests with other government agencies. In Malaysia, Uganda and Zimbabwe, drug regulatory authorities likewise do not regulate drug prices. Among the 10 countries, only Cyprus states specifically in its official drug regulation mission statements that "rationally priced" drugs should be available. The Zimbabwean drug regulatory mission statement specifies the notion of "sustainable cost", but does not regulate drug prices.

Table 4.1   Regulatory functions performed by the 10 drug regulatory authorities

Functions	Australia (TGA)	Cuba	Cyprus	Estonia	Malaysia	Netherlands	Tunisia	Uganda	Venezuela	Zimbabwe
Licensing of manufacturing	●	●	●	●	●	●	●	●	●	●
Licensing of importation	□	□	□	●	●	●	●	●	●	□
Licensing of wholesale	□	□	□	●	●	●	●	●	●	●
Licensing of retail	□	□	●	●	●	□	●	●	●	●
Product assessment & registration	●	●	●	●	●	●	●	●	●	●
GMP inspection	●	●	●	●	●	●	●	●	●	●
Inspection of distribution channels	●	□	●	●	●	●	●	●	●	●
Import control	●*	●**	●	●	●	●**	●	●	●**	●**
Quality control of products	●	●	●	●	●	●	●	●	●	●
Control of drug promotion & advertising	●	□	●	●	●	●	●	●	●	●
Price control	□	□	●	□	□	□	●	□	□	□
Generic substitution	●	□	□	□	□	●	□	□	●	□
Control of prescribing	●	●	□	●	●	□	□	□	●	●

● = yes   □ = no
* Special permit for biological products, steroids and others.
** Permit required for investigational products and products for personal use.

Prescribing practice is the least widely regulated activity. It is regulated in six of the 10 countries, namely Australia, Cuba, Estonia, Malaysia, Venezuela and Zimbabwe.

4.2.1 Regulatory policy spheres

The existence of a regulatory function in a country does not necessarily mean that the function covers the entire range of pharmaceutical products and/or activities. Nor does it mean that the control described in the country's legislation is always fully executed in practice.

Moreover, a country may choose to enact laws to regulate only certain areas of its drug supply system. Figure 4.1 depicts the conceptual framework of theoretical and actual domains of drug regulation. For example, the universe of all the products claimed to have effects on human health (therapeutic, preventive, etc.) can be thought of as the area within the boundary of the outermost circle — the **global sphere**. The DRA may choose to register all products, or only certain categories. It may decide not to register herbal medicines, but to require that all other pharmaceutical products be registered. The exempted products thus fall into area A, while other drugs are within the boundary of the next circle, area B—the **regulatory sphere.**

Figure 4.1   Conceptual spheres of regulatory control

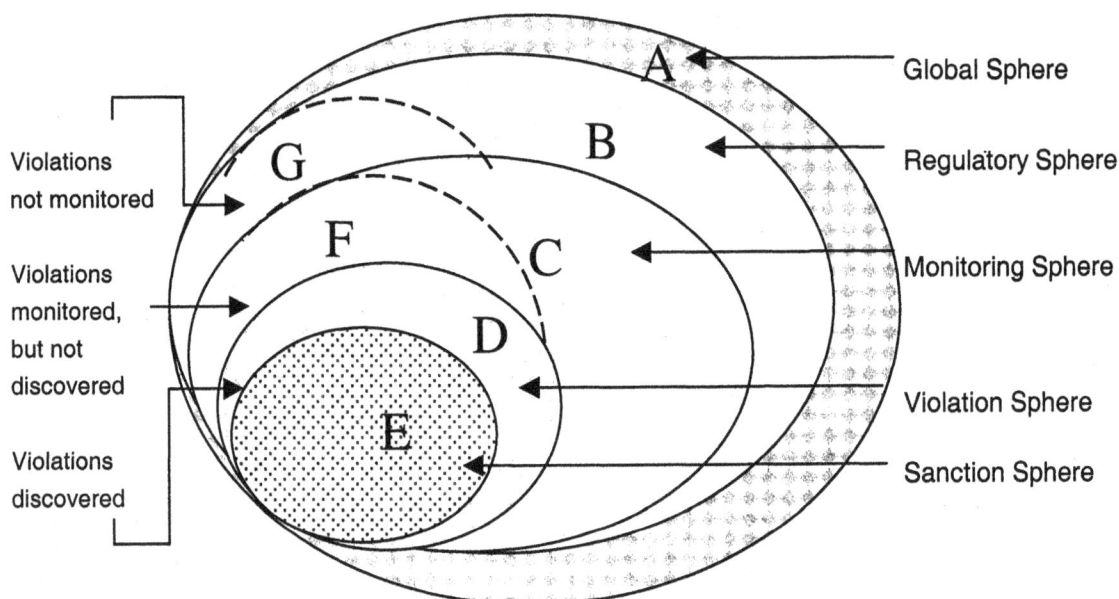

In any given year, the DRA may be able to inspect manufacturing, importation and distribution facilities and to collect samples for quality testing in a limited number of product categories. These products can then be considered as being contained within the third largest circle—the **monitoring sphere**. Some of these drugs pass the quality test, represented by area C, while a percentage of them may be found substandard or counterfeit, or else are not registered. These failed/illegal products can be visualized as falling within the next area, area D—the **violation sphere.** Legal sanctions may be imposed in all or a proportion of the violation cases found, which are contained in the smallest circle, area E—the **sanction sphere.** Violations discovered do not necessarily represent all the violations that exist. There are likely to be violations that are beyond the reach of regulatory authorities and other monitoring mechanisms (area G). It is also possible that monitoring fails to uncover a number of violations within the monitoring sphere (area F).

28

Additionally, although violations are not indicated for area A, this does not imply that all products that fall within this area are effective, safe and of good quality. It is rather that the relevant legislation currently does not cover this area. The regulatory sphere can be expanded once it is deemed necessary for society to regulate additional products contained in area A, and when its capacity to do so is adequate.

The four main regulatory functions—product registration; licensing of manufacturing, importation and distribution, control of drug promotion and advertising; and price control—are conceptually presented in Figure 4.2. Each of the core drug regulatory functions is placed in a segment within the conceptual sphere. (This figure is for illustrative purposes only, since some details, e.g. those related to violations, have been omitted.)

Figure 4.2   Conceptual spheres of the four main regulatory functions

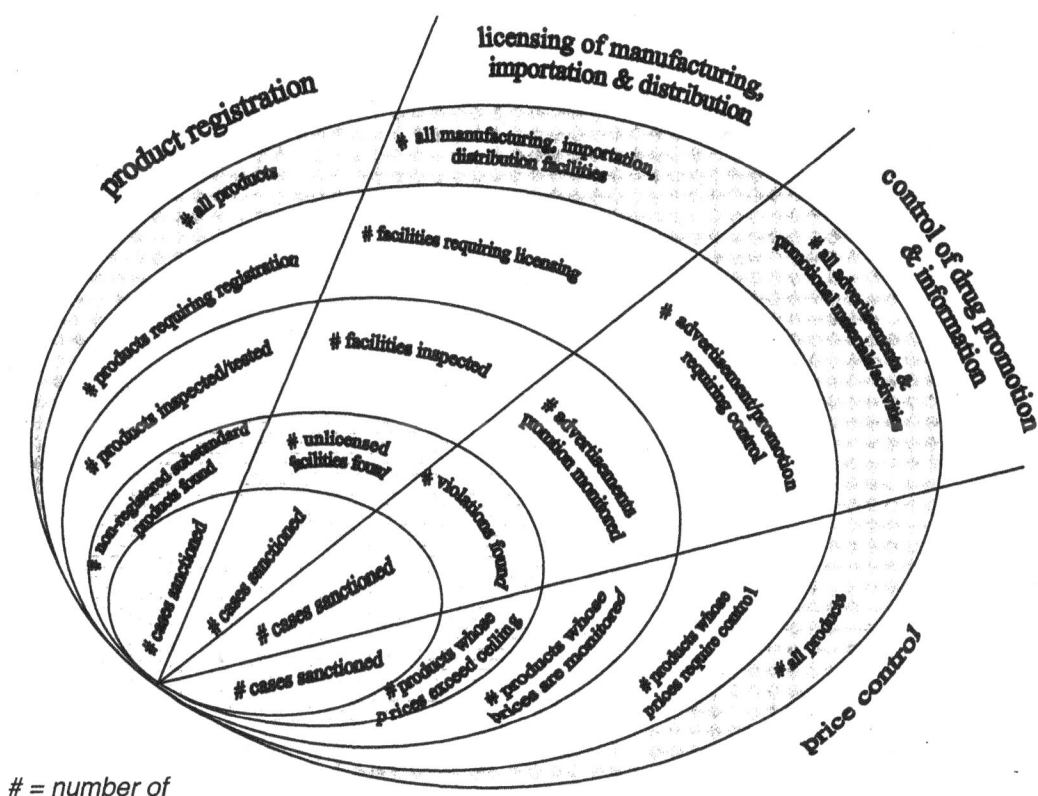

= number of

The outer layer of the second segment of the diagram covers all facilities engaged in the activities of pharmaceutical manufacturing, import and distribution. The next layer of the segment represents those where a licence is required to operate. The third layer represents the manufacturing, importation and distribution facilities inspected. Cases of violation of GMP, GDP and other requirements are represented in the fourth layer, while sanctioned cases are found in the innermost layer. Similar diagrammatic representations can be made for product registration, control of drug promotion and information and price control.

The lines that set the boundary between the spheres may not be at the same level from one segment to the next, since government regulation may be more extensive, monitoring more thorough, violations more rampant and sanctions more strictly imposed in one functional area than in others. If quantitative data are available for each of the subsegments in the spheres, the size of each subsegment can be computed and a map of the drug regulatory system drawn for visualizing the legal domains and the extent to which drug regulation is undertaken.

Table 4.2 shows the details of the regulation of different components of the four main regulatory functions in the 10 countries.

All 10 countries have a registration system for allopathic/modern drugs, but only seven countries (Australia, Estonia, Malaysia, Netherlands, Tunisia, Uganda and Venezuela) make registration of herbal medicines compulsory.

Table 4.2 Domains of regulation

Functions	Australia	Cuba	Cyprus	Estonia	Malaysia	Netherlands	Tunisia	Uganda	Venezuela	Zimbabwe
1. Product registration										
1.1 Product types										
- Allopathic (modern) drugs	●	●	●	●	●	●	●	●	●	●
- Herbal medicines	●	□	□	●	●	●	●	●	●	□
1.2 Sources of products										
- Private manufacturers	●	N/A	●	●	●	●	●	●	●	●
- Government manufacturers	N/A	●	□	●	N/A	●	●	●	●	●
- Government imports	N/A	●	□	●	●	●	●	□	●	●
2. Licensing										
- Manufacturer's licences	●*	●	□	●	●	●	●	●	●	●
- Importer's licences	-	□	□	●	●	●	●***	●	●	□
- Retailer's licences	●	□	●	●	●	□**	●	●	●	●
-Wholesaler's licences	-	□	□	●	●	●	●	●	●	●
3. Inspection and surveillance										
-GMP	●	●	●	●	●	●	●	●	●	●
-Distribution channels	●	□	●	●	●	●	●	●	●	●
4. Price control										
- General sales	□	●	●	●	□	□	●	□	□	□
- Insurance reimbursement	●	-	□	-	□	●	-	□	□	□

● = Yes □ = No N/A = not applicable - = information or data not available
* A manufacturing licence is issued for each product, rather than to the manufacturer.
** Pharmacies do not need a formal licence, but must register with the Healthcare Inspectorate. Dispensing physicians must be licensed.
*** Importation is centralized and State-operated.

Under the provisions of the Australian Therapeutic Goods Act, all goods about which a therapeutic claim is made must be registered, including herbal and complementary products. The level of evaluation that is carried out varies according to the type of product. In the Netherlands, registration of herbal and homeopathic drugs has been required since 1995. However, registration of these drugs applies only to quality and safety, not to efficacy. Herbal products which have no medical claims or indications are not registered as medicines. Similarly, Malaysia has mandated registration of traditional medicines since 1992, but largely for safety and quality, and only partially for efficacy.

Zimbabwe has rules regarding the practice of traditional medicine, but not for registration of traditional medicinal products. In future, however, the Medicines control agency can be expected to exert some control over this category of product. In Cyprus, there are no legislative provisions for herbal, dietary or homeopathic medicines, but some herbal medicines are registered as allopathic medicines.

Ownership also determines regulation. In Cyprus, Government drug supplies, including those manufactured by the Government-owned Pharmaceutical Laboratory, as well as imported drugs, are exempt under Law 6/67 and do not have to be registered. In Cuba, because all drug distribution channels are owned by the Government, inspection of these channels is not required by law.

Price controls also illustrate differences in regulatory emphasis. Many countries regulate drug prices through other government agencies or through health insurance systems, but not through the DRA. In Australia, the Pharmaceutical Benefits Scheme, which reimburses more drug costs than any other body, sets the prices for prescription products covered by the scheme. In addition, control is exerted over wholesalers' margins, retail mark-ups and dispensing fees for pharmaceutical benefits. Similarly, in Estonia, the Government, but not the SAM, sets the gross margins for wholesale and retail trade, and also reimburses drugs at a percentage discount. Drug price controls are also exercised through the Public Health Insurance Scheme in the Netherlands. Once the Medicines Evaluation Board (MEB) has allowed a medicine to enter the market, the Government decides whether it should be included in the public health care insurance package. For such medicines, it is the Medication Reimbursement System that determines the level of reimbursement.

Drug price-setting in Cyprus is an integral part of registration. Law 6/67 (Control of Quality, Supply and Prices) stipulates that prices of controlled pharmaceutical preparations should be fixed before they are sold on the market. This applies to imported as well as locally manufactured products. A 30% mark-up is added to wholesale and retail prices. In Tunisia, price regulation is also tied to registration. Any national or international manufacturer must submit a price proposal when applying for registration. The drug price is then determined by a committee consisting of officers from the health and trade ministries. In Venezuela, prices of products with only one formulation or form are regulated at retail pharmacy level by the Government, through the Ministry of Commerce and Industry. Prices are not set for drugs with more than one formulation, but are left to market mechanisms. Drug prices in Cuba are controlled by the Ministry of Finance. The Government also subsidizes drug costs to bring prices down, with the result that some drug prices are no higher than they were 30 years ago.

4.3 Other non-regulatory pharmaceutical functions

Some governments not only regulate, but also manufacture, purchase and distribute drugs.

Cuba, Cyprus, Tunisia and Venezuela have government pharmaceutical manufacturing facilities operating as public enterprises. Cuba has over 50 pharmaceutical manufacturing facilities throughout the country. In Cyprus, the Pharmaceutical Laboratory has a manufacturing unit that is responsible for producing and repacking drugs for use in public hospitals and pharmacies. As stated above, products manufactured by the Laboratory do not need to be registered. The Ugandan Government undertakes manufacturing through its sole pharmaceutical public enterprise—the National Enterprises Corporation. Tunisia, by contrast, has a number of public enterprises that manufacture pharmaceuticals. In Venezuela, too, various Government organizations are responsible for producing various types of products for the health service.

The Australian and Malaysian governments currently do not undertake pharmaceutical manufacturing. Formerly, the Australian Government owned the Commonwealth Serum Laboratories, but it privatized this operation in the early 1990s. Similarly, the Malaysian Government ended its role in pharmaceutical manufacturing in 1993. In view of the trend towards privatization of public enterprise, more governments can be expected to follow the examples of Australia and Malaysia.

4.4 National drug policy

In many countries, the national drug policy defines public policy relating to the pharmaceutical sector, including regulation. However, of the 10 countries studied, only four (Australia, the Netherlands, Uganda, Zimbabwe) have a written national drug policy document.

Countries nevertheless spell out their policy intentions in their drug legislation, or incorporate their pharmaceutical policy into national planning documents. For example, Tunisia's national pharmaceutical policy is incorporated into its five-year economic development plan. In Malaysia, drug legislation and regulations and a system for selection, procurement and distribution of essential drugs all serve to describe that country's policy regarding the pharmaceutical sector.

4.5 Historical development of drug regulation

Drug regulation structures in existence today—drug laws, drug regulatory agencies, drug evaluation boards, QC laboratories, drug information centres, etc.—have developed over time. In some countries, such developments began centuries ago; in others, they are relatively recent, having started only in the 1990s. A timeline of drug regulatory events is shown in Figure 4.3 below.

Figure 4.3   Timeline of drug regulation events

Australia	Cuba	Cyprus	Estonia	Malaysia	(time scale)	The Netherlands	Tunisia	Uganda	Venezuela	Zimbabwe
	1998	1997			2000					1997
	1995		1996			1995		1993	1993	
	1996		1993			1996				
1991	1991		1990				1990		1990	
	1992		1991							
1989	1989			1989			1984			
							1985			
	1983	1983	1983				1981		1982	
			1984							
	1979			1978	1975		1978			
		1970					1973	1970	1971	1971
1967		1967					1969			1969
1965						1963	1961	1963		
								1960		
		1959	1956			1958				
			1952		1950			1952		
1948									1946	
							1942		1943	
									1944	
									1938	
									1928	
					1925					
	1920									
					1900					
	1912								1904	
									1983	
	1833									
					1800					
	1709									
					1700					

4.5.1 Different evolutionary paths

Cuba has a long history of drug regulation. The first regulation relating to drugs, the royal act *Real Tribunal Protomedicato* was enacted in 1709. This law did not, however, attempt to control "drugs" themselves, but rather aimed to regulate pharmacists and medical activities. In 1833, the enactment of the Superior Royal

Board of Pharmacy Regulation was aimed not only at regulating pharmacy and the medical profession, but also at regulating drugs. After the 1959 revolution, private manufacturers and pharmacies were nationalized. The current drug regulatory structures were established only recently. The National Regulatory Authority and NCDQC were created by ministerial decree in 1989. Rules for drug registration were instituted in 1995, also by ministerial decree.

Venezuela developed its drug regulation system relatively early. Its first drug-related law was issued in 1883 as the Ordinance of the Council of Physicians on Secret Medicines and Patents. Drug laws have been revised regularly; a significant number of drug laws were adopted over the course of the 20th century. The law which established the drug registration system—the Law on the Exercise of the Pharmacy—was passed in 1928, before the Ministry of Health was set up in 1936. The National Institute of Hygiene was established in 1938 to serve as the nation's DRA. Over the years, new rules and organizations have been created to expand the scope of regulation and to add capacity for executing the laws. The section on pharmacological advice, the Laboratory for Pharmacological Analysis and the Centre for Pharmacological Surveillance were established in 1944, 1946 and 1962, respectively. Rules for GMP were drawn up in 1990.

Tunisia first introduced drug regulation in 1942, in the form of a decree on medical and pharmaceutical promotion and drugs control. All finished pharmaceutical products, whether manufactured in Tunisia or imported, must undergo a technical committee review and obtain a certificate of approval from the Ministry of Health before they may be placed on the market. Registration is also required for homeopathic drugs, and some herbal medicines are registered with the status of allopathic medicines. Key legislation includes the 1961 Law on Inspection of Pharmacies and Manufacturers, the 1969 Poisonous Drug Law and the 1985 Law on Production of Drugs for Human Use. Between 1985 and 1991, several legal texts were promulgated concerning GMP, clinical trials, medical and scientific information, procedures to obtain licensing of manufacturing and registration. New organizations were also created by law, for example the Pharmacy and Medicines Directorate in 1981, the National Pharmacovigilance Centre in 1984 and the National Medicines Control Laboratory in 1990.

Regulatory controls over the pharmaceutical sector in **Malaysia** were introduced in the 1950s, starting with the promulgation of three ordinances: the Sales of Food and Drugs Ordinance of 1952, the Poisons Ordinance of 1952 and the Dangerous Drugs Ordinance of 1952. These were followed by the Medicines (Advertisement and Sale) Ordinance of 1956. Combined, the laws provided a legal framework to regulate the general handling of pharmaceuticals, including poisons and narcotics, in respect of importation, manufacture, compounding, storage, distribution and transportation. They also covered advertising, sales, record-keeping and use of pharmaceuticals.

The next wave of major legislative activities and capacity-building relating to drug regulation came in the late 1970s and 1980s. The National Pharmaceutical Control Laboratory was set up in 1978 for the purposes of regulatory control. New legislation was introduced in 1984 in response to increased concerns about the infiltration of products into the market and the inaccuracy of information provided by the pharmaceutical industry. This legislation was promulgated under the Control of Drugs and Cosmetics Regulations 1984. This Act provided for the establishment of the Drug Control Authority (DCA), which started registering pharmaceutical products in January 1985. But the initial implementation of this law was limited only to the states of Peninsular Malaysia (West Malaysia). In 1990 the law was extended to cover the states of Sabah, Sarawak and the Federal Territory of Labuan (in East Malaysia). The Poisons Ordinance, revised to become the Poisons Act 1952, was again revised in 1989, to include the Poisons Regulations (Psychotropic Substances Act 1989). Similarly, the Sales of Food and Drugs Ordinance was revised in 1959 to become the Sales of Drugs Act 1952 (revised 1989).

In the **Netherlands**, the legal basis for licensing of pharmaceutical manufacturing and distribution was established in 1956. The Medicines Act of 1958 thereafter regulated the admission of medicines to the Dutch market through the MEB. But the Board started to operate only after 1963, triggered by the thalidomide disaster of 1961. European drug regulation is now playing a growing role. In 1995, the European Medicines Evaluation Agency was founded to co-ordinate the tasks of the drug regulatory authorities of European Union Member States. Certain aspects of Netherlands drug regulation now follow European Union rules. For example, GMP inspection is based on the 1983 European Union guidelines for GMP. Since 1 January 1995, a European procedure for registration has operated in the Netherlands. Now two types of trade licences exist: a European licence and a national licence. Products with a European licence may be sold throughout the whole European Union, while the national licences are only valid for the country in which the licence was issued by means of the national registration procedure.

In **Cyprus**, the Pharmacy and Poisons Law was first promulgated in 1959. It established the framework for regulation of pharmacy practice, drug distribution, prescription and labelling. The principal legislation regulating pharmaceuticals today—the Drug Law—was introduced in 1967 following the thalidomide disaster. Several major regulatory activities, e.g. drug registration and licensing of manufacturers, began in 1970.

The "thalidomide disaster" was also a key factor in the development of the **Australian** drug regulatory system. Before the 1960s, drug regulation was predominantly the responsibility of the states and territories, rather than the Australian Commonwealth. There was considerable diversity in the level of control exercised. The first advisory committee to review drugs was set up by the state of Victoria in 1948. This committee reviewed all products sold in the state of Victoria, but had no jurisdiction over other states in Australia. The first Commonwealth advisory committee in Australia was established in 1964. Because of the legislative process, the Commonwealth limited its control to imported products and those included in the Government reimbursement list. The National Biological Standards Laboratory (the forerunner of the mechanisms established under the Therapeutic Goods Act) was established to test drugs provided on the Schedule for Quality. The first federal act relating to therapeutic goods was enacted in 1965. Lack of control over locally manufactured products emerged as a public policy issue in the mid-1980s, and the Therapeutic Goods Act was changed in 1989 in response.

Under the terms of the Act, the TGA was created. It combined the old Therapeutics Division within the Department of Health with the National Biological Standards Laboratory.

Uganda passed its first drug regulation law, *Eddagala Luwangula*, in 1952. A poisons guide was issued in 1960, a dispensary tariff imposed in 1962 and a trade guide issued in 1963. In 1970, the Pharmacy and Drugs Act was enacted to regulate the pharmacy profession. Currently, the major piece of drug regulatory legislation in use is the National Drug Authority Statute of 1993.

Regulation of medicines in **Zimbabwe** started in 1969, with the promulgation of the Drugs and Allied Substances Control Act, Chapter 320. This Act created the Drugs Control Council (a body corporate), which started operations in 1971. The 1997 amendment transformed the Drugs and Allied Substances Control Act into the Medicines and Allied Substances Control Act (MASCA), Chapter 15:03, which established the Medicines Control Agency of Zimbabwe (MCAZ), with increased authority.

Estonia's drug regulatory framework has begun to take shape only over the last decade, since the country gained independence. However, the pace of regulatory development has been rapid. The Licensing Board of Pharmaceutical Activities and the Centre of Medicines were both created in 1991. Registration and licensing were introduced that year. In 1993, the SAM was created to become the DRA. The main legislation—the Medicinal Products Act—came into force in 1996.

4.5.2 Patterns of development

Some observations can be made on the basis of the country data relating to the historical development of drug regulation.

Objectives of the first drug law

Cuba, which has the longest drug regulation experience in this group, issued its royal act *Real Tribunal Protomedicato* in 1709 to control the conduct of professionals, rather than pharmaceutical products themselves. Before the industrialization of pharmaceutical production, drugs were made up and dispensed to individual patients in pharmacies. Accordingly, attempts to protect patients were aimed first at the activities of the professionals who practised pharmacy rather than at the products themselves, which at that time were being manufactured on a small scale only.

The first **Venezuelan** drug law, the Ordinance of the Council of Physicians and Secret Medicines and Patents (1883), stated its objective as the control and registry of medicines, in order to develop a pharmacopoeia of drugs with established pharmacological properties, composition, indication and dosage, for the purposes of standardization. A product registration system was developed and the DRA was created some decades later.

The specific feature of **Tunisia's** first drug law—the 1942 Decree related to Medical and Pharmaceutical Promotion and Drug Control—was the control of drug information. It required authorization of product information on leaflets before a drug could be marketed.

Countries that developed their drug regulation more recently generally began with one or more relatively comprehensive pieces of legislation, which covered a larger number of functions relating to control of the pharmaceutical sector than legislation developed earlier. The drug laws of Australia, Malaysia and Zimbabwe are examples of such development.

Patterns of historical development

The 10 countries appear to follow some general patterns of development in their drug regulatory systems. Most countries started out with the enactment of a law specifying the scope of control, followed by institutionalization—the creation of a specialized organization to execute the law. They then built up capacity by establishing QC laboratories and other facilities to strengthen regulation. In some countries, for example Zimbabwe, the first law included comprehensive provisions for areas of control, as well as the creation of specialized drug regulatory institutions. The scope of drug legislation was then gradually expanded to cover such areas as manufacturing practice, drug promotion and drug prices.

In brief, drug laws in these 10 countries evolved, and regulatory capacities developed over time, to meet the growing complexity of the pharmaceutical sector, and to respond to societal concerns.

Crisis-led change

Regulatory policies are often developed in response to problems.

As mentioned above, significant changes in drug regulation in Australia, Cyprus and the Netherlands, were made as a result of the thalidomide disaster that occurred in Europe in 1961. This is a classic example of a crisis-led change. The disaster increased public concerns about pharmaceutical safety: governments responded by imposing more stringent controls on the pharmaceutical sector, and with less resistance from the industry than would normally have been the case.

Discrete versus continuous drug regulation development

Two distinctive patterns of drug regulation development can be identified from the timeline map in Figure 4.3: discrete development versus continuous development. Cuba, Tunisia and Venezuela offer examples of the latter: their laws were promulgated at more or less regular intervals. Australia, Malaysia and the Netherlands have displayed a pattern of discrete development, alternating between periods of massive change and relative quiet. For example, in Malaysia, several laws were enacted in the early 1950s, which laid the groundwork for drug regulation in the country. But the country's drug laboratory was not established until 1978, with subsequent major amendments to the 1950s laws being adopted in the 1980s.

In Figure 4.3, the major milestones in drug regulatory development in the 10 countries are presented as a time-scale, to illustrate discrete development versus continuous development of drug regulation.

Trend towards harmonization

International collaboration in drug regulation has led to the creation of international instruments to facilitate cross-border drug control, particularly for narcotics. All the 10 countries in this study have signed a number of international conventions. The most commonly endorsed of these conventions relate to narcotic drugs and psychotropic substances, and illicit trafficking.

Recent regional activities indicate a trend towards harmonization of standards and laws. The European Union is the most advanced in fostering regional harmonization of drug regulation. In 1995, the European Medicines Evaluation Agency was created to co-ordinate drug regulatory affairs in its Member States. The influence of European Union guidelines and rules is evident in Estonia and the Netherlands. Because its drug regulatory structures have been developed recently, Estonian drug regulation has made rapid progress towards harmonization with European Union structures. In the Netherlands, on the other hand, the main regulatory framework was created in the 1960s, so that the country currently recognizes two drug regulation systems. Drugs registered by the MEB, and those registered by the European Commission (on the recommendation of the European Medicines Evaluation Agency) are both available on the Netherlands market. For GMP inspection, the Dutch regulatory body follows the relevant European Union guidelines. The Netherlands is also involved in the process initiated by the International Conference on Harmonization of Technical Requirements for Registration of Pharmaceuticals for Human Use (ICH) by virtue of its membership of the European Union.

Venezuela also observes harmonization decisions made by a regional body, namely the Andean Community.

Australia has a formal process for adopting European guidelines for drug development and evaluation, including the ICH guidelines. It also has bilateral agreements with a number of countries, and its membership of the Pharmaceutical Inspection Convention allows it to exchange GMP information with other members.

Members of the Association of South-East Asian Nations (ASEAN), **Malaysia** included, have yet to formulate common rules for drug regulation. Nonetheless, efforts have been made towards harmonization in terms of voluntary standards. Through the ASEAN Technical Cooperation Project in Pharmaceuticals, a number of reference substances and guidelines have been developed (17). Furthermore, agreements made for the ASEAN Free Trade Area have harmonized and reduced import tariffs on a number of goods, including pharmaceutical raw materials and finished products.

5. Regulatory capacity

The task of government is generally carried out by a multitude of agencies, mostly organized along functional lines. Execution of legal requirements for drug control is generally performed by specialized organizations authorized by law. Of particular interest in this chapter are the scope and authority of the main DRA, how it is organized, how it is financed, the human resources available to perform the regulatory tasks, and the authority's accountability.

Many factors influence how a policy is implemented and whether it achieves its objectives effectively. Experience in policy implementation in many areas indicate the importance of good organization. A number of organizational attributes, such as a sound structure, efficient procedures, well-trained personnel and adequate financial resources, are considered crucial for effective policy execution (18, 19, 20, 21).

5.1 Legal basis, organizational structure and authority

In all the countries studied, laws form the foundation from which drug regulatory powers are derived. The implementation of these laws relies on the creation of agencies specifically responsible for drug regulation. The DRA is organized differently, however, in different countries. In some countries, all drug regulatory functions are assigned to a single agency. In others, specific functions are performed by different organizations.

In the countries reviewed, the drug regulatory authorities:

- all belong to the government
- are all specialized agencies
- all have centralized authority
- all employ advisory boards/committees to provide technical support.

In most of the countries, a single national agency is responsible for drug regulation.

Table 5.1 summarizes the drug regulatory authorities in terms of: main regulatory authority; its legal status; existence of a central council structure; supervisory body; links with other regulatory agencies; unity of command; power to hire and dismiss staff; financial independence; performance of non-regulatory functions. The various regulatory functions and names of agencies responsible for carrying out those functions are listed in Table 5.2.

Table 5.1 Key aspects of the 10 drug regulatory authorities

	Australia	Cuba	Cyprus	Estonia	Malaysia	Netherlands	Tunisia	Uganda	Venezuela	Zimbabwe
Legal status of regulatory authority	Executive dept.	Executive dept.	Council	Exec. agency	Executive dept.	Board	Executive dept.	Statutory authority	Executive dept.	Statutory authority
Main regulatory authority	TGA	NCDQC	Drug Council	SAM	DCA NPCB	MEB	DPM	NDA	• INH • MSDSC	MCAZ
Supervisory body	Ministry of Health & Aged	Ministry of Health	Ministry of Health	Ministry of Social Affairs	Dept. of Health	the Crown	Ministry of Health	Ministry of Health	Ministry of Health	Ministry of Health & Child Welfare
Links with other drug regulatory agencies	State govt. with limited linkage to federal govt.	National Pharmacy Division Pharmaco-epidemiology Development Centre	N/A	N/A	State government with linkage to federal	• Health Inspectorate • RIVM • LAREB	N/A	N/A	N/A	N/A
Unity of command and control	• Fed-state • Single agency at fed. level	Single agency	Single agency	Single agency	• Fed-state • Single agency at fed. level	Multiple agencies	Multiple agencies	Single agency	Multiple agencies	Single agency
Power to hire and fire personnel	●	□	□	●	□	●	□	●	●	●
Financial independence	●	Partly	□	Partly	□	●	□	●	□	●
Non-regulatory functions	□	□	• Procurement • Manufacturing	□	• Procurement • Hospital pharmacy management	□	□	□	Production of biological products (INH)	□

● = Yes □ = No N/A = not applicable

40

Table 5.2   Agencies responsible for various drug regulatory functions in the 10 countries

Drug regulatory function	Australia	Cuba	Cyprus	Estonia	Malaysia	Netherlands	Tunisia	Uganda	Venezuela	Zimbabwe
Licensing of manufacturing	TGA	NCDQC	Drug Council	SAM	DCA/NPCB	Ministry of Health, Welfare & Sports (MoHWS)	DPM	NDA	DDC	MCAZ
Licensing of importation	□	National Pharmacy Directorate	Drug Council/ Pharm. Services Div.	SAM	DCA/NPCB	MoHWS	DPM	NDA	DDC	-
Licensing of wholesale trade	State	National Pharmacy Directorate	□	SAM	NPCB	MoHWS	DPM	NDA	DDC	MCAZ
Licensing of retail trade	State	National Pharmacy Directorate	Pharmacy Board	SAM	Pharmaceutical Services Dept.	MoHWS	DPM	NDA	DDC	MCAZ
GMP inspection	TGA	NCDQC	Drug Council	SAM	DCA/NPCB	Healthcare Inspectorate	DIP	NDA	DDC	MCAZ
Inspection of distribution channels	State government	Provincial health authorities	Inspectorate, Pharm. Services Div.	SAM	Pharm. Services Dept.	Healthcare Inspectorate/ MoHWS	DIP	NDA	DDC + states	MCAZ
Product assessment & registration	TGA	NCDQC	Drug Council	SAM	DCA/NPCB	Medicines Evaluation Board	DPM	NDA	INH	MCAZ
Quality control	TGA	NCDQC	Pharm. Serv. Div/ General Laboratory	SAM	DCA/NPCB	RIVM	LNCM	NDA	INH	MCAZ
Control of promotion & information	APMA + TGA co-regulation	□	Drug Council/ Pharm. Services Div.	SAM	Pharm. Services Dept.	KOAG	DPM	NDA	INH	MCAZ
ADR monitoring	ADRAC	National Centre for Pharm. Surveillance, Min. of Health	●	SAM	DCA/NPCB	MEB +LAREB	National Pharmaco-vigilance Centre	□	INH	MCAZ
Price regulation	Pharmaceutical Benefits Scheme + Pharm. Benefits Advisory Committee, Pharmaceutical Benefits Pricing Authority	Min. of Finance	Pharm. Serv. Div.	Govt.	□	MoHWS	Min. of Trade + Min. of Health + Central Pharmacy	□	Min. of Industry and Commerce + DDC	□

● = Yes   □ = No   - = information or data not available

5.1.1 Structural arrangements for regulatory administration

The DRA is entrusted with ensuring the efficacy, safety and quality of medicines, and is expected to carry out its tasks by applying the best available scientific knowledge and skills without bias. Competent human resources, adequate financial resources and freedom from the influence of politics and the interests of individuals, groups and the public are therefore critical. A sound organizational structure, the power to acquire and use resources and to appoint and dismiss staff and determine the level of their remuneration are essential for ensuring independent and unbiased decision-making regarding drug regulation.

This section assesses the drug regulatory authorities of the 10 countries from the perspective of organizational structure, particularly organizational forms, human resources and financing.

The way a regulatory administration is organized has implications for the execution of drug regulatory functions. Two common organizational forms for a regulation authority are the commission/board format and the executive department format. These two forms differ mainly in their degree of independence in carrying out their functions.

The distinctive feature of a commission or board format is that it is headed by a number of commissioners or board members who form a non-partisan body, and typically hold fixed and staggered terms of office. The purpose of this arrangement is to insulate the workings of the regulatory commission or board from electoral politics. It provides a degree of stability and continuity in the commission or board, and protects the members from rapid changes in leadership when the partisanship of the executive or legislative branch changes. The commission or board is designated, in the public interest and in the long term, to regulate a particular sector of the pharmaceutical economy, or an aspect of pharmaceutical commerce. It should, therefore, function independently of politics.

Alternatively, the regulatory authority may be a department or division of the executive branch. Authorities of this type are headed by a director, who is appointed by the head of the executive branch or ministry. This structural arrangement allows the head of the executive branch/ministry greater influence or control over the decision-making and enforcement activities of a regulatory authority (22).

Analysis of the study reports shows that the MEB in the Netherlands and the drug regulatory authorities of Uganda and Zimbabwe are organized in a board format. The MEB, which is the main DRA in the Netherlands, is organized as a board whose members are appointed directly by the Crown. This appointment procedure makes it relatively free from the influence of other Government bodies. The MCAZ and the Ugandan NDA are also established as statutory authorities, with executive committees plus some specialized advisory committees. Although board members are appointed by the Minister of Health, their independence is established by statute.

In Cuba, Tunisia and Venezuela, the drug regulatory authorities are departments within the executive branch, the Ministry of Health, which possesses decision-making powers regarding drug regulation. Expert committees are consulted on technical issues, rather than as decision-making bodies. Under this structure, the superior agency (the Ministry of Health) theoretically has the authority to alter a decision if it chooses to do so.

The Cypriot and Malaysian drug regulatory authorities employ a mixed structure. Regulatory functions are administered through an executive department, with an additional structural arrangement in the form of a central committee, whose role is not limited to advising the authority, since it also has some decision-making powers regarding drug regulation. Generally, the main DRA serves as the central committee's secretariat. Under such a central committee, a number of subcommittees are responsible for different regulatory areas. Additionally, advisory committees may provide scientific advice on specific issues. The appointment and composition of this type of committee ties it more closely to the executive branch than in the board format, and hence makes it less "free".

Malaysia has the DCA, whose members are appointed by the Minister of Health. The National Pharmaceutical Control Bureau (NPCB), within the Pharmaceutical Services Division, is the secretariat to the DCA. Advisory boards are "semi-independent" structures whose chairperson is either the Director-General of Health or the Director of the Pharmaceutical Services Division. These advisory boards report to the Minister of Health.

In Cyprus, drug regulation is also organized under the Pharmaceutical Services Division. The Drug Council serves as the central committee, with the Drug Control of Quality and Supply Sector (DCQSS) under the Pharmaceutical Services Division as its Secretariat. Drug Council members are drawn from both the public and private sectors, and are appointed by the Ministerial Council.

The organizational format, however, is only one of the factors that determine the level of independence of an organization. An executive department can also be highly independent in terms of decision-making if it is invested by law with full authority. The TGA of Australia is an example of such an executive department.

The power to hire and dismiss the organization's personnel and generate and use revenue are also important in determining an authority's degree of independence. Because all laws have to be interpreted when they are applied to a particular case, those who are appointed to make decisions regarding drug regulation must possess discretionary powers. For example, when considering whether an application for registration of a pharmaceutical product should be accepted or rejected, a staff member of the DRA has to make a judgement about the validity and reliability of the efficacy and safety information submitted, and probably also about several other issues, before reaching a decision.

The appointment and dismissal, as well as the remuneration, of those whose decisions influence drug regulation are therefore key factors in the independence of the DRA and determine its freedom (or otherwise) from political influence.

The drug regulatory authorities of Australia, Cyprus, Malaysia and Tunisia are all organized as an executive department. The last three do not have the power either to hire and dismiss their own personnel or to determine their own financing, while the drug regulatory authorities of Australia, the Netherlands and Zimbabwe have full authority over the recruitment and dismissal of their staff, and are also self-financing. It should be pointed out that the Australian TGA is autonomous, even though it is organized as an executive department. Estonia comes close to being self-financing, with fees and charges making up 88% of its income. The Venezuelan and Ugandan drug regulatory authorities have the power to hire and dismiss their personnel, but lack the power to secure financial resources. Most of Uganda's income comes from foreign aid—60% in 1997. This reliance on foreign sources of funds raises serious concerns about the sustainability of drug regulation in this country.

In the two countries with a federal system of government—Australia and Malaysia—drug regulatory powers are divided between the federal and the state levels. Implementing a public policy through multiple levels of government with autonomous authority requires a concerted effort between the agencies at both levels in order to attain the same regulatory objectives throughout the entire country. In Malaysia, coordination between the federal and state regulatory authorities has been created by establishing a Deputy Director of Health in each state, who reports directly to the Pharmaceutical Services at federal level. In Australia, the TGA has two committees: the National Coordinating Committee on Therapeutic Goods and the National Drugs and Poisons Schedule Committee, whose role is to ensure adequate and appropriate communication between federal and state levels.

Divided lines of command are also observable in the Netherlands and Venezuela. In the Netherlands, drug registration is undertaken by the MEB, while other activities are carried out by other institutions, including the Ministry of Health, Welfare and Sports (MoHWS). Under this type of structural arrangement, command and control regarding regulation must be exerted across different government agencies. Coordinating a multitude of drug regulatory functions to ensure that overall objectives are achieved is an enormous and sometimes difficult task. In extreme cases, such an arrangement can limit policy coherence and effectiveness, and lead to unclear accountability and failures of communication. The multiple functions across multiple agencies can be streamlined by establishing inter-agency SOPs or creating a central coordinating and supervisory body. In the former case, SOPs should be designed with the focus on the goals of quality, efficacy and safety, rather than the relative authority or existing routines of the agencies involved.

If regulatory control is fragmented among agencies, responsibilities overlap, the involved agencies have different perspectives and missions and act independently, and there is no strong and authoritative mechanism for coordinating regulatory activities at national level, regulatory power and effectiveness will suffer.

The country data also show that some drug regulatory authorities are assigned non-regulatory functions, in addition to drug regulation. In Malaysia, the Pharmaceutical Services are responsible not only for drug regulation, but also for procuring and distributing drugs and managing hospital pharmacies. Similarly, in Cyprus, the Pharmaceutical Services Division is responsible for public sector drug manufacturing and supply activities.

The fact that an authority performs multiple functions is not in itself a cause for concern, provided that there are no conflicts of interest and all the functions are carried out according to procedures and plans aimed at achieving all the authority's objectives. Thus deviation from the normal, set course of action, for example following a change in priority among the various functions, owing to political considerations or shortage of resources, could lead to a shift in personnel and budget from one function to another, and compromise performance.

However, putting drug regulatory responsibilities and drug manufacturing and supply responsibilities under one management will undoubtedly contribute to conflicts of interest, as seen in some of the countries included in the study. For instance, in Cyprus, drugs manufactured or imported by the public sector are not subject to assessment and registration, unlike those imported or manufactured by the private sector, thus creating double standards in drug regulation.

5.2 Human resources

Many different factors determine how well a drug regulatory policy will be implemented. These factors include the number of personnel and their qualifications and competence, their attitude to their work in general and to the drug regulatory policy in particular, their level of pay and career structure, as well as the culture within the organization.

This study used a small number of objective variables to provide a preliminary picture of the human resources and managerial capacity of the drug regulatory authorities in the 10 countries. Although they were inadequate for establishing causal relationships between human resource factors and the effectiveness of regulation, they nevertheless helped to identify common characteristics across countries and pointed to areas requiring further investigation.

Table 5.3 presents an overview of the human resources within the drug regulatory authorities in the 10 countries. These drug regulatory authorities differ greatly in the number of staff they employ. The Australian TGA has 500 full-time employees, while the Cyprus DRA has only 12.

Cyprus is the only country in the group whose public employees are better paid than their private counterparts. Drug regulatory authority personnel in the Netherlands and Australia receive remuneration comparable with that which they would receive in the private sector. However, medical practitioners working with the TGA are paid less than their peers in clinical practice. For the rest of the group, with the exception of Cuba, which does not have a private sector, government employees receive lower pay than private-sector employees. The lower level of remuneration generally leads to two problems in personnel management: difficulty in recruiting qualified people and difficulty in retaining them. In extreme cases it may also lead to corruption.

Staff shortages appear to be a serious problem in all 10 countries. Difficulty in recruiting staff was cited in six countries, while there was difficulty in retaining staff in four countries. The study indicated that in Malaysia, Venezuela and Zimbabwe these problems are due to the lower pay rates prevailing in the public sector in general. The MCAZ, although independent in managing its funds and recruiting staff, cannot increase the salaries of its staff without Government approval. At the time of the study, 19 of its 70 posts (27%) were vacant. The NPCB in Malaysia had 36 of its 150 posts unfilled (24%). The average annual staff turnover rates in the past five years for Malaysia, Venezuela and Zimbabwe were 5%, 5% and 4%, respectively. However, difficulties in recruiting and retaining staff are not due only to lower salary levels.

Table 5.3   Overview of human resources in the drug regulatory authorities

	Australia	Cuba	Cyprus	Estonia	Malaysia	Netherlands	Tunisia	Uganda	Venezuela	Zimbabwe
No. of staff working in DRA	500*	67	12	34	170	168	86	40	272	51
Salary compared with private sector	Comparable, but lower than clinical practice	**	Higher	Lower, but higher than other public agencies	Lower	Comparable	Lower	Lower than in manufacturing, higher than in private pharmacies	Lower	Lower
Staff shortages	●	●	●	●	●	●	●	●	●	●
Difficulty in staff recruitment/ number of vacant posts	●	-	●	●	●/36	N/A		●	●	●/19
Problem in retaining staff	●	□	□	□	●	N/A	□	□	●	●
No. of staff who resigned within five years	600	2	-	4	30	N/A	2 (promoted)	2	5%	10
Average turnover	24%	1%		2%	5%	N/A	1%		5%	4%
Power to hire/ dismiss personnel	●	□	□	●	□	●	□	●	●	●
Job description	●	●	□	Partly (SOP)	●	●	●	●	● (SOP)	●
Training	Required and available	Plans exist	Opportunity given, no plan, depends on funds	Opportunity given, no plan, depends on funds	Opportunity given	Plans exist	No plan	Required, planned but not always achieved	Several courses carried out in 1994-95. (training plans)	Planned and executed

● = Yes □ = No - = information or data not available

* Therapeutic Goods Administration only.

** Cuba does not have a private sector.

In Cyprus and Estonia, there is a lack of qualified specialists. In Cyprus, the inflexibility of the recruitment procedure is also cited as a problem, especially in relation to appointing specialized personnel. What is interesting, however, is that both Cyprus and Estonia have more drug regulatory personnel per 1 million population than the other countries, except Australia (Figure 5.1). Whereas Australia, Cyprus and Estonia have 21.4, 18.2 and 23.5 drug regulatory staff per 1 million population, respectively, Uganda and Zimbabwe have only 3-4 drug regulatory staff per 1 million population. Given the small size of both the DRA and the populations of Cyprus and Estonia (the two smallest in the group), the figures suggest that a higher proportion of human resources may be invested in drug regulation in small countries than in larger countries.

Figure 5.1   Number of drug regulatory staff per 1 million population (1998)*

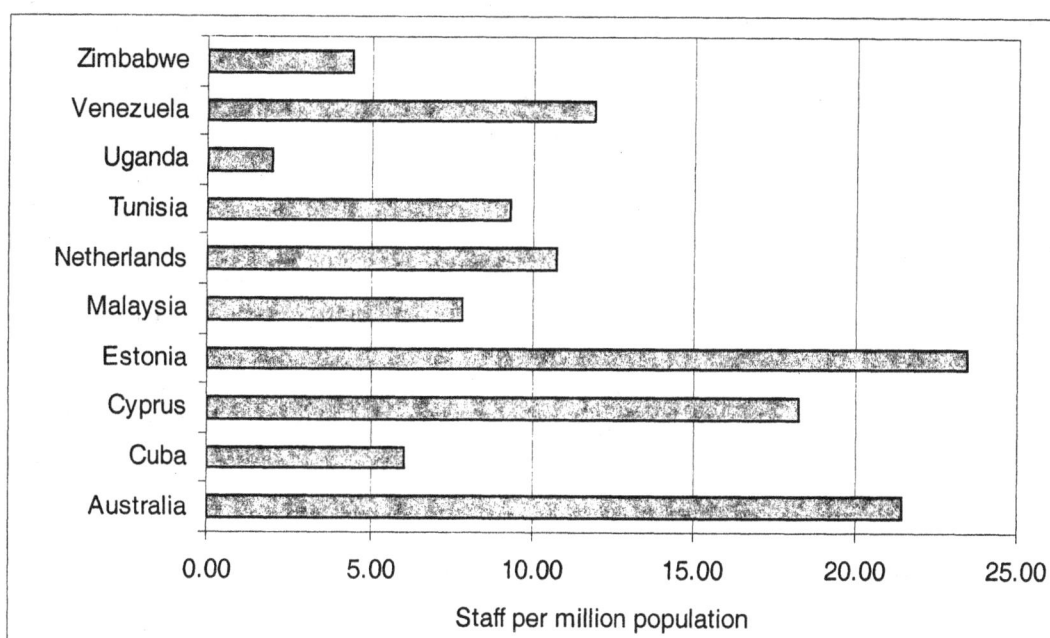

* Australia: TGA only.

During 1997/98, the Australian public service was extensively restructured, and many staff were redeployed. Attracting people to work in some parts of the country, such as Canberra, adds to the difficulties faced by the TGA in managing personnel. In 1996/97 and 1997/98, the number of permanent staff leaving the TGA was 58 and 59 respectively, representing an average turnover of 12%.

Training is a mechanism for developing employees' skills and specializations, as well as advancing their careers. The provision of training varies among the countries (Table 5.3). In Venezuela and Zimbabwe several courses have been offered to DRA employees during recent years. In Australia, Training is both required and made available. In other countries, training opportunities are provided subject to availability of funds. Although policies and plans regarding training are generally available, information is scarce about the specific courses offered to DRA employees in each country.

As for job specifications, drug regulatory authorities in all the countries provide written job descriptions for their employees, with the exception of Cyprus and Venezuela, although in the latter written SOPs are available.

5.3 Financing drug regulation

The sustainability of financial resources of a government agency is a key concern. Having a specific budget assigned to drug regulation is one means of safeguarding funding for drug regulation against the competing needs of other government agencies.

All the countries in this group, with the exception of Cyprus and Tunisia, are assigned a specific budget for drug regulation (Table 5.4). Both the Cypriot and Tunisian drug regulatory authorities, which are organized as executive departments, rely entirely on government funding for their regulatory activities. Although the Malaysian and Venezuelan drug regulatory authorities are allocated a separate budget for drug regulation, they too receive 100% of their financial resources from the Government. This does not mean, however, that the drug regulatory authorities in these countries provide their services free of charge. They do collect fees and charges for the services they provide. But those fees are transferred to the Government central treasury, and the authorities do not have the power to use the revenue they generate. In some of the countries, fees and charges are set arbitrarily, instead of being linked directly to the cost of providing the services. For example, the fees and charges set by the drug regulatory authorities in Cyprus, Malaysia and Uganda for registration of pharmaceutical products containing new active ingredients are lower than those set by the other seven countries (Table 5.5). Furthermore, a number of time-consuming services and items of information are offered free of charge.

Table 5.4   Overview of drug regulatory authorities' financial resources

	Australia	Cuba	Cyprus	Estonia	Malaysia	Netherlands	Tunisia	Uganda	Venezuela	Zimbabwe
Specific budget for drug regulation	●	●	□	Not specific	●	●	□	●	●	●
Sources of finance (%)	Fees (100)	Govt (66) Fees (27) Aid (1)	Govt. budget (100)	Fees (88) Govt. (6) Aid (4)	Govt. budget (100)	Fees (100)	Govt. budget (100)	Aid (60) Govt. (20) Fees (20)	Govt. budget (100)	Fees (100)
Fees charged for services	●	●	●	●	●	●	●		●	●
Fees reflect costs	●	●	□, lower flat rate	●	□, lower flat rate	●	●	□, lower flat rate	□	●
Use of fees collected by DRA	●	●	No	●	□	●	□	●	● (partial)	●
Financial sustainability problems	□	□	□	□	● (but not serious)	□	●	●	□	□

● = Yes □ = No

49

Table 5.5   Examples of fees and charges levied (US$)

	Australia	Cuba	Cyprus	Estonia	Malaysia	Netherlands	Tunisia	Uganda	Venezuela	Zimbabwe
Product registration fees										
New product	5 000 -120 000	700	120	785	100	15 000	1 200	300	1 270	1 000
Renewal/annual retention fee	645	350	60	571	100		600	200		600
Registration domestic product		700			100		600	200		38
OTC/generic (imported)	2 500	700			100	5 000		300	215	1 000
Manufacturing										
Premises licence								217-362		125
Manufacturing licence				357	100					
Product manufacturing licence			50							
Wholesale and retail										
Wholesale dealer licence/suitability of premises				71-357	40			108-180		38
GMP inspection										
Licence application fee	325									
GMP inspection/other than initial	215/hr/ auditor							20-35		25
Certificates										
Export licence/free sale certificate	42/hr/ auditor								61	
GMP certificate	43/hr/ auditor				10					
Clinical trial fees	660-8 100				40				182	37-500

The TGA in Australia, the MEB in the Netherlands and the Medicines Control Agency in Zimbabwe are financed entirely by the fees and charges they collect. Unlike the countries mentioned above, these drug regulatory authorities have full powers to dispose of the revenue they collect. And because their financial viability depends on the revenue they generate, fees and charges reflect the real cost of services.

Australia is an example of a DRA that has transformed itself from a government-financed to a self-financed agency (Figure 5.2). It has been the policy of several successive Commonwealth Governments that the TGA should provide its own funding entirely from fees and charges, and this policy has been phased in over several years. Fees for evaluation of applications were introduced in the late 1980s. At that time, the industry accepted the introduction of fees because "it understood that the TGA was unable, with its existing staff levels and resources, to provide a reasonable service or to remove or reduce the delay in evaluations"(23). The original agreement with the industry was that the TGA would recover 50% of the cost of all its activities (i.e. not only industry-related activities) from fees and charges.

As shown in Figure 5.2, the Government budget accounted for 53% of the Administration's budget in the fiscal year 1994/95. This was reduced to 22% in 1997/98, and by 1999 the TGA was financed entirely by the fees and charges it levied for its services. Under the present fee system, the fee schedules are reviewed annually in consultation with the industry.

Figure 5.2   Sources of funding of the TGA, Australia, 1994-1999

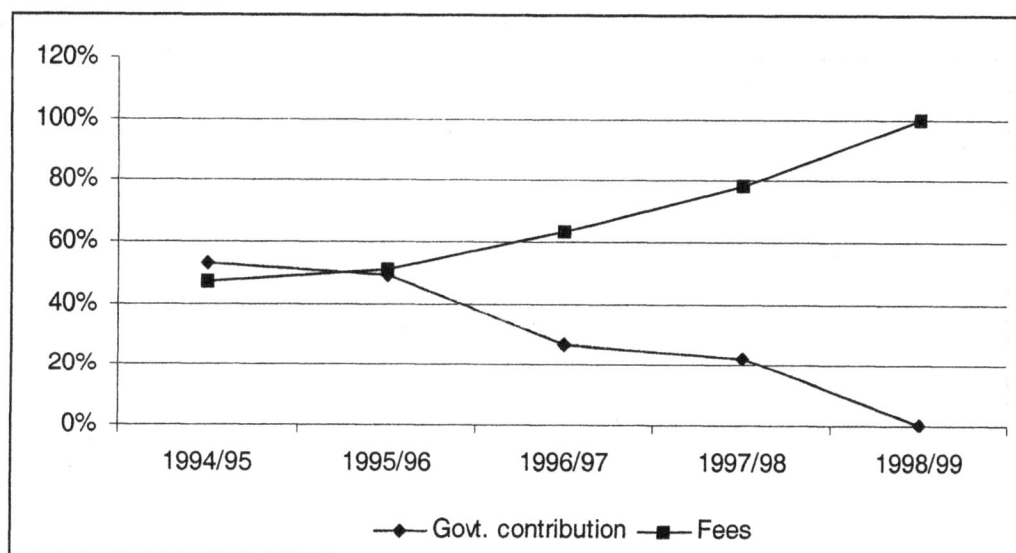

The Cuban, Estonian and Ugandan drug regulatory authorities have mixed sources of funding: all three rely on government budgets, fees and foreign aid for funding, but in significantly different proportions. In Cuba, the Government budget remains the largest source of finance at 66%, fees account for 27%, and aid for a minimal 1%. In Estonia, fees constitute 88% of the budget of the SAM, while the Government provides 6% and foreign aid 4%. The Ugandan DRA relies heavily on foreign aid at 60% in 1997, down from 100% in 1995. Government budget and fees make up only 20% each.

Because of its heavy reliance on aid for the funding of regulatory activities, the Ugandan DRA is faced with a serious problem of financial sustainability. The financial resources are not only beyond its own control, but also beyond the control of the Government itself. When donors finally withdraw their funding, some of the DRA's activities may have to cease. However, the NDA has invested in real estate which generates rent and has also placed short-term, fixed deposits with local banks, which may solve the financial problem in the long term. The MCAZ has also made similar investments in order to generate income for its activities. Studies have found financial sustainability problems in the drug regulatory authorities in Malaysia and, to a lesser degree, in Tunisia. These are due mainly to inadequate funding for functions deemed necessary to implement regulation.

Figures 5.3 and 5.4 compare the DRA's budget as a percentage of national drug expenditure and per capita for the 10 countries.

Figure 5.3   Drug regulatory budget as a percentage of national drug expenditure*

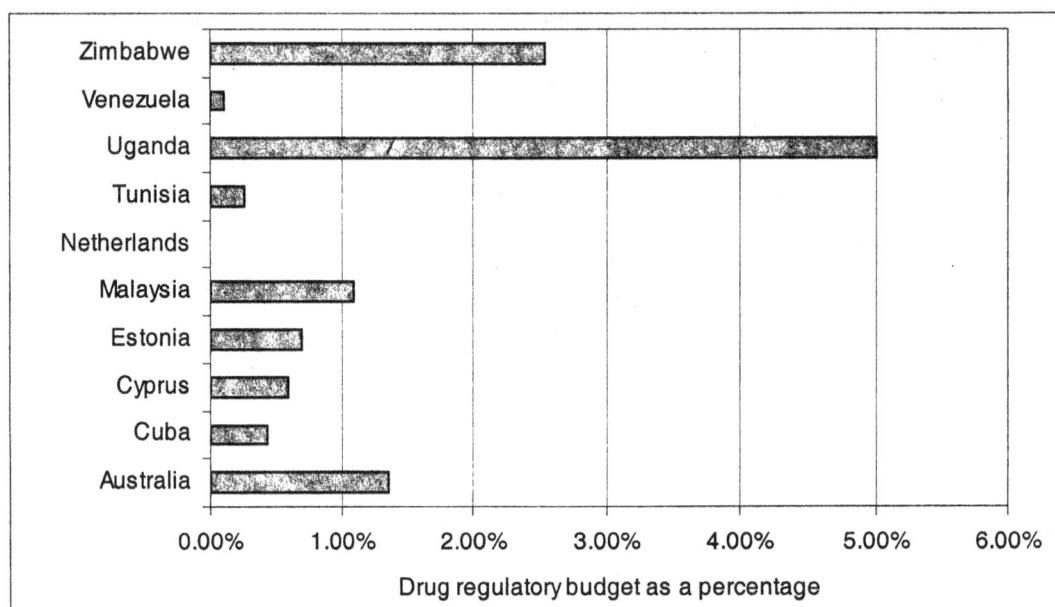

* Data for the Netherlands not available.

The DRA budget as a percentage of national drug expenditure is highest in Uganda (5%), followed by Zimbabwe (2.5%) and Australia (1.36%). This is because Uganda and Zimbabwe have very low national drug expenditure. For Venezuela, the percentage is a mere 0.1%. In Australia, Uganda and Zimbabwe, drug regulation is financed through a fee-based system. The drug regulatory authorities in these three countries have autonomy over their own budget, while their counterparts in other countries do not. In terms of per capita expenditure on drug regulation, the TGA budget is the highest (US$1.43), that of Cyprus and Estonia (US$0.57 and US$0.30 respectively) is also high, indicating that these small countries (in terms both of size of the country and of population) spend comparatively more money on drug regulation.

Figure 5.4   Per capita drug regulation expenditure (average 1994-97)*

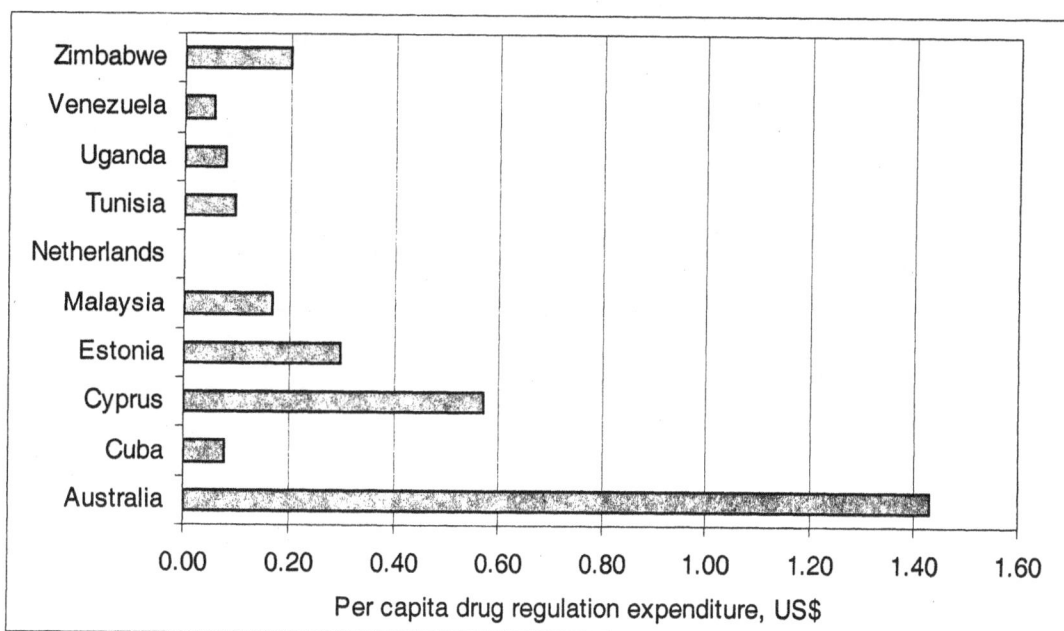

* Data for the Netherlands not available.

The above analysis is by no means an attempt to specify or establish some "best" or "optimal" ratios for each pair of parameters. It is intended only to put into perspective the resources made available for drug regulation in relation to the society from which they are drawn.

The amount of resources—human as well as financial—used for drug regulation is affected not only by the type and the extent of regulatory functions performed in each country, but also by many other factors, such as methods used for resource allocation and efficiency of resource management.

5.4 Planning, monitoring and evaluating implementation

The studies indicate that, in eight out of the 10 countries, regulatory activities are performed on the basis of workplans (see Table 5.6). In Australia, Cuba, Malaysia, the Netherlands, Uganda and Venezuela, the activities of the DRA are guided by official plans. The TGA's activities are guided by clear and explicit SOPs. The SAM in Estonia uses a short-term plan only when needed. Tunisia's Pharmacy and Medicines Directorate bases its activities on a consolidated five-year national economic plan. In Cyprus, there is no monitoring or evaluation of plans. In the other countries, a process for monitoring and evaluating implementation exists. The DRA in Zimbabwe does not prepare a workplan.

Table 5.6   Existence of mechanisms for planning, monitoring and evaluation

	Australia	Cuba	Cyprus	Estonia	Malaysia	Netherlands	Tunisia	Uganda	Venezuela	Zimbabwe
Regulation activities based on workplan	●	●	●	Partly, short-term plans	●	●	●	□	●	□
Monitoring and evaluation	□	●	□	Partly	●	●	●	●	●	□
Annual report	●	●	●	●	●	●	●	●	●	●

● = Yes   □= No

Drug regulatory authorities in each of the countries produce an annual or quarterly report, the contents of which vary. The study in Cyprus specifically pointed out that the annual reports of its DRA are mostly activity reports, with no comments about the extent to which the set objectives have been achieved.

Australia has a well-organized system of performance evaluation. The TGA submits a report as part of the Department of Health and Aged Care's annual report to Parliament. In addition, quarterly performance reports are issued, which are reviewed by the Therapeutic Goods Consultative Committee. This Committee is represented on the TGA, the Department of Finance, the Department of Industry, Science and Technology, and the industry organizations representing the regulated parties, i.e. manufacturers of prescription drugs, non-prescription drugs, medical devices and herbal and nutritional products (24).

5.5   Problems encountered and strengths identified

5.5.1 Problems faced by drug regulatory authorities

The principal investigators of most of the country studies invariably pointed to the shortage of qualified personnel as the main problem faced by drug regulatory agencies. This phenomenon is primarily due to the lower salaries paid by the drug regulatory authorities, which causes difficulties in attracting and retaining staff. Another factor (discussed in Chapter 5.2 above) is the limited pool of pharmaceutical professionals in some small countries, owing to the fact that training is available in only a few educational establishments. Other problems revealed in the country studies include limited financial resources and problems relating to the legal and organizational structures of drug regulation.

Lack of funding is mentioned as a problem for the drug regulatory authorities in Tunisia and Venezuela. Inadequate facilities for regulation, due to a lack of funds for the purchase of equipment, were cited by Cyprus, Malaysia and Uganda.

The Netherlands drug regulatory system is currently being restructured to accommodate European Union regulations and allow greater transparency within the national system. For Cuba, the exemption of importers from licensing and the exemption of distribution channels from inspection were identified as problems. In Venezuela, drug regulatory functions are divided between the National Institute of Health and the Drugs and Cosmetics Directorate (DDC). The latter comes under a different department in the Ministry of Health, namely the Main Sectorial Directorate of Sanitary Comptrollership. Coordination between these two agencies to enable drug regulation to be carried out coherently has been a major concern.

5.5.2 Strengths

Some aspects of the legal and organizational structures are described as system strengths in Cuba, Malaysia and Venezuela. The centralized system of drug regulation in Cuba allows the controls to be carried out under direct command of the Government. Implementation therefore follows the requirements of the Government's regulatory policies. Strict controls and clear norms and procedures are also quoted as factors in the effective implementation of drug regulation in Venezuela. In addition, computerization of the drug regulation systems is said to have facilitated the work of the Australian and Venezuelan drug regulatory authorities. In Malaysia, the restructuring of the drug regulation system in the 1980s and its continuous development have resulted in increasing upgrading of regulatory standards. In Tunisia, the centralized drug importation system operated by the Central Pharmacy of Tunisia is considered to have many advantages for the work of the Pharmacy and Medicines Directorate in terms of ensuring the efficacy of drugs and controlling drug prices.

5.6 Political influence and accountability

5.6.1 Political influence

A distinction should be made between the different levels of political influence operating at different levels of policy. At the macro level, the body politic is regarded as representative of the public or the electorate. Hence, politics is a means by which society decides which regulatory direction is ethically acceptable, socially preferable, economically beneficial and scientifically reliable. From the perspective of representative democracy, therefore, it is desirable for politics to determine the overall legal frameworks within which drugs are regulated. But at the micro level, where decisions are made which apply those legal frameworks to specific cases, it is not desirable for politics to exert influence on individual cases.

Drug regulatory issues which provoke political interest primarily involve ethical, religious or social concerns. In Australia, two classes of drugs, abortifacients and contraceptives, generate significant political interest. But political representatives can influence drug regulation only via questions in Parliament concerning specific drugs. The power to register drugs lies with the department, not the minister, with the exception of abortifacients, which require the approval of a minister and a secretary (i.e. a head of department). In the late 1980s and early 1990s, considerable political pressure was applied to the system by HIV/AIDS lobby groups, but this has now effectively disappeared.

In Malaysia, interference from the outside, political or otherwise, regarding decisions of the regulatory authority is rare. A recent exception was the debate over the registration of sildenafil (Viagra®), for the treatment of erectile dysfunction.

In the Netherlands, political interests are more concerned with the reimbursement system than with traditional drug regulatory functions, such as registration and inspection.

At the micro level, all the country reports maintained that political pressure has little influence, if any, on drug regulatory decisions.

The structural arrangements of the drug regulatory authorities were cited as the key factor in preventing politics from influencing drug regulation. The level of independence assigned to the DRA, a clear decision-making framework and transparency of procedures together enable the drug regulatory authorities to base their decisions on scientific factors and maintain their technical integrity.

5.6.2 Transparency and accountability

Regulation imposes restrictions upon the behaviour of certain target groups in a society, for the public good. Although the public good is a value that all societies cherish, it is not the only value which they pursue. Public policies must seek to balance collective and individual interests. Regulatory policies of all kinds are, therefore, almost always accompanied by concerns about the transparency and accountability of government actions.

In response to such concerns, mechanisms are often instituted to ensure government accountability. There is a range of "instruments of accountability" that governments can use. Peters (13) groups these "instruments" into three categories: organizational, political and judicial methods of control.

The mechanisms provided for transparency and accountability of the drug regulatory authorities in the 10 countries are listed in Table 5.7. These mechanisms are summarized below according to the group for whose benefit accountability is sought.

Industry

Information dissemination: General information regarding DRA guidelines and other matters is disseminated regularly through a newsletter (Australia) and websites (Australia, Estonia, Malaysia, Tunisia), to which the industry has full access. Specific information regarding the acceptance or rejection for registration and licensing of a particular product is given either directly to the pharmaceutical companies as feedback information, including reasons for the decisions, or published in official gazettes (Australia, Uganda, Venezuela and Zimbabwe), or on websites (Australia, Estonia).

Regular contacts and seminars: Maintenance of regular contacts between the DRA and the industry is indicated as a means of accountability in Australia, Estonia, Malaysia and Uganda.

Appeals system: An official appeals system allowing the pharmaceutical industry to voice disagreement with decisions made by the DRA exists in all 10 countries.

Membership of committees: Australia is the only country in the group with a system for including pharmaceutical industry representatives on committees which have the power to consider applications.

Consumers/general public

Only two of the 10 countries have devised specific measures for the benefit of consumers. The Australian drug regulatory system also provides for the inclusion of consumer group representatives on various drug regulatory committees. The appeals system in the Netherlands is not limited to industry, but is also open to consumers.

Table 5.7   *Mechanisms used by drug regulatory authorities to ensure transparency and accountability*

Countries	Targets vis-à-vis regulated firms/ industry	Targets vis-à-vis consumers/ general public
Australia	• Newsletter • Inclusion in committees • Seminar with industry	• Inclusion in committees • Website • Recommendations of expert committees made public • Annual report
Cuba	Clear standard procedures for registration	No specific mechanism
Cyprus	Appeals system	No specific mechanism
Estonia	Regular contacts	• Information on registered products and licence on website • Quarterly annual report • Violations of drug promotion standards publicized on website
Malaysia	• Official venues for appeal • Self-regulation • Disciplinary committee	No specific mechanism
Netherlands	Appeals system	Appeals system
Tunisia	Information on regulatory decisions provided	No specific mechanism
Uganda	• Reasons given for decisions • Close contact and seminar	Major decisions publicized on radio and in print
Venezuela	Information provided to interested parties	Regulatory decisions published in official gazette
Zimbabwe	• Decisions published in official gazette • Appeals system	No specific mechanism

For the general public, the mechanisms, where they exist at all, are limited to provision of information. As described above, regulatory information is made available regularly via government gazette, reports, website or radio. In addition, clear SOPs are cited as a means of achieving transparency.

Almost all these mechanisms for accountability are limited to organizational instruments, namely publicity (through websites, reports, gazettes, radio); citizen participation (inclusion of interest groups on the committees); and internal discipline (transparent SOPs). Four countries apply a judicial control approach: an appeals system operates in Cyprus, Malaysia, the Netherlands and Zimbabwe.

Of the 10 countries, the Australian TGA has developed a relatively more explicit and comprehensive range of accountability mechanisms. Registration decisions are not made public, but recommendations of the expert committees are. In addition, a list of approved products is published in the *Commonwealth*

Government Gazette, issued monthly. Negative decisions are not published, although they are often the subject of public debate, in the media or in Parliament. Details of numbers of applications, type, processing times, refusals, etc. are published in the Administration's quarterly reports. These are made available on request to industry, Parliament and interested parties. The reports contain full details of all the Administration's activities, which are audited by the Therapeutic Goods Consultative Committee. Reports are also submitted to Parliament.

6. Licensing of manufacturing, distribution and retail sale

Specifications regarding pharmaceutical premises, personnel and procedures must be followed by pharmaceutical manufacturers, distributors and retailers if they wish to obtain and retain their licence to operate. By means of these licences, drug regulatory authorities control the activities of pharmaceutical manufacturers, importers and distributors and companies engaged in drug promotion and advertising.

6.1 Power and process

This section briefly summarizes the licensing system in each of the 10 countries, focusing on: the power the drug regulatory authorities in each country have over pharmaceutical facilities; the sources of that power; and the licensing process.

Table 6.1 lists legal and professional requirements for each type of licence issued in each country, as well as requirements regarding import permits for different types of pharmaceuticals. The numbers in each category of pharmaceutical establishment licensed in the 10 countries are presented in Figure 6.1.

The four major areas in which licensing is required by drug regulatory authorities in most of the countries are: manufacturing; importation; wholesale sale of drugs; retail sale of drugs. Additional types of licensing are also required in some countries. For instance, Estonia requires licensing of blood units and facilities which handle the packaging of medicinal plants and gases. In Zimbabwe, industrial clinics, private clinics, dispensing physicians, dispensing veterinarians and veterinary outlets are required to be licensed. In Malaysia and the Netherlands, dispensing physicians need a licence to operate.

The basic criteria for granting a licence are the qualifications of the technical personnel and the adequacy of the premises, processes and equipment. Some countries add further criteria to serve purposes other than those associated with quality of pharmaceutical functions. These criteria may promote economy and equity. For example, the Tunisian DRA restricts the number of pharmacies per inhabitant in order to achieve a fair distribution of pharmacies. Uganda's regulations generally permit the manufacturing and importation only of products listed on the essential drugs list, which are considered a national priority. Some exceptions are spelled out by law. In the Netherlands, dispensing physicians are allowed to open dispensaries in places where pharmacies are lacking. In Estonia, any individual is permitted a licence for only one activity. In Malaysia, health assistants, nurses and pharmacy assistants can dispense drugs in peripheral areas.

6.2 Human resources

The lack of human resources is a major constraint for drug regulatory authorities in all 10 countries, and the licensing function is no exception. Some countries have sought to lessen the problem by, for example, multi-skilling (in Zimbabwe) and risk management (in Australia) (see Chapter 7.4).

Figure 6.1   Licensed pharmaceutical establishments, 1998

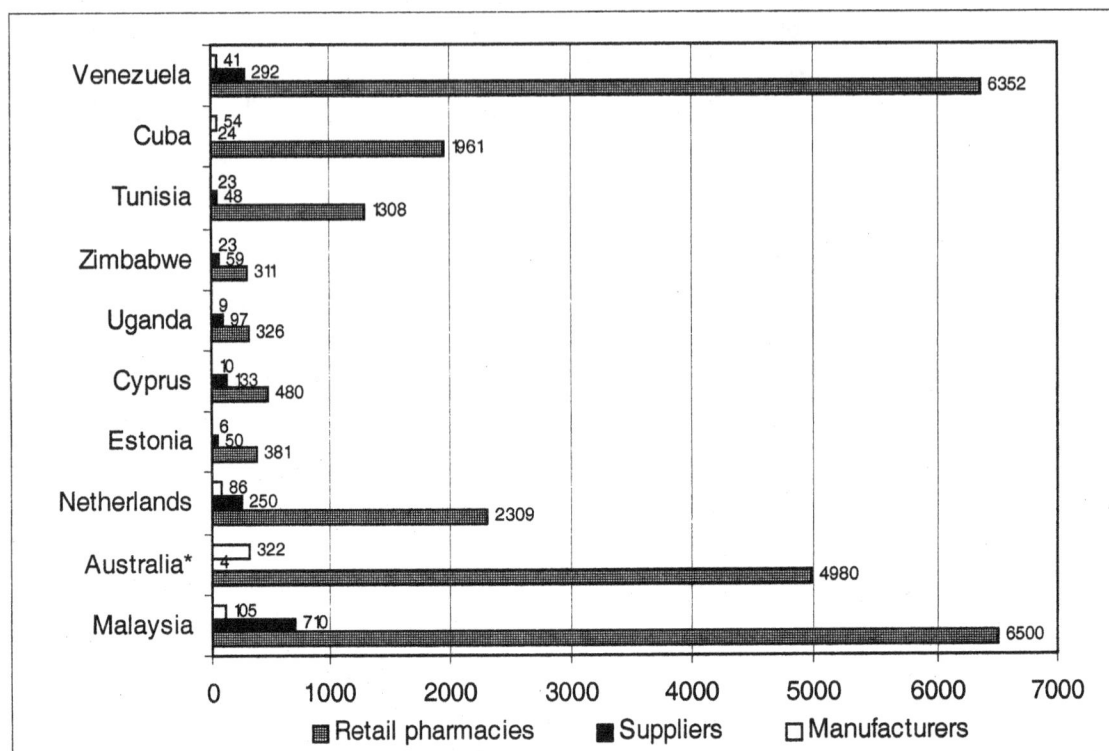

Venezuela: Manufacturers 41, Suppliers 292, Retail pharmacies 6352
Cuba: Manufacturers 54, Suppliers 24, Retail pharmacies 1961
Tunisia: Manufacturers 23, Suppliers 48, Retail pharmacies 1308
Zimbabwe: Manufacturers 23, Suppliers 59, Retail pharmacies 311
Uganda: Manufacturers 9, Suppliers 97, Retail pharmacies 326
Cyprus: Manufacturers 10, Suppliers 133, Retail pharmacies 480
Estonia: Manufacturers 6, Suppliers 50, Retail pharmacies 381
Netherlands: Manufacturers 86, Suppliers 250, Retail pharmacies 2309
Australia*: Manufacturers 322, Suppliers 4, Retail pharmacies 4980
Malaysia: Manufacturers 105, Suppliers 710, Retail pharmacies 6500

■ Retail pharmacies   ■ Suppliers   □ Manufacturers

*   Retail pharmacies do not include hospital and health centre drug outlets, dispensing physicians, etc.

6.3 Paying for licensing

Sources of finance for licensing activities are the same as those for overall drug regulation (see Chapter 5.3).

Budgets for licensing activities are provided from the overall budget of the drug regulatory authorities in each of the 10 countries. The countries differ, however, in how budgets are allocated. In Australia, the Netherlands and Venezuela, a specific sum is allocated to the division/section conducting this particular function. Others have no specific licensing budget, but expenses are paid from the overall budget. For instance, in Australia, the Conformity Assessment Branch derives its budget from the overall budget of the TGA, which is generated through industry fees. In contrast, in Malaysia, the expenses for licensing and related activities are fully funded by the Government through the Ministry of Health. Uganda and Zimbabwe levy fees for licensing of pharmaceutical premises.

Table 6.1   Legal and professional requirements for obtaining a licence to operate

Activity/product:	Australia	Cuba	Cyprus	Estonia	Malaysia	Netherlands	Tunisia	Uganda	Venezuela	Zimbabwe
Manufacturing	Qualified person	GMP qualified person	Pharmacist/ Chemist	Pharmacist or other relevant university degree	Pharmacist(s)	Qualified person	Pharmacist	Pharmacist	Pharmacist	Pharmacist
Importation	N/A	-	Not required	Same as above	Pharmacist(s)	Pharmacist	Pharmacist	Pharmacist	Pharmacist	N/A
Wholesale distribution	State Health Dept. requirements	-	Not required	Same as above	Pharmacist	Pharmacist	Pharmacist	Pharmacist	Pharmacist	Pharmacist/ Pharmacy technician
Retail pharmacy	Pharmacy Board criteria, plus Health Insurance Commission	-	Pharmacist	Pharmacist	Pharmacist (for drug items only)	Pharmacist	Pharmacist	Pharmacist (annual renewal)	Pharmacist	Pharmacist
Hospital pharmacy	State health dept. & National Hospital accreditation criteria	Pharmacist	Pharmacist	Pharmacist	Pharmacist	Pharmacist	Pharmacist	Dispenser	Pharmacist	Pharmacist
Other health care facility drug outlet	-	Varies	Physicians	Pharmacist	Variable	-	-	Varies	Varies	Dispensing physicians
Import permit required:										
Registered product	□	□	●	●	●	□	●	●	□	□
Unregistered product	□	●	□	●	□	●	●	●	●	●
Investigational product	□	●	●	●	●	●	●	●	●	●
Unregistered product for individual patient	●	□	●	●	□	●	●	●	●	●

● = Yes   □ = No   N/A = not applicable   - = information or data not available

61

6.4 Performance

This section focuses on licensing activities, unlicensed illegal facilities, problems related to legal structures and implementation problems.

6.4.1 Licensing activities

Licensing-related activities include the issuing, renewal, suspension and revocation of licences. These can be considered as outputs of the licensing system. Measuring outputs is the fundamental and least complicated aspect of evaluating policy and performance of an organization. However, data for the various licensing activities carried out between 1994 and 1997 are not always readily available or accessible. Even when they do exist, they may have been compiled using different systems of categorization, making comparison across countries difficult. For example, the Australian TGA has a good data system for licensing of manufacturing, but licences are grouped under a product-type system, rather than an establishment-type system, as in most of the other countries. In Malaysia, the list of licensed manufacturers, importers and wholesalers of registered products is available on the DRA's website. However, the website does not give the profiles of premises whose licences have been revoked.

In some countries data on licensing is not centrally available.

6.4.2 Unlicensed/illegal establishments

Another means of evaluating policy and organization performance is by measuring actual outputs against expected outputs. When asked whether unlicensed drug establishments and persons had been detected in their countries, five of the 10 countries responded that they had indeed detected such establishments and persons, but were unsure of their actual numbers.

For Malaysia, the official records indicate that there are no unlicensed establishments engaged in the pharmaceutical trade. However, the Malaysian Organization of Pharmaceutical Industries believes that this is not, in fact, the case. In Australia, Cyprus, Estonia, the Netherlands, Tunisia, Uganda and Venezuela, the great majority of — if not all — manufacturers, importers, wholesalers and retailers are licensed. However, unlicensed persons engaged in the pharmaceutical trade have been detected in most of these countries. In Australia and the Netherlands, their numbers are reported to be small, but in Uganda and Venezuela the numbers are much larger. In Cuba in 1998, only 25 out of 54 manufacturing laboratories had a licence, although this does not mean that the others were necessarily illegal establishments.

6.4.3 Problems related to legal structures

The studies revealed that problems in licensing pharmaceutical establishments can be grouped into those relating to legal structures and those relating to implementation.

The absence of mandatory manufacturer licensing in Cyprus is believed to be a factor in the establishment of small packaging units to bypass price-fixing procedures. Moreover, the procedure for issuing a licence to manufacture a product is, to a certain degree, retrospective, since the application is submitted after the manufacturer has built the facility. Ensuring that any requested modification of the facility is carried out is therefore difficult.

Another problem arises from the way in which the laws grant different responsibilities to different authorities, leading to coordination problems. In Cyprus, the licensing body for manufacturing and marketing is the Drug Council, which is an independent body with the DCQSS as its secretariat. The same body is responsible for GMP inspection. But inspections of distribution channels are undertaken by another department of the Pharmaceutical Services Division — the Inspectorate Sector — which is not related to the Drug Council. To make matters even more complex, the authority to issue licences to pharmacists and pharmacies rests with the Pharmacy Board, which is a consultative board to the Minister of Health.

In Zimbabwe, the employment of unlicensed pharmaceutical sales representatives by some importing companies can perhaps be attributed to the fact that no import permit is required for importing registered drug products. Therefore, once a company registers a product, any other company can also import and distribute that product using unregistered sales representatives.

6.4.4 Implementation problems
As shown in Chapter 4, the fact that laws exist to regulate a pharmaceutical function does not necessarily mean that they will be complied with, as can be seen in the following example from Uganda.

According to the law of Uganda, a medicine should never be dispensed in a retail pharmacy if the authorized person is absent. But given Uganda's low number of qualified pharmacists, this requirement is not met anywhere in the country other than in the capital, Kampala. Moreover, many of Uganda's drug shops, particularly those in rural areas, are neither licensed nor operated by medically trained personnel, and some drug shop premises are in poor condition.

More problems relate to the sale of drugs. Although Uganda's wholesalers are required to sell drugs based on previously placed orders, wholesale pharmacies commonly operate like retail pharmacies, selling drugs to any purchaser at any time. Similarly, in spite of the fact that an import licence is required by law, a large number of drugs enter Uganda illegally.

7. Inspection and surveillance

Inspection and surveillance enable drug regulatory authorities to monitor whether pharmaceutical operations are carried out in accordance with approved standards and guidelines. In so doing, they uncover weaknesses and actual errors in drug production, QC, storage and distribution of drugs. Activities include physical inspection and quality-testing of product samples. In order to perform these duties, inspectors should be assigned the necessary legal powers. They should also be suitably qualified and free from conflicts of interest and political pressure.

This chapter assesses the situation in the 10 countries with respect to GMP inspection and inspection of distribution channels.

7.1 Power and process: comparing structures and processes

7.1.1 Legal structure

In all 10 countries, there are laws giving drug regulatory authorities (in the person of their inspectors) the power to inspect manufacturing plants and distribution channels. In each country, inspection and surveillance are the responsibility of the government and are carried out by specialized agencies. These activities are never contracted out to the private sector. In some countries, Ministry of Health staff working in the regions and districts who are not members of the DRA are delegated to carry out inspections, but this delegation is not supported by legal provisions.

In Estonia, the Netherlands, Tunisia, Uganda, Venezuela and Zimbabwe, inspections both of GMP and of distribution channels are organized under one unit or agency. In Cyprus, GMP inspection is the responsibility of the DCQSS, but distribution channels are inspected by the Inspectorate Sector, both of which come under the Pharmaceutical Services Division. A similar arrangement is found in Malaysia. The GMP inspection function has been assigned to the GMP and Licensing Division of the NPCB, while distribution-channel inspection is the responsibility of the Licensing and Enforcement Unit of the Pharmaceutical Services Division. Both functions come under the Pharmaceutical Services Division, but are carried out by different inspectors. In addition, inspection of distribution channels in the states is delegated to state-level employees.

Australia has a GMP Licensing and Audit section within the TGA at the Commonwealth level. Inspection of distribution channels is carried out by each state or territory. The federal and state levels are linked through the National Coordinating Committee on Therapeutic Goods and the National Drugs and Poisons Schedule Committee. In Cuba, even though inspection of distribution channels is not required by law, the function is performed by three different supervisory agencies: the National Centre for Drug Quality Control, the Pharmaceutical Industry Union and the Pharmacy Division of the Public Health Ministry. Table 7.1 presents an overview of the laws, organizations and guidelines for GMP and distribution-channel inspection in the 10 countries.

Because distribution channels are usually dispersed throughout a country, inspection is sometimes delegated to the public administration at lower levels. This is the case in Australia, Malaysia, the Netherlands, Tunisia, Uganda and Venezuela. The remaining countries do not decentralize this function. In general, an inspectorate at central headquarters level is responsible for GMP inspection and inspection of distribution channels located in the capital city and ports. Distribution channels located in state and regional administrations are supervised by an inspectorate at the state level.

Table 7.1   Legal framework and tools for inspection of GMP and distribution channels

	Australia	Cuba	Cyprus	Estonia	Malaysia	Netherlands	Tunisia	Uganda	Venezuela	Zimbabwe
Law requiring GMP inspection	•	•	•	•	•	•	•	•	•	•
GMP inspectorate	•	•	•	•	•	•	•	•	•	•
Written GMP guidelines	•	•	•	•	•	•	•	•	•	•
Manuals/SOPs for GMP inspectors	•	•	□	•	•	•	•	•	•	•
Laws requiring inspection of distribution channels	•	•	•	•	•	•	•	•	•	•
Distribution-channel inspectorate	•*	□	•	•	•	•	•	•	•	•
Written guidelines for GDPs	□	□	□	•	□	•	•	□	□	•
Manual/SOPs for inspectors of distribution channels	-	-	□	•	•	•	•	•	□	□

• = Yes   □ = No   - = information or data not available
* There is a system for inspection of pharmacies in each state.

In Australia and Malaysia, which have a federal system of government, the delegation of inspection responsibilities and reporting systems is organized in different ways. In Malaysia, inspection of distribution channels in the states comes under the authority of the State Deputy Director of Health (Pharmacy), and there is a direct route for reporting between the states and the federal agencies.

Several countries (Cyprus, Estonia, Venezuela and Zimbabwe) have adopted the WHO GMP guidelines (25) as their statutory GMP standards. Australia has its own GMP guidelines. Malaysia uses the GMP guidelines of the ASEAN (26). The Netherlands has adopted the European Union guidelines on GMP inspection (27). The majority of the countries have also developed SOPs for their inspectors, as indicated in Table 7.1. Australia, Cuba, Cyprus, Malaysia, Uganda and Venezuela have not developed guidelines for GDP.

7.1.2 GMP certificates

Only three countries, Tunisia, Uganda and Zimbabwe, do not issue a GMP certificate. The drug regulatory authorities in these three countries do conduct GMP inspections, but do not issue a specific document which indicates that a manufacturing plant has attained GMP standards. The MCAZ does, however, provide a GMP certificate at the manufacturer's request to facilitate international registration and export of products. In Malaysia, various types of certificates are issued: GMP certificates; Certificate of Pharmaceutical Product for export; and Certificate of Free Sale for medical devices and cosmetic products. Cyprus has no clear criteria for issuing a GMP certificate: instead, the inspectors make a decision which they must then justify to the Drug Council. In Australia, compliance with the national GMP code is required in order to obtain a GMP certificate. In Venezuela, four types of certificates are issued: general certificates for all areas of manufacture; certificates for production; certificates for partial fabrication; and certificates for export of pharmaceuticals.

7.1.3 Appeals procedures

Procedures for appealing against decisions resulting from GMP and distribution-channel inspections exist in each of the countries. Some countries employ administrative procedures to handle appeals, some employ judicial control, while others combine both approaches.

7.2 Human resources

7.2.1 Qualifications and training

In each of the countries, inspectors of both manufacturing plants and distribution channels are professionals, mostly pharmacists. Some countries also employ pharmacy assistants as inspectors. Uganda, in particular, has a large number of assistant drug inspectors stationed in the regions.

In terms of qualifications, Australia appears to have the most demanding recruitment requirements for GMP inspectors. The TGA's GMP auditors need to have worked in industry before their appointment and undergo 6-12 months' formal training after appointment. Similarly, GMP inspectors in the Netherlands must have acquired experience in the pharmaceutical industry.

GMP inspectors generally receive greater formal training than distribution-channel inspectors. In Cyprus, Malaysia and Venezuela, for instance, specialized training courses (or even training abroad) plus on-the-job training are offered to GMP inspectors, while distribution-channel inspectors receive on-the-job training only. Conversely, the MCAZ has provided a formal training course for distribution-channel inspectors, as well as for inspectors of other countries in the region. In Tunisia, inspectors are reported to lack training.

7.2.2 Salary levels

In most of the countries studied, the salaries of GMP and distribution-channel inspectors are lower than those of the professionals working in the facilities which they inspect. In Figures 7.1 and 7.2, the average monthly salaries of GMP inspectors and distribution-channel inspectors are shown, together with those of their counterparts in the private sector.

Figure 7.1   *Salaries of GMP inspectors compared with their private-sector counterparts, 1998*

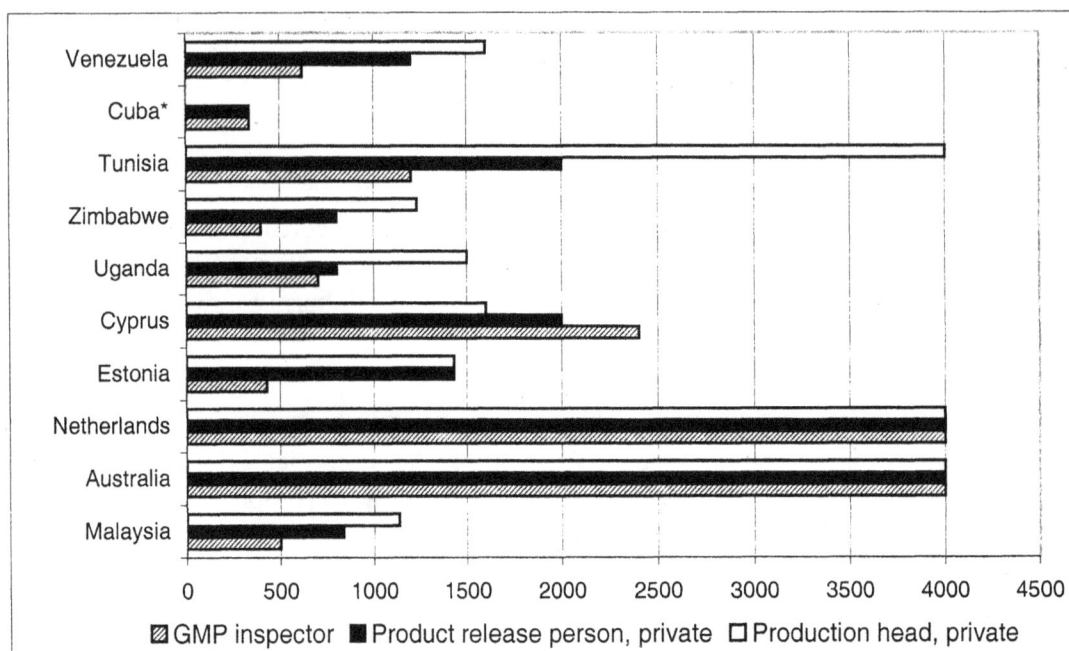

* *Private sector does not exist in Cuba*
Note: Product release person: person responsible for the release of batches of finished products in a manufacturing plant

Figure 7.2   *Salaries of distribution-channel inspectors compared with their private-sector counterparts, 1998*

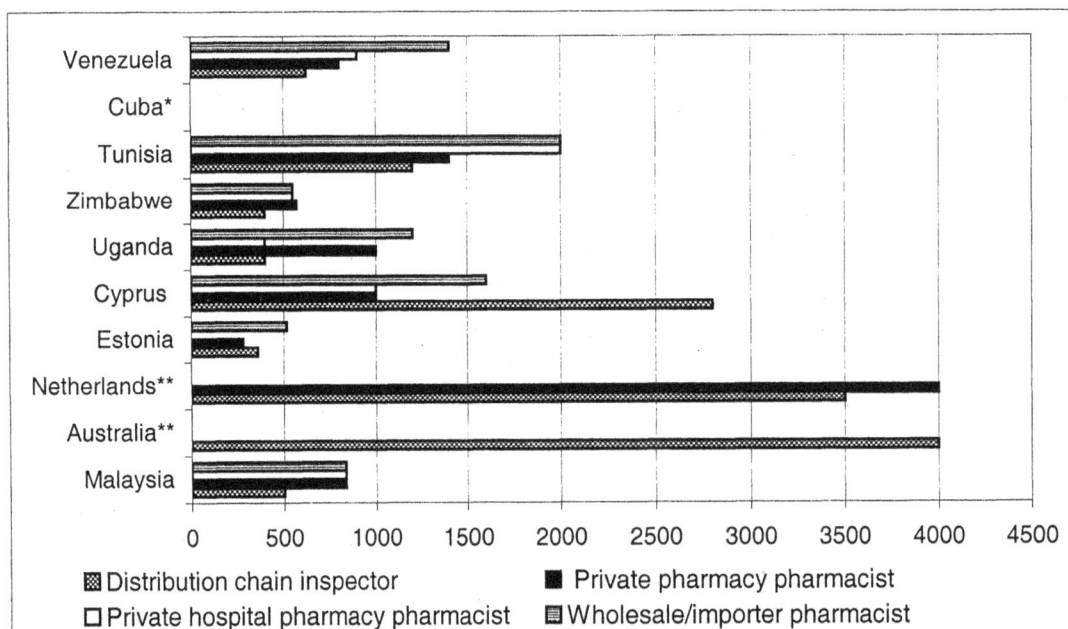

* *Private sector does not exist in Cuba and data for inspector of distribution channels not available.*
**Data for Australia and the Netherlands not complete.*

The difference between the monthly salary of a GMP inspector and of a head of production in a private pharmaceutical plant is considerable. The salary of a head of production is 3.3 times greater than that of a GMP inspector in Tunisia, and double that of a GMP inspector in Uganda. In these two countries, the gap between the monthly salary of a distribution-channel inspector and that of a pharmacist working in a retail pharmacy is smaller, but still significant. In Australia and the Netherlands, salaries for pharmaceutical professionals in the public and private sectors are comparable. Only in Cyprus are GMP and distribution-channel inspectors better paid than their private-sector counterparts.

7.2.3 Human resources management

Human resources management systems for inspection differ among countries. In Australia, the same group of personnel is responsible both for licensing of manufacturers and for GMP inspection. In Cyprus, Tunisia, Venezuela and Zimbabwe, GMP inspectors also carry out other drug regulatory functions. One of the results of such an arrangement is that the different functions must compete for the employees' time. Cuba, Estonia and Tunisia employ both full-time and part-time inspectors for both functions. Other countries have full-time employees only.

7.2.4 Workload

Ideally, in order to understand how many staff are required to perform a particular function satisfactorily, human resources should be compared with workload figures. However, comparing the workload of personnel for inspection and other regulatory functions across countries is not straightforward. This is because the actual tasks may not be exactly the same for each function. Furthermore, in many countries the same personnel carry out more than one function. For example, in Australia, GMP inspectors undertake both licensing and GMP audit. They also conduct a training programme for domestic and foreign inspectors. Accurately estimating the number of full-time employees required specifically for the inspection function is therefore difficult.

An attempt is made in Figure 7.3 to give a crude picture of the human resources required in the various countries. For Australia, however, estimating the workload is not possible, owing to a lack of data about the number of distribution-channel inspectors.

Of the 10 countries, Australia has the highest number of staff (18 inspectors) for GMP inspection. Malaysia and the Netherlands come next, with six inspectors each. The inspectors in these three countries are also responsible for the largest numbers of manufacturing firms. In terms of human resources for distribution-channel inspection, Malaysia has the largest number (52), followed closely by Uganda (45). But the number of distribution channels per inspector differs greatly: the figure for Malaysia is five times that for Uganda. The country with the highest number of distribution channels per inspector is the Netherlands, with more than 500 distribution channels to be taken care of by, on average, one inspector, followed by Venezuela (417), Cuba (330) and Cyprus (205).

Figure 7.3   Workload of GMP and distribution-channel inspectors, 1998*

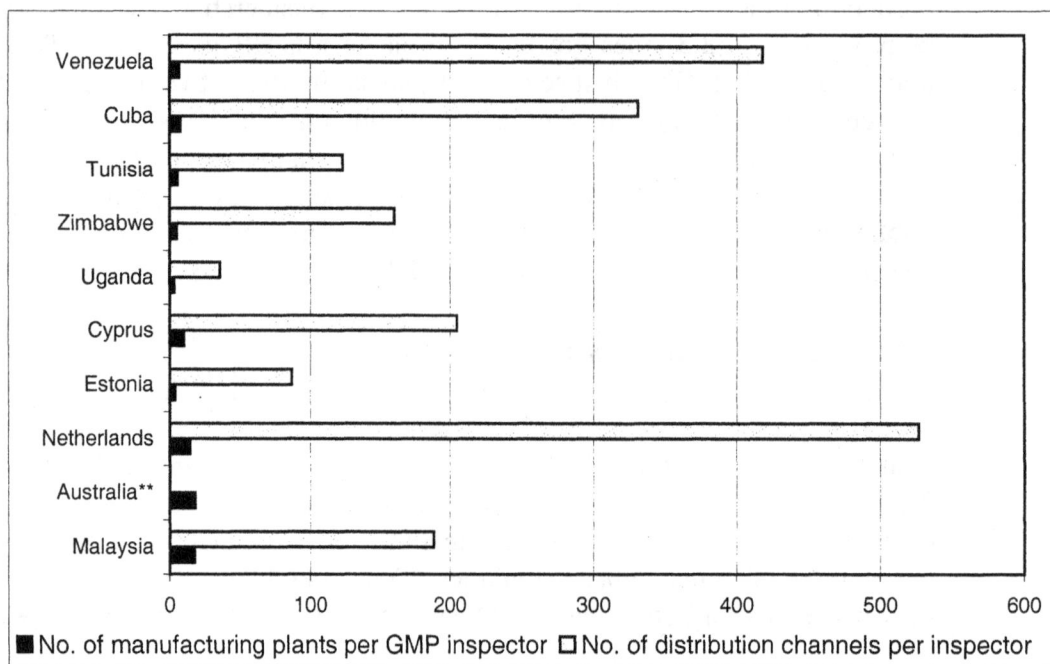

* Distribution channels — includes all types of drug outlet.
** For Australia, no data are available about the number of distribution-channel inspectors.

7.3 Paying for inspection

The financing of inspection activities is basically the same as the financing of overall regulatory functions (see Chapter 5). Budgets for GMP and distribution-channel inspection—irrespective of whether they are allocated separately—are allocated in the same way as budgets for licensing, with the exception of the Netherlands. In the Netherlands, GMP inspection activities are funded by a combination of fees and Government budget, while inspections of distribution channels are financed solely from the Government budget.

In Australia, Malaysia, the Netherlands, Uganda and Zimbabwe, a fee is charged for GMP inspections. Uganda and Zimbabwe also charge fees for inspection of distribution channels. The fee system in Australia is based on the number of hours staff spend on an inspection, whereas the other countries charge a fixed rate (see Table 5.5).

7.4 Planning, process and performance

7.4.1 Planning and implementation of plan

The survey showed that all the countries have planned GMP inspections. These plans are generally based on regulatory requirements relating to frequency of inspection. For instance, in the Netherlands, manufacturing plants are inspected at least once every two years. For Venezuela, the plan is activity-based: it is set in terms of the number of inspections to be conducted per month. But most drug regulatory authorities determine statutory frequencies for GMP inspection by considering the number of manufacturing plants.

The TGA uses a more refined system for setting inspection frequency, based on product type and on manufacturer type. The risk-management approach applied to licensing is also applied to GMP inspection. Products are classified according to their relative "risk", i.e. as high-risk, medium-risk or low-risk. Similarly, manufacturers are classified by their GMP compliance, i.e. acceptable, marginal or unacceptable GMP. The frequency of GMP inspection then depends on which category a particular product or manufacturer belongs to. Frequent inspections are made of plants producing high-risk products, and of manufacturers with marginal or unacceptable GMP compliance. Figure 7.4 shows GMP compliance status in Australia from 1994 to 1998. [The number of manufacturers with unacceptable GMP dropped to almost zero (0.9%) in 1997/98.]

Figure 7.4   Status of GMP compliance in Australia, 1994-98

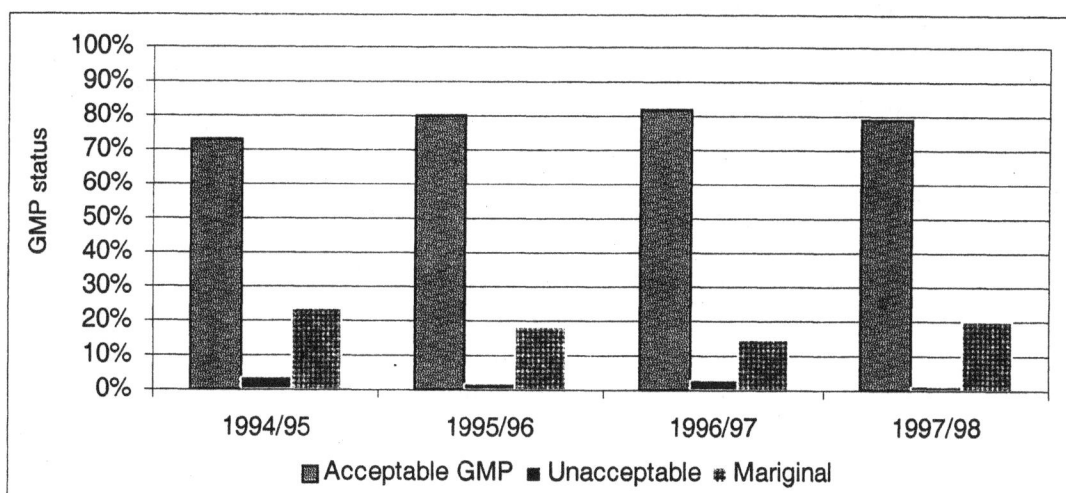

In Malaysia, inspections are scheduled by the category of product — i.e. whether the product is low-risk, medium-risk or high-risk — and the manufacturer's GMP compliance status (categorized as good, marginal or low). Schedules for routine inspections are prepared yearly and monitored six-monthly under the Quality Assurance Programme. Malaysia also has a strategy for improving GMP compliance, particularly aimed at those applicants who wish to set up new premises or renovate existing facilities. The DRA has established a one-stop information centre for customer-friendly services. In addition, dialogue sessions are held with the various manufacturers and associations.

Information on implementation of GMP inspection plans is available in only some of the countries. Where data exist, they indicate that plans were successfully followed or even exceeded their targets. This applies to Cuba, Malaysia, the Netherlands, Uganda, Venezuela and Zimbabwe. For Cyprus, however, inspections of domestic plants fell short of the planned values. Cyprus has 10 domestic manufacturers, and nine inspections were planned, but in 1997 only seven were carried out. The Netherlands has 86 manufacturers and 28 inspections were planned in 1998; all of them were carried out. Venezuela has 41 manufacturers and 23 inspections were planned in 1997, of which 35 were carried out. So a low implementation rate does not necessarily indicate a low inspection rate. Enforcement measures are available in case of non-compliance in Cyprus, Estonia, Malaysia, Tunisia, Uganda, Venezuela and Zimbabwe. In Cuba, no enforcement measures are specified for failure to comply with GMP standards.

Comparatively speaking, there is less likely to be a workplan for inspection of distribution channels than there is for GMP inspection. Only four countries — Cyprus, Estonia, Uganda and Venezuela — carry out inspection of distribution channels based on such a plan.

The range of enforcement measures following violation of distribution-channel regulations includes: warnings; fines; suspension of licence; closure; and imprisonment. Cypriot inspectors, however, do not have as many options as their counterparts in other countries: they can either issue a warning, or refer violations to the courts (through the police) or to the Pharmacy Board, depending on the seriousness of the offence.

Box 2

Strategies used by the DRA of Malaysia to improve GMP compliance

- one-stop information centre for customer-friendly services
- technical guidance
- dialogue sessions and regular training for industry personnel
- Technical Working Group on GMP, including NPCB and industry representatives
- recommendation of sources of financial support for manufacturers seeking to improve their GMP status
- encouragement of foreign partnerships for transfer of technology and "smart" alliance

---

7.4.2 Compliance and law enforcement

Figures 7.5a and 7.5b below provide information on the number of manufacturing plants and distribution outlets monitored, violations found and sanctions imposed. The data indicate the scope of monitoring, the seriousness of violations and the severity of the sanctions imposed.

Figure 7.5a indicates the total number of licensed manufacturing plants, GMP inspection coverage, number of violations detected and number of sanctions imposed. The ratio between the number of manufacturing plants inspected in a given year and the total number of manufacturing plants for these countries indicates a range of approximately 22% of manufacturing plants inspected in Zimbabwe (the lowest) to 100% in Australia and Cuba (the highest). The percentage of violations in the manufacturing plants inspected varied widely, from around 1% in Australia to 60% in Uganda and 83% in Estonia. Although GMP standards and criteria for determining the degree of compliance differ from country to country, these figures reflect the serious problems of GMP implementation in countries such as Estonia, Uganda and Venezuela and the effectiveness of GMP inspection in Australia. As indicated earlier, data on the coverage of distribution-channel inspections, the number of violations detected and sanctions imposed were not readily available for every country. Figure 7.5b gives only a partial picture of the situation. In 1997, for instance, Estonia's coverage for distribution-channel inspection was relatively high (63% of total licensed channels). Venezuela, on the other hand, inspected only around 14% of its distribution channels. In terms of violations, data from a number of countries show higher figures for sanctions than for violations. This may be due to the fact that one violation leads to more than one sanction. For example, a warning letter may be issued immediately after a violation has been detected, to be followed by other sanctions such as seizure of products or a fine. In addition, since these are cross-sectional figures, they may include carry-over cases from the previous year.

Figure 7.5a   GMP inspections, violations and sanctions, 1997

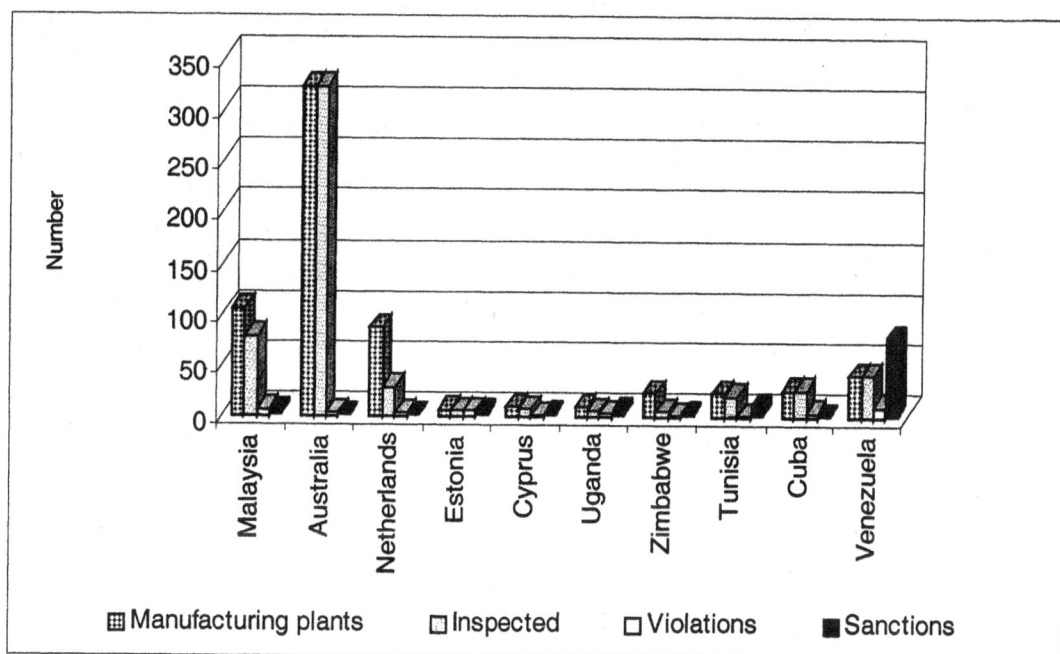

Figure 7.5b   Inspection of distribution channels in four countries: coverage, violations and sanctions, 1997*

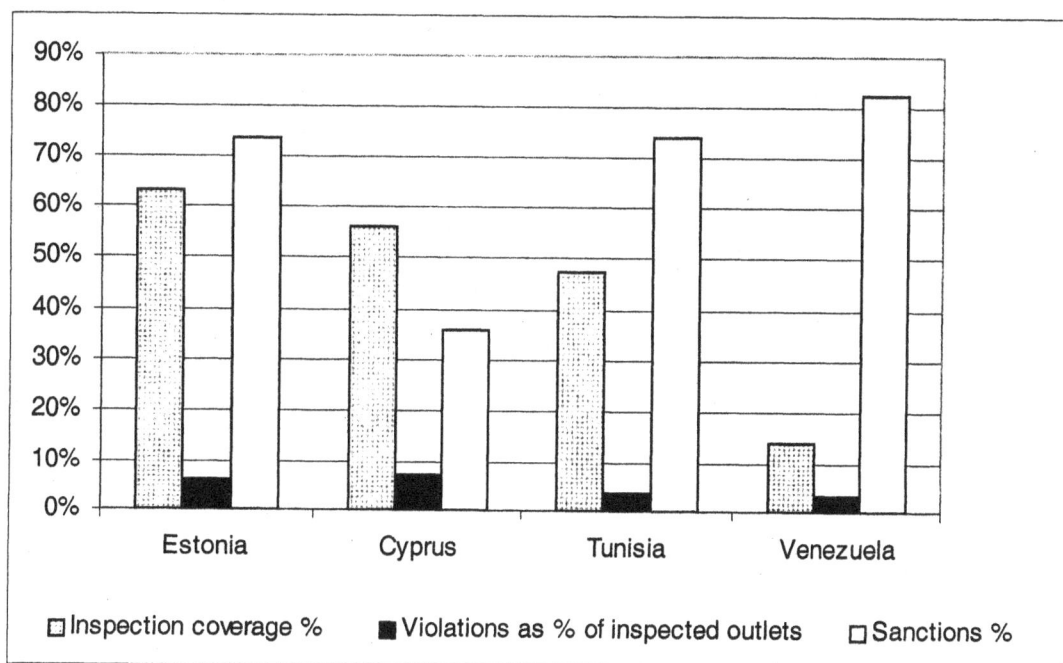

*   Violation data only for importers/wholesalers (data for the other countries not available).

The types of violation found by inspecting distribution channels, and the types of enforcement measure used by countries are summarized in Table 7.2.

Table 7.2   Types of violation and enforcement measures

Types of violation	Types of enforcement measure
• Unlicensed pharmaceutical premises	• Warning letters
• Premises operated without professionals	• Seizure of products
• Unrenewed/expired licence	• Product confiscation
• Counterfeit products	• Product destruction
• Illegally imported products	• Public admonition
• Expired products being sold	• Fines
• Unregistered products on the market	• Temporary/permanent closure
• Products stored under improper conditions	• Suspension of licence
• Sale of those products not authorized in that establishment	• Revocation of licence
• No record-keeping/book-keeping	• Imprisonment
• Dispensing prescription products without prescription	
• Absenteeism	

7.4.3 Audit system

Only four of the 10 countries—Australia, Estonia, Malaysia and the Netherlands —operate an audit system to evaluate the GMP performance of inspectors or the inspectorate. Auditing of distribution-channel inspection is carried out by Malaysia, the Netherlands, Uganda and Venezuela. In Australia, GMP audit is both internal and external, and involves an extensive review of process and technical approach. Further training, advice, revision of job description, legal proceedings and dismissal of inspectors are some of the means used to correct any weaknesses observed.

8. Product assessment and registration

Product assessment and registration (also known as marketing authorization and product licensing) are carried out by drug regulatory authorities to ensure that a pharmaceutical product has been adequately tested and evaluated for safety, efficacy and quality and that the product information provided by the manufacturer is accurate. They involve evaluating technical and administrative data submitted about a drug product, deciding whether to approve or reject the product, issuing a marketing authorization (certificate) and conducting ADR monitoring. The overall process requires a legal foundation, an adequate number of qualified staff, sustainable resources, a data retrieval system and a system to ensure freedom from conflicts of interest, accountability and transparency. GMP inspection and QC services are also necessary to ensure that GMP requirements are adhered to and to carry out quality testing. This chapter describes the drug assessment and registration situation in the 10 countries.

8.1 Power and process

An official product assessment and registration system for pharmaceuticals exists in each of the 10 countries. Their functions are determined by legal provisions. Systems for registration of pharmaceutical products came into operation at quite different times in the 10 countries — as early as 1942 in Tunisia and as late as 1993 in Uganda. Some of the systems have evolved in response to drug-related crises such as the thalidomide disaster, public pressure to expand the scope of drug assessment and the pressure from industry and consumers to expedite the registration process.

8.1.1 Scope of product assessment and registration
A review of the country reports indicates that each country requires registration of some categories of pharmaceutical products, but not others. Countries define regulation differently, depending on such factors as historical development, major adverse drug accidents, political influence, industry influence and regulatory capacity. For example, herbal medicines are registered in Australia, Malaysia, the Netherlands and Venezuela, but are not registered in Cuba, Cyprus, Estonia or Zimbabwe. In Australia, Malaysia and the Netherlands, the drug laws require herbal and homeopathic medicines to be registered. In Uganda and Zimbabwe, veterinary drugs, but not traditional medicines, are subject to registration.

Assessment and registration are not the same for all categories of products, even in the same country. How extensive the assessment should be depends on a number of factors and varies from country to country. For instance, in Australia, the potential risks of the product and the availability of human resources are taken into account in setting priorities and deciding the depth of the review. On the basis of these parameters, prescription products, some specific alternative products and some medical devices are subject to extensive pre-marketing evaluation and registration to ensure safety, efficacy and quality. Low-risk products are evaluated only for safety. For some product groups, the manufacturer's declaration of safety is accepted and the product is then subjected to more intensive post-marketing checks, as necessary.

In addition to exemptions based on type, products may also be exempted from registration on the basis of their source. In Cyprus, for example, drugs manufactured or imported by the Government need not be registered. In Australia, drugs produced by unincorporated companies and not traded between states are not registered or controlled. Similarly, drugs for export are not evaluated to the same extent as those sold in Australia.

8.1.2 Changes in scope and process

The scope and process of registration may change over time owing to changes in government policy, political considerations or industry or consumer pressure. In recent decades, three key changes in the registration of pharmaceutical products have occurred in many countries. These are: expansion of the scope of registration; introduction of a fast-track process; and institution of time-limit requirements.

Expansion of scope of registration

New drug laws were introduced in Malaysia in the mid-1980s, which revised registration procedures and greatly expanded the scope of registration. Under the new laws, traditional medicines, veterinary medicines, cosmetics and pharmaceutical raw materials must all now be registered. The new laws were phased in gradually, so that the pharmaceutical industry could prepare for the new legal requirements and regulators could prepare themselves for their additional responsibilities. Implementation of the new laws, which started in 1985, was carried out in four phases. The initial two phases of registration, covering scheduled and non-scheduled drugs, have been successfully completed. The third phase of registration, which started in 1992, covers registration of traditional medicines. The final phase — Phase 4 — covering registration of cosmetics started in 2001. Regulatory control will be extended later to cover medical devices, veterinary medicines and pharmaceutical raw materials.

In Australia, there was considerable political debate about the extension of registration to cover herbal products and vitamin supplements. Politicians who opposed the idea of regulation of non-prescription drugs, as well as those who supported the establishment of appropriate standards of evidence for the efficacy and safety of such products, showed great interest in the issue. In general, consumer groups were in favour of ensuring the quality of non-prescription products, although it has also been suggested that the registration process will hamper the consumer's right to self-medication. The Complementary Medicines Evaluation Committee was established in 1998 for the further development of appropriate standards for evaluation and registration of non-prescription products.

Fast-track registration

In many countries, a fast-track registration system has been introduced as a result of pressure on the DRA from both the consumer and the client. Consumer groups, especially those involved with HIV/AIDS issues, have demanded that products with potential for the treatment of currently incurable diseases should be approved rapidly. The pharmaceutical industry, eager to introduce new products to the market, has been keen to reduce the costs resulting from delays in registration. In other countries, accelerated registration procedures have been introduced to serve the government's need to make certain drugs available to the public more quickly.

Fast-track registration systems now exist in Australia, Cyprus, Estonia, Malaysia, the Netherlands, Tunisia and Zimbabwe (see Table 8.1), although probably not all of them were established as a result of political pressure. Different fast-track systems serve different purposes. In Australia, Cyprus and Malaysia, fast-track registration is intended to facilitate the assessment and registration of new drugs for treating serious, life-threatening diseases or conditions. In Malaysia, pharmaceutical entities can be registered for additional indications more quickly. The Netherlands has a fast-track registration system for clones and products qualifying for parallel importation. Estonia allows drugs approved by the European Commission to be registered through its fast-track system. In Tunisia and Zimbabwe, fast-track procedures are linked to government procurement. Each fast-track system is, therefore, a mechanism for modifying regulatory procedures in order to accommodate other government policies.

In Venezuela, there is no official fast-track system. However, "brief-mode" registration is available for generic products for which a bioavailability study has been undertaken. Similarly, Malaysia has an "abridged procedure" for registration of products classified as non-scheduled poisons. This type of simplified procedure does not, in essence, differ from the use of less stringent registration requirements for certain categories of products as seen, for example, for herbal medicines in Australia and the Netherlands.

Time-limits

In many countries the pharmaceutical industry has pushed for time-limits for registration as a means of making regulatory agencies more accountable. The country reports indicate that time-limits operate in all the countries with respect to assessment and notification of the results of applications for registration. However, among the 10 countries, only Australia, Cuba, Cyprus, Estonia, Malaysia and the Netherlands have included time-limits in their drug legislation. In Australia, Malaysia and the Netherlands, different time-limits have been set for registration of different types of products (new chemical entities, generic drugs and fast-track drugs). In Cuba, Cyprus, Estonia and Venezuela, a single time-limit has been set for all products. In practice, the average time taken to register a product containing a new chemical entity (NCE) ranges from six to 19 months, from two to 18 months for generic drugs and from two to six months for fast-track products (see Table 8.1).

Countries vary in their policy towards the application of sanctions if the regulatory authorities do not meet the time-limit for processing applications and notifying the result to the applicant. In Cyprus, the time-limit has been established by legislation, but no sanction is in fact applied if the time-limit is not met by the authority. In Malaysia, there are no statutory sanctions — applicants can only resort to lodging a complaint with the authority. A similar situation applies in the Netherlands. However, in Australia (in the case of a category 3 minor-variation application only) and Venezuela, the drug in question is automatically considered as registered if the time-limit is passed and no official decision has been made. In between these two extremes lies a range of variation. In Cuba, negotiations would take place between the parties involved. In Estonia, the applicant could ultimately take legal action against the DRA, although this has never been done in practice.

Table 8.1   Drug assessment and registration structures and processes

	Australia	Cuba	Cyprus	Estonia	Malaysia	Netherlands	Tunisia	Uganda	Venezuela	Zimbabwe
Standard application form	●	●	●	●	●	●	●	●	●	●
SOPs for staff	●	●	□	●	●	●	●	□	●	□
Written criteria for registration	●	●	●	●	●	●	●	●	●	●
External expert/ committee support	●	●	●	●	●	●	●	●	●	●
Final decision-maker	Dept. Secretary or delegate	NCDQC	Drug Council	SAM	DCA	MEB	Min. of Health	Committee	RBPP	MCAZ
Document of approval issued	●	●	●	●	●	●	●	●	●	●
Registration valid for (years)	Indefinite	5	5	5 & 3	5	5	5	1	7	Indefinite
Re-registration	●	●	□	□	-	□	□	□	□	□
DRA initiates re-evaluation	●	●	●	●	●	●	●	●	●	●
Fast-track registration	●	□	●	●	●	●	●	□	□	●
Criteria for combination products	●	□	●	●	●	□	●	□	●	●
Fees	●	●	●	●	●	●	●	●	●	●
Months taken to assess new drugs	12-16	12	5	9	6	19	18	6	6	18
Months taken to assess generic drugs	6	6	5	9	6	19	6	6	2	18
Months taken to assess fast-track products	N/A	N/A	3	1	6	2	3	6	1	6

● = Yes   □= No   - = information or data not applicable

In Australia, the authority would have to forfeit 25% of its fee in all cases except that of a minor variation, which would be automatically registered on expiry of the time limit, as described above.

8.1.3 Registration requirements and process
Information required and degree of assessment

Applications for registration of pharmaceutical products are classified in different categories, for example, products containing new chemical entities, generic products, fast-track products, applications for variation and applications for renewal. The requirements for these categories of application differ from country to country and even within the same country. In Australia and the Netherlands, new chemical entities are fully evaluated and dossier requirements are similar to those of the European Union, namely administrative information, chemical and pharmaceutical information, pharmacological-toxicological data and clinical data. In Malaysia, in addition to documentation supporting safety, efficacy and quality, the applicant's company incorporation or registration certificate, a letter of authorization from the manufacturer (if the applicant is not the manufacturer), a Certificate of Free Sale from the country of manufacture and a GMP certificate are also requested. In Estonia, in addition to submission of documentation supporting safety, efficacy and quality, the applicant must be resident in Estonia.

For non-prescription and generic drugs, the documentation required is simplified and is mostly concerned with chemical and pharmaceutical data. In general, the documentation required for registering products containing new chemical entities is more extensive than that for products in other categories (see Table 8.2). Countries that have the capacity to make an independent assessment of the safety, efficacy and quality of products, such as Australia, Estonia and the Netherlands, do not request the WHO-recommended Certificate of Pharmaceutical Product. Only Cyprus and Tunisia request price information.

Ensuring transparency

Registration requirements, SOPs and decision criteria are documented to ensure transparency of the regulatory process and to facilitate communication between the regulatory authority, the pharmaceutical industry and the public.

While written application forms for registration are used in all countries, only seven countries have a written SOP for staff involved in drug registration (see Table 8.1). In Cyprus, Uganda and Zimbabwe, the absence of a written SOP probably reflects the fact that only a few staff are responsible for registration. In Cyprus, the two pharmacists working in the DCQSS carry out not only registration and licensing, but also GMP inspections. They do not have either a job description or an SOP. In Zimbabwe, a total of nine technical and professional staff perform multiple regulatory functions for the Medicines Control Agency. All 10 countries have documented their criteria for assessing a registration application.

Decision-making

As shown in Table 8.1, all the countries employ an expert committee to support their assessment of applications for registration. The structures and roles of the committees vary between the countries, however. Those drug regulatory authorities with a board or a mixed/hybrid structure possess final decision-making powers, while for drug regulatory authorities with a departmental structure, the final decision-making power normally rests with the head of the department, unless it is delegated. In Australia, the legal power to make the final decision resides with the Secretary of the Department of Health. However, the Secretary has delegated the decision-making authority to senior technical staff within the TGA.

Table 8.2 *Technical information and documentation required for registration of products containing new chemical entities*

	Australia	Cuba	Cyprus	Estonia	Malaysia	Netherlands	Tunisia	Uganda	Venezuela	Zimbabwe
Product characteristics and label	●	●	●	●	●	●	●	●	●	●
Chemical/pharmaceutical information	●	●	●	●	●	●	●	●	●	●
Clinical data	●	●	●	●	●	●	●	●	●	●
Pharmacological and toxicological data	●	●	●	●	●	●	●	●	●	●
GMP certificate	●	●	●	●	●	●	●	●	●	●
WHO-type certificate for imported products	□	●	●	□	●	□	●	●	●	●
Manufacturing process	●	●	●	●	●	●	●	●	●	●
Quality certificate for raw materials	●	●	●	●	□	●	●	●	●	●
Quality specification for containers	●	●	●	●	●	●	●	●	●	●
Bioavailability data	●	□	●	●	●	●	●	●	●	●
Stability data	●	●	●	●	●	●	●	●	●	●
Applicant information	●	●	●	●	●	●	●	●	●	●
Samples for analysis	●	●	●	●	●	●	●	●	●	●
Price information	□	□	●	□	□	□	●	□	□	□

● = Yes □ = No

Registration validity and review

Once an application has been approved for registration, an official document is generally issued to the applicant upon payment of a registration fee, to prove that the drug may be sold. The period of validity of the registration licence or certificate varies. Australia and Zimbabwe allow a "life-long" licence, while other countries set a time-limit. In Australia and Zimbabwe, mechanisms other than licence renewal are used to evaluate the product. In Australia, a new product is reviewed for safety every year during its first three years on the market. Thereafter it is reviewed if a new application is made or a question of safety arises. In Uganda and Zimbabwe, an annual retention system operates for all registered pharmaceutical products (although documentation is not reviewed). If the retention fee is paid late or not at all, fines will be imposed or the product removed from the registry. In all the countries, registration agencies have the authority to initiate a change in the registration status of a pharmaceutical product. In other words, they can take regulatory action following evaluation of an individual drug or product category (see Table 8.1).

Appeals system

There is an appeals system for resolving disputes about registration decisions in each of the 10 countries. Some countries have a number of levels of mechanism for the settlement of disputes. Under these systems, the first step is usually submission of a complaint to the registration body or the supervisory body for a new ruling. If the new ruling is not satisfactory, the case can be forwarded to another level, which may be an independent administrative court, as is the case in Australia, Estonia, the Netherlands and Zimbabwe. In others, the registration body and/or ministry also has the power to determine whether the previous decision should be overturned (see Table 8.3).

Table 8.3   Appeals system

Country	Appellate body
Australia	First level: Minister of Health Second level: Administrative Appeals Tribunal Third level: court
Cuba	Minister of Health
Cyprus	Minister of Health
Estonia	First level: Registration Committee Second level: administrative court
Malaysia	Minister of Health
Netherlands	First level: MEB Second level: administrative court
Tunisia	Minister of Health
Uganda	National Drug Authority
Venezuela	Minister of Health Revisory Board of Pharmaceutical Products (JRPF)
Zimbabwe	Medicines Control Agency administrative court

8.2 Human resources

In each country, management of human resources for registration operates on the same basis as for the entire regulatory authority.

Figure 8.1 shows the number and proportion of professional and administrative staff responsible for registration, and the equivalent number of full-time personnel. For part-timers, if there are no data on the amount of work-time, it has been assumed that they work half-time (0.5). For Cyprus and Zimbabwe, where staff perform multiple functions, the total numbers of staff have been used.

The Australian TGA is by far the largest in terms of the number of staff. Venezuela and the Netherlands rank second and third, respectively. Cyprus has the smallest number of registration staff—two pharmacists and three administrative staff—who are also responsible for licensing and GMP inspection. Of all the drug regulatory authorities, only those of Australia, Cyprus and Tunisia have more administrative staff than professional staff. The drug regulatory authorities of Estonia, Uganda and Zimbabwe do not employ administrative staff for the registration unit, and it is not clear whether administrative matters are handled by the professionals.

All the countries use external experts or committees to help with the assessment of applications. However, their number and area of expertise differ from country to country. In most countries, the experts merely provide advice, while in some they also have a decision-making role. From the point of view of management, it would be interesting to analyze the assignment of technical and administrative tasks among the staff and its effect on efficiency. Such data are not, however, available in the present study.

Figure 8.1   Human resources for registration, 1998*

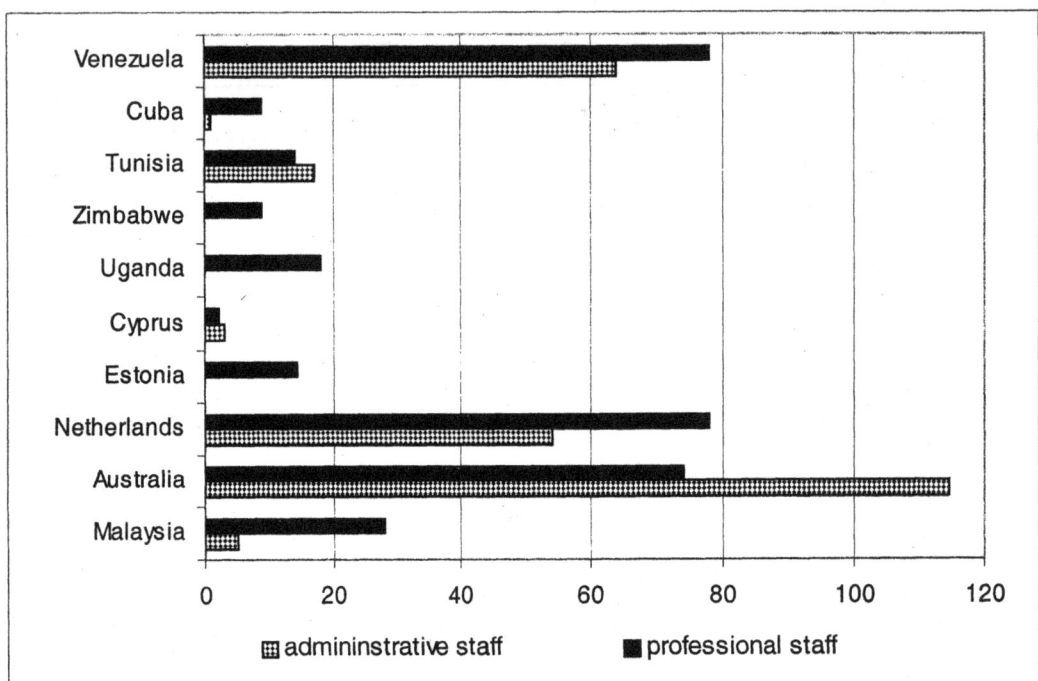

* No administrative staff for Estonia, Uganda and Zimbabwe

8.3 Paying for registration

The unit responsible for assessment and registration generally comes within the same organizational structure as other drug regulatory units. The financing of the registration function in each of the countries is therefore the same as the financing of other regulatory functions, as discussed in Chapter 5.

Each of the countries collects fees for carrying out registration. Different rates generally apply for registration of products in different categories. Registration fees for new chemical entities are higher than those for generic and fast-track products. Some countries—Uganda and Zimbabwe, for example—have different rates for domestic and foreign products. For instance, Zimbabwe charges US$1 000 for an imported product and only about US$40 for a domestic product (see Table 5.5).

Registration fees vary significantly between countries (see Figure 8.2). Registering a new drug can cost the applicant as much as US$120 000 in Australia or as little as US$100 in Malaysia. The fees charged by the Australian TGA are eight times higher than those charged by the MEB in the Netherlands, even though both countries request similar documentation and both perform an independent assessment.

Figure 8.2   Fees charged for registration of products containing new chemical entities

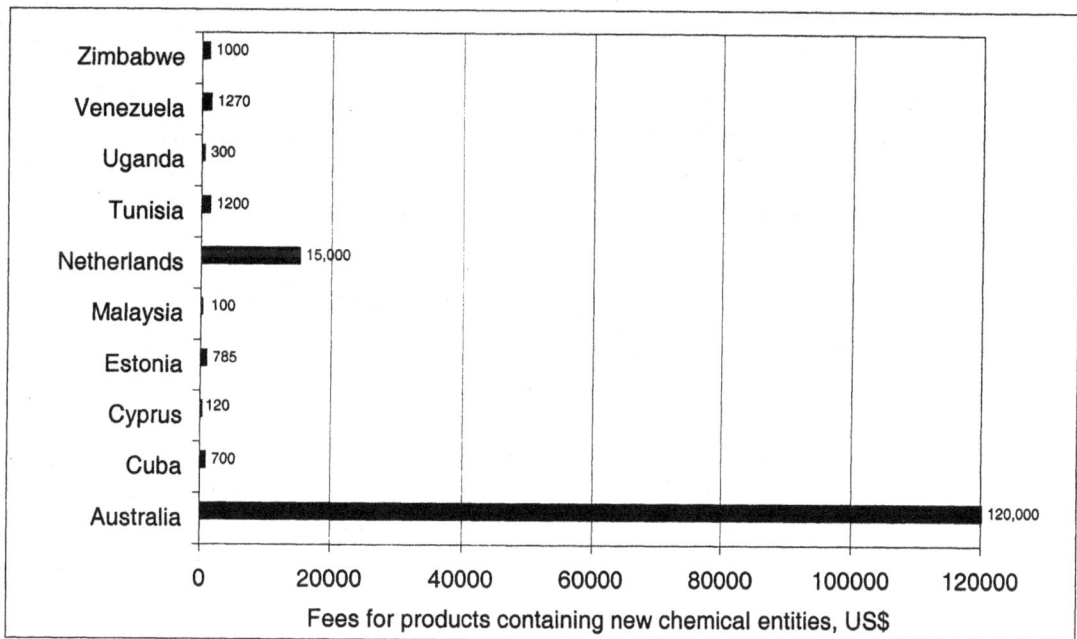

As indicated in Chapter 5, the Zimbabwean and Australian drug regulatory authorities rely entirely on the fees they charge for their services to cover all their operating costs. The level of registration varies enormously between the two countries and probably reflects significant differences in regulation costs. The MCAZ has only 51 staff, whereas the Australian TGA has 500 (Table 5.3). And only nine people are responsible for multiple regulatory functions, including registration, at the Medicines Control Agency, while 188 people (full-time equivalent) carry out registration for the TGA. Salary level is another key determinant of fee level. Information on the average salary of registration staff was not available for this study, but the salary of inspectors provides some insight. A GMP inspector at the TGA earns 10 times more than his/her Zimbabwean counterpart.

Despite their high level, the fees charged by the TGA are based on an agreement between the Administration and the pharmaceutical industry. Although the Australian pharmaceutical industry pays high costs in terms of registration fees, it does not benefit in terms of registration time. Registration of a drug that contains a new chemical entity in Australia takes 12-16 months on an average (Figure 8.4).

8.4 Performance

Empirical data are rarely suitable for assessing the effectiveness of a system's outcomes and impacts on public health. Nonetheless, certain measures can serve as proxies for evaluating the efficacy of drug regulation.

From this set of comparative data, several parameters can be computed to allow an assessment of some aspects of regulatory impact. For example, assuming that similar products are put forward for assessment and registration, indicators such as registration approval and rejection rates, number of ADR reports per number of drugs registered and registration times can be used for quantitative comparison of registration systems. For other aspects, however, for which quantitative measurements are lacking, the analysis has to rely on qualitative descriptions, such as action taken on the basis of ADR reports, system transparency and customer satisfaction (3).

The following sections compare systems of product assessment in the 10 countries in terms of effectiveness, efficiency and transparency. However, the existing data allow only a partial, incomplete analysis.

8.4.1 Approval and rejection rates

The purpose of registration is to assess drugs for efficacy, safety and quality and to ensure that they are of an acceptable standard for use. When similar products are processed, the rates of registration approval and rejection reflect the ability of the registration system to prevent questionable products from gaining market access (3).

An application filed for registration may be approved or rejected, or withdrawn before the final decision is made. Data used for the analysis here have been computed from the number of new applications assessed, including those for which marketing authorization was issued or refused, or withdrawn prior to a final decision. The average figures for new applications for 1994-97 indicate that the Netherlands has the highest approval rate (95%), and Cuba the lowest (65%) (Figure 8.3). Approval rates range from 70% to 85% for most countries. Of the applications which were not approved for registration, some were rejected at the end of the process, and others withdrawn before the application reached the final stage, presumably because the applicants predicted a low probability of success. According to this set of data, applications filed in the Netherlands and Estonia are very rarely rejected.

In Estonia, however, as many as 17% of the applications are withdrawn from the process. Rejection rates are highest in Venezuela and Malaysia (30% and 29%, respectively). In both countries, withdrawal rates are small (0% and 3%, respectively). In Australia in particular, the number of applications withdrawn before a final decision has increased significantly in the past four years. This increase in withdrawals is probably a result of the way in which the registration system now operates, with a *proposed* decision to reject being made by the Delegate, prior to obtaining formal advice from the Australian Drug Evaluation Committee.

Figure 8.3   Approval/rejection/withdrawal rate of applications for registration

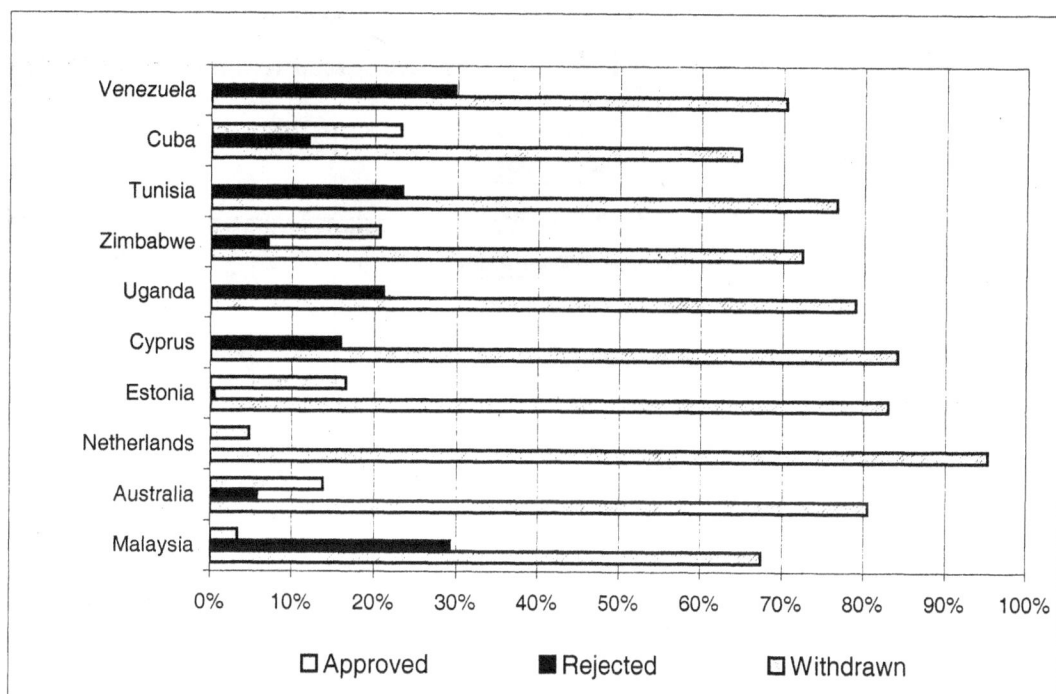

8.4.2 Registration time

The time taken to assess and register a product should be long enough to ensure that drugs are effectively assessed for safety, efficacy and quality. However, if this process takes too long, much-needed drugs will not be available and lives may be lost. Delay is also a disincentive to research and development. On the other hand, if too little time is allocated to these activities, the safety, efficacy and quality of drugs may be compromised, endangering the health of patients and the public.

This section examines the amount of time taken to register a pharmaceutical product—i.e. from the time an application is submitted to the time when the final decision is reached—and attempts to clarify how workload and fees affect registration time.

Total registration time

Figure 8.4 shows the average registration time for three categories of pharmaceutical products (products containing new chemical entities, generics and fast-track drugs) in the 10 countries, for 1994-97. In practice, registering a new drug takes 18 months in Tunisia and Zimbabwe and five months in Cyprus. The average time needed to register a generic product ranges from two to 18 months. In Cyprus, Estonia, Malaysia, the Netherlands, Uganda and Zimbabwe, the time taken to register a generic drug is no different from that taken to register a new drug. It takes about 18 months to register a generic product in the Netherlands and Zimbabwe. In general, a fast-track registration system shortens the registration process, particularly in Estonia, the Netherlands, Tunisia and Venezuela.

Figure 8.4 *Average time taken to register different categories of drug (months)*

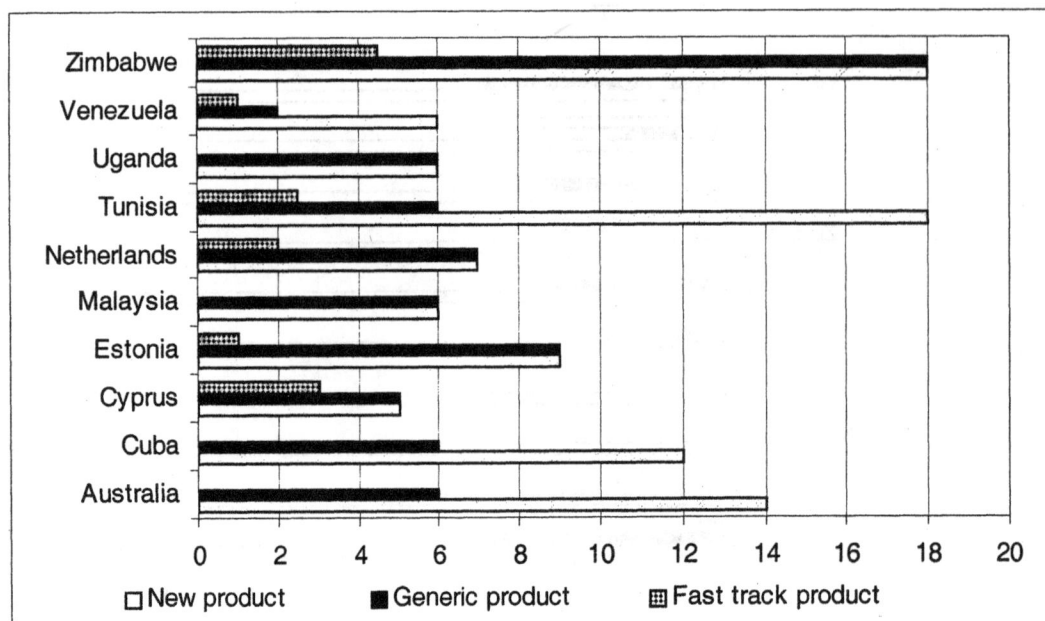

Chart legend: □ New product   ■ Generic product   ▦ Fast track product

Countries (top to bottom): Zimbabwe, Venezuela, Uganda, Tunisia, Netherlands, Malaysia, Estonia, Cyprus, Cuba, Australia

X-axis scale: 0, 2, 4, 6, 8, 10, 12, 14, 16, 18, 20

Registration workload

In order to assess the workload of staff in product assessment and registration, we took as a proxy the average number of applications during the period 1994-97 in the following categories: products containing new chemical entities, generics, fast-track registrations and variation registrations. It should be noted, however, that the data used for the analyses in this subsection and the next have limitations, for the following reasons:

- The number of applications used to calculate the registration figures does not include all applications dealt with by the registration staff, but only categories considered to require more intensive evaluation.

- The way in which tasks are assigned to staff differs greatly between the countries, making the computation of staff numbers not entirely comparable.

- The volume and complexity of the work carried out was not the same in all countries.

- The qualification and competence of the staff differs between countries.

- Some countries may carry out the assessment independently, while others request decisions from other countries, particularly for imported products.

- Work environments vary.

Such difficulties are common in comparative studies which use cross-country data. The graphs and discussion should therefore serve purely as an illustration of a conceptual approach for examining how workload, organization and financial factors can affect efficiency.

Figure 8.5 shows the number of applications per staff member (professional plus administrative staff) and the number of applications per professional staff member. The workload per person related to registration varies greatly among the drug regulatory authorities. Cyprus has the largest load per individual professional staff member, and ranks second in workload per staff member of any grade.

Figure 8.5   Registration workload

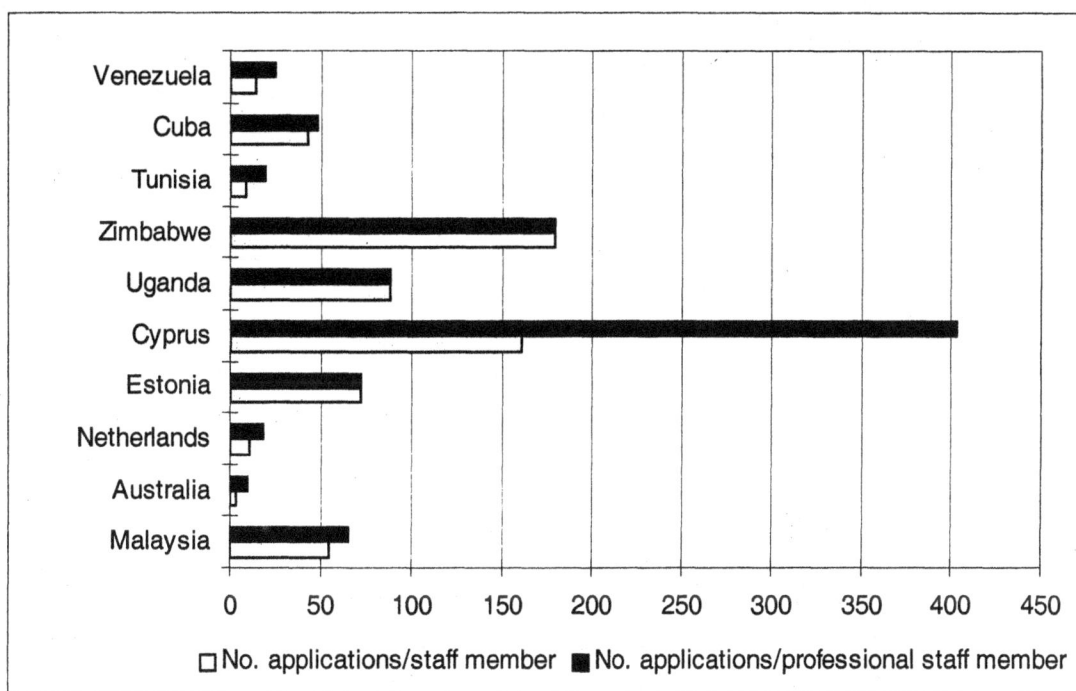

This is not surprising, considering that the DCQSS has only two pharmacists and three administrative staff, who carry out not only registration functions, but other regulatory functions as well. The same is true of Zimbabwe, where staff also work as inspectors. Conversely, staff working on product assessment and registration in the TGA in Australia and the MEB in the Netherlands have a comparatively light registration workload. This is because these authorities carry out their own assessments, i.e. they do not depend on information provided by other drug regulatory authorities (as Cyprus and Zimbabwe do). The volume and complexity of work to be done and hence the time required to assess one application will therefore be greater and the number of applications dealt with by one staff member correspondingly lower.

Effect of workload on registration time

Does workload affect the time taken for assessment and registration? Since the registration of products containing new chemical entities requires the most extensive review and expertise, it is used for this analysis. The data are the same as those presented in Figure 8.5.

Figure 8.6 is a scatter graph showing the average time (in months) taken to register new drugs and the number of applications per professional staff member involved in registration. Judging from the overall data, the number of applications per professional staff member does not appear to affect the average time taken for registering new drugs across the 10 countries.

Figure 8.6   Average time vs. number of applications per professional

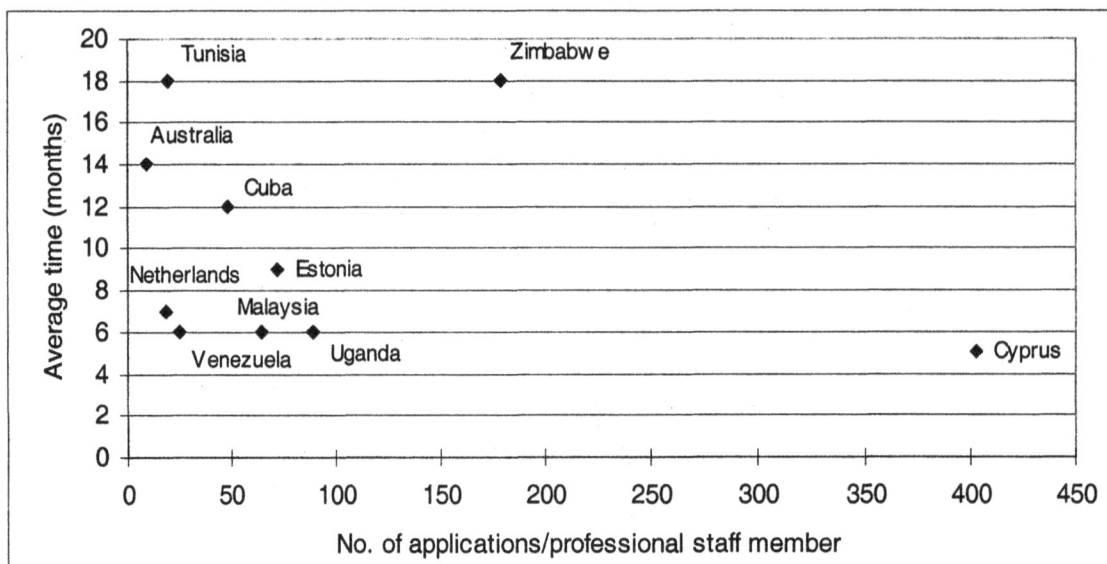

Effect of fees on registration time

Charging fees for registration is a policy set by law, or through negotiation as in the case of Australia. It is not intended as an instrument for expediting registration. However, it would be interesting to analyse whether higher fees do in fact facilitate the registration process in such a way as to shorten the total time taken.

Figure 8.7 plots registration fees against the average time taken to register a product containing a new chemical entity. Because the fees charged vary enormously between the countries, the figure shows a cluster of points representing countries charging relatively low registration fees, and two separate points, representing Australia and the Netherlands, which charge relatively higher fees.

It does not appear from the graph that the level of fees charged affects the registration time. Several reasons could account for this. Firstly, the registration function in the majority of countries is financed not by fees, but by government budget, so that the fee levels have little influence on how, or how quickly, the work is carried out in these countries. Secondly, the fees are fixed by policy, instead of reflecting the true costs involved.

It should be emphasized that the registration process must not be expedited at the expense of a thorough evaluation of the efficacy and safety of drugs. If fees are to be used as a tool to finance the registration process, they should be used to pay for resources — for example, expert reviewers — which enable applications to be adequately reviewed. Since the registration fee is negligible as a component of drug development and marketing costs, a higher fee should help provide the DRA with sufficient resources to retain competent staff and remunerate external experts, but without unduly increasing costs for either the pharmaceutical industry or the consumer.

Figure 8.7 **Average registration time vs. registration fees for new chemical entities**

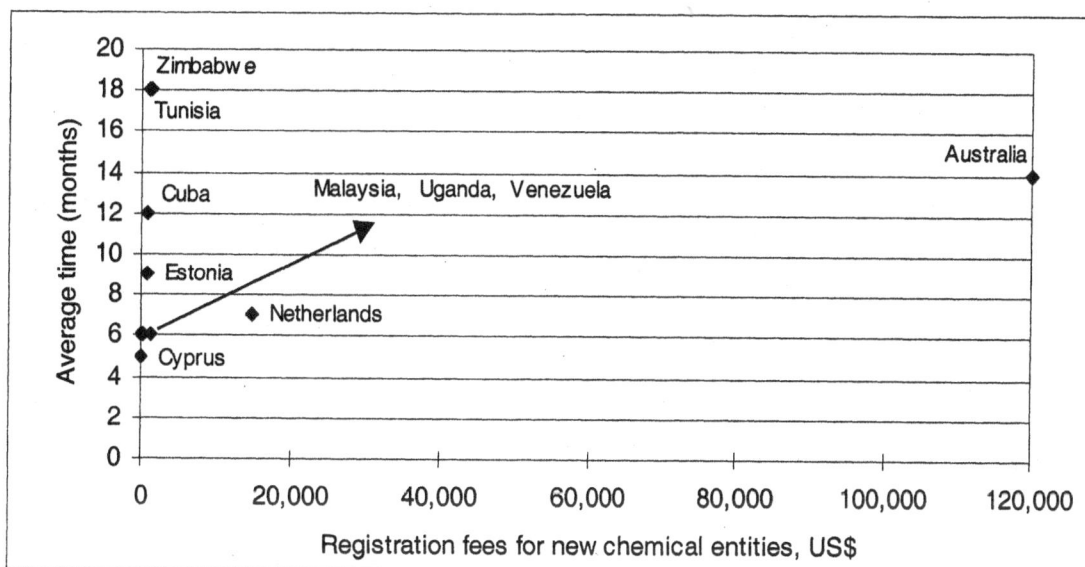

Effect of registration time on adequacy of drug evaluation

The above analyses treat registration time as an independent variable and ask whether other factors affect time taken for registration. Another question can be raised in relation to registration time as an independent variable: whether a shorter registration time risks compromising the adequacy of drug assessment for registration. In other words, is quality compromised for the sake of speed? The data from this comparative study are insufficient to answer this question: however, recent research in the United States of America found no evidence of a relationship between withdrawal of drugs from the market because of reported ADR and the expedited procedures for drug registration (28).

8.4.3 Transparency

Transparency refers to the degree of openness of the authority in its handling of the product assessment process, and its responsiveness to the concerns of clients and consumers. This area has been evaluated only qualitatively by the principal investigators.

The general assessment indicates that the pharmaceutical industry experiences problems with transparency of drug registration in two out of the 10 countries—Cyprus and Uganda. The main problems cited involve communication between the DRA and the industry regarding clarity of procedures and adequacy of official explanations for the rejection of an application. In Cyprus, the Drug Council also raised issues concerning the fairness of treatment of foreign versus domestic industry, and the arbitration of contradictory quality analysis results provided by different laboratories, both belonging to the Drug Council.

As shown in Table 8.1, all the countries have written registration application forms, as well as written criteria for drug assessment and registration. It is unclear, however, whether written documents detailing the registration procedures are available for the applicants, in addition to the application forms.

As for consumers, in the three countries where consumers might be considered to experience problems regarding transparency of registration (Australia, the Netherlands and Uganda), the problems cited related mainly to access to information from the DRA about drugs registered or registration decisions. But these seem to refer to communication problems between the DRA and the consumers, rather than to transparency in the strict sense.

Indeed, the major problems presented as problems of transparency, as perceived by the industry and consumers, appear to bear more relation to communication. Better communication, in the form of clearly written documents on processes and criteria, regular publications, face-to-face explanations and regular meetings, would doubtless help to ameliorate the perceived lack of transparency of the drug registration process.

8.5 Adverse drug reaction monitoring

Overseeing the conduct of clinical trials and monitoring adverse reactions to drugs are important mechanisms for assessing the safety and efficacy of pharmaceutical products. The former helps to ensure the integrity of research design and protect trial subjects from potential harm from new drugs. The latter is an essential form of post-marketing surveillance for drugs already on the market. The existence and operation of these two mechanisms are important components of drug regulation and reflect the authority's ability to regulate the entire process of pharmaceutical product assessment.

This section examines ADR monitoring systems in the 10 countries. An ADR monitoring model, as depicted in Figure 8.8, was developed for the analysis.

Figure 8.8   ADR monitoring model

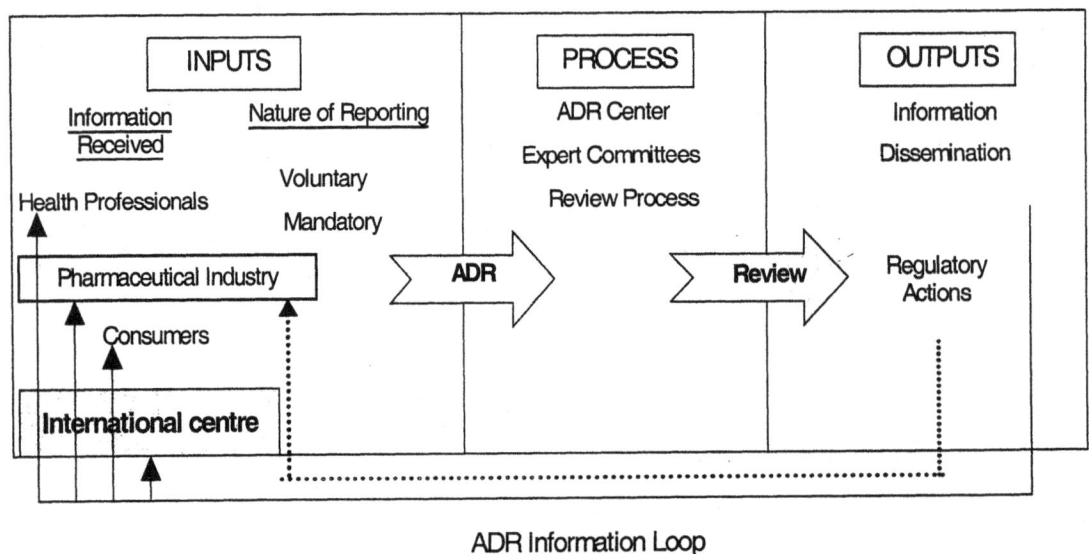

ADR Information Loop

8.5.1 ADR monitoring model

The model is based on an input–process–output framework. It basically addresses the following components of monitoring of ADR:

- **inputs**: how an ADR monitoring system acquires necessary information; who reports ADRs; whether reporting is voluntary or mandatory

- **process**: how ADR reports are handled; whether reports are validated; whether there is an expert committee to carry out validation

- **outputs**: what happens after the analysis; whether information from the review is fed back to the reporters; which parties receive the information; the kind of regulatory actions taken, if any, as a result of ADR review.

Information on drug reactions is the main input into the ADR monitoring system. The information may come from various sources, and by various means. Generally, health professionals — particularly physicians and pharmacists — are key persons in the discovery and preliminary identification of adverse reactions resulting from use of a drug. The marketing authorization holder, who possesses information on the ingredients of a product and the processes of manufacturing, packaging, storage and distribution, is another key source. In addition, multinational corporations should also have mechanisms for collecting information on the use of their products in the countries where they are marketed. Consumers can be considered another important source of information, since they experience any adverse effects at first hand. However, it can be difficult for consumers to identify an adverse reaction, and their accuracy of reporting may be doubtful, owing to the technical nature of pharmaceuticals.

ADR reporting may be either voluntary or obligatory. Spontaneous reporting by health professionals is often favoured, since it is very difficult to make reporting compulsory. But in many countries, considerations of ethical responsibility and/or technical expediency have inclined governments to make reporting mandatory for the holders of marketing authorizations.

The next element is processing ADR reports. Generally the ADR reports are sent to a single organization. The way the reports are handled there determines how effectively and fully the information will be used. Tracing and following up the incidents and identifying whether there is evidence for the effects of the drug in question helps to validate the information and establish the epidemiological pattern of adverse reactions.

A centralized system is more suitable for ADR monitoring than a decentralized system. The larger the number of reports a centre gathers, the easier it is to ensure accurate validation. Furthermore, organizing a single, centralized system facilitates the creation of a pool of expertise for analysing the reports. For the same reasons, an international centre, such as the WHO Collaborating Centre for International Drug Monitoring in Uppsala, Sweden, has a key role in ADR monitoring and assisting countries with collection of cross-national information and analysis.

The main aim of post-marketing surveillance is to enable identification of problematic products and to take action to prevent problems recurring. Results from the analysis of ADR reports should be used to raise awareness of the problem or potential problem among users and to serve as the basis for regulatory action, where appropriate. Conclusions from the ADR analysis should be disseminated to the parties involved, including the ADR reporters and marketing-authorization holders. The flow of ADR information should be a loop rather than one-way. If the problem is confirmed, regulatory action should be considered where applicable, and where deemed useful in preventing potential harm.

The ability of an ADR monitoring system to help prevent drug-induced injury depends on three factors:

- there must be a high probability that potential adverse drug effects will be identified and reported

- reports must be reviewed and validated by experts

- review results must be fed back to the relevant parties and appropriate regulatory action must be taken.

8.5.2 ADR monitoring systems at work

Uganda is the only one of the 10 countries that does not have a system for monitoring ADR. Each of the other nine countries uses a spontaneous reporting system for health professionals — i.e. health professionals send reports on a voluntary basis. Reporting by the pharmaceutical industry, by contrast, is mandatory in most of the countries. Australia, Cuba, Estonia, Malaysia, the Netherlands, Tunisia and Venezuela all require marketing authorization holders to report any ADRs for their drug products (see Table 8.4). In Cyprus and Zimbabwe, reporting by marketing authorization holders is voluntary. No data are available to evaluate the relative effectiveness of voluntary versus mandatory reporting by the pharmaceutical industry.

Consumer ADR reports are collected in the Netherlands, although as a result of consumer participation rather than by design. The drug information telephone line of the Royal Dutch Association for the Advancement of Pharmacy was initially created merely to provide information to the public on all aspects of drug use, but it has also become an additional source of ADR reports. In Australia, an ADR reporting system for consumers is planned.

In those countries where reports are evaluated and recorded, specialized bodies have been set up to review ADR reports. Each country has a different set of operating procedures for this body. In Australia, Malaysia and Zimbabwe, a specialized committee is employed as part of the DRA to carry out the review task. The Adverse Drug Reactions Advisory Committee in Australia, for example, has a system for following up and validating the reports, classifying the reported incidents as "possible", "probable" or "certain" and then referring them to the appropriate parties for further action.

The countries use similar means for disseminating information from the review. In Australia, Cyprus, Estonia and Venezuela, ADR information and the results of report evaluation are published in bulletins which are distributed to physicians and pharmacists. In Tunisia, such information is disseminated at health professionals' workshops. In Malaysia, review information is also sent to the reporters and the marketing authorization holders as information feedback. In every country, review information is forwarded to the DRA. Each of the countries also sends reports to the WHO Collaborating Centre for International Drug Monitoring.

Table 8.4 ADR monitoring systems

	Australia	Cuba	Cyprus	Estonia	Malaysia	Netherlands	Tunisia	Uganda	Venezuela	Zimbabwe
ADR monitoring system exists	●	●	●	●	●	●	●	□	●	●
Date of commencement	1968	1976	1997	1993	1987	1963	1990	□	1998	1994
Reporting by health professionals	Voluntary	Voluntary	Voluntary	Voluntary	Voluntary	Voluntary	Voluntary	□	Voluntary	Voluntary
Reporting by marketing authorization holder	Mandatory	Mandatory	Voluntary	iMandatory	Mandatory	Mandatory	Mandatory	□	Mandatory	Voluntary
Name of ADR Centre/dept. of DRA	●/ADRAC	National Centre for Pharm. Surveillance/●	DIPC/●	National Pharmaco-vigilance Centre/●	MADRAC/●	LAREB/No	National Pharmaco-vigilance Centre/●	□	CENAVIF/Yes	ADR Committee/●
Review process	●/ADRAC	-	-	●	●/ADR Advisory Committee	●	-	□	●/ CENAVIF	●/ ADR Committee
Information dissemination	Published & distributed to physicians	Report to MOH, DRA and industry	Reported to Drug Council Published in newsletters	Published in Drug Information Bulletin	Advised to DCA Feedback sent to registration holders	Info. to prescribers	Information disseminated in local workshops	□	DRA is informed Published in CENAVIF bulletin	Published in quarterly Drugs and Toxicology Bulletin
Reporting to WHO Centre	●	●	●	●	●	●	●	□	●	●
Regulatory actions taken	●, inclusion of ADR in product information, withdrawal	Some batches of drugs have been retained for quality control	None	□, decisions are based on international experience.	●, indication restrictions, inclusion of warnings, labelling changes	●, adaptations to the summary of product characteristics & patient leaflet, suspension/ withdrawal	●, withdrawal from registration & reclassifi-cation	□	●, prohibitions, restrictions on indications Suspension from market	●, drug recategorized, labelling modified, recalled, withdrawn

● = Yes   □ = No   - = data or information not available

Regulatory action has been taken in most countries as a result of ADR reports. This ranges from modification of drug labels, to reclassification, to withdrawal from the market.

In Estonia, however, regulatory action is not taken on the basis of ADR reports sent by health professionals. This is because the SAM considers that the small number of reports made in Estonia forms an inadequate basis for regulatory decision-making.

Since a large database of reports is essential to the verification of ADRs, the role of an international ADR centre in assisting drug regulation and drug use in member countries, particularly the smaller ones, cannot be overemphasized.

8.5.3 Performance

The voluntary nature of ADR reporting by health professionals means that the number of reports received by an ADR centre depends very much on the awareness and active participation of physicians, pharmacists and other health personnel. The number of ADR reports sent to the responsible bodies in these countries increased between 1994 and 1997. The Adverse Drug Reactions Advisory Committee in Australia receives the largest number of reports each year, with a four-year average of 8 354 reports. The Netherlands and Cuba rank a distant second and third (3 300 and 1 560 reports per year, respectively). The numbers of ADR reports received per year by responsible agencies in Cyprus, Estonia, Venezuela and Zimbabwe are strikingly small — less than 100 reports for all four countries. Figure 8.9 presents an overall picture of ADR reporting in these countries, with the average figures for 1994-97.

Figure 8.9   Average number of ADR reports received, 1994-97

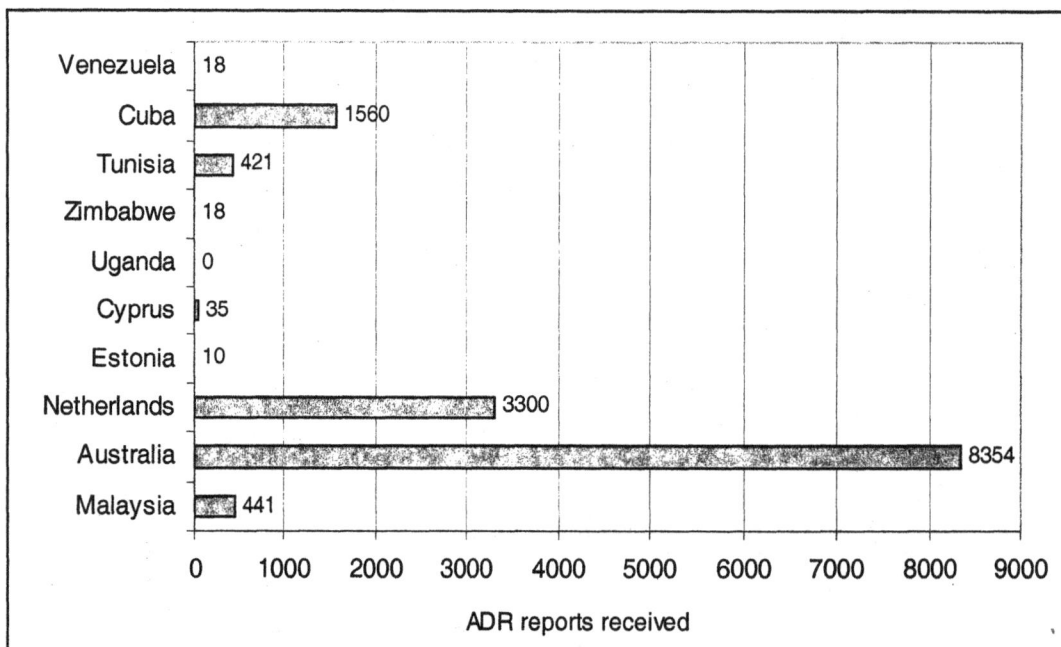

Because countries differ in the size of their human resources for health and in the number of drugs available to them, the performance of an ADR reporting system should be investigated in terms of both those variables. Two parameters were computed for the analysis: the ratio of the average number of ADR reports to the number of physicians and pharmacists; and the ratio of the average number of ADR reports to the number of drugs registered in each of the countries (Figure 8.10). For the first parameter, the Netherlands ranks first, with a ratio of 0.147, closely followed by Australia with a ratio of 0.142. Cuba has the largest number of reports per registered drug, followed by the Netherlands and Australia.

Figure 8.10   ADR reports per physician, pharmacist and number of registered drugs*

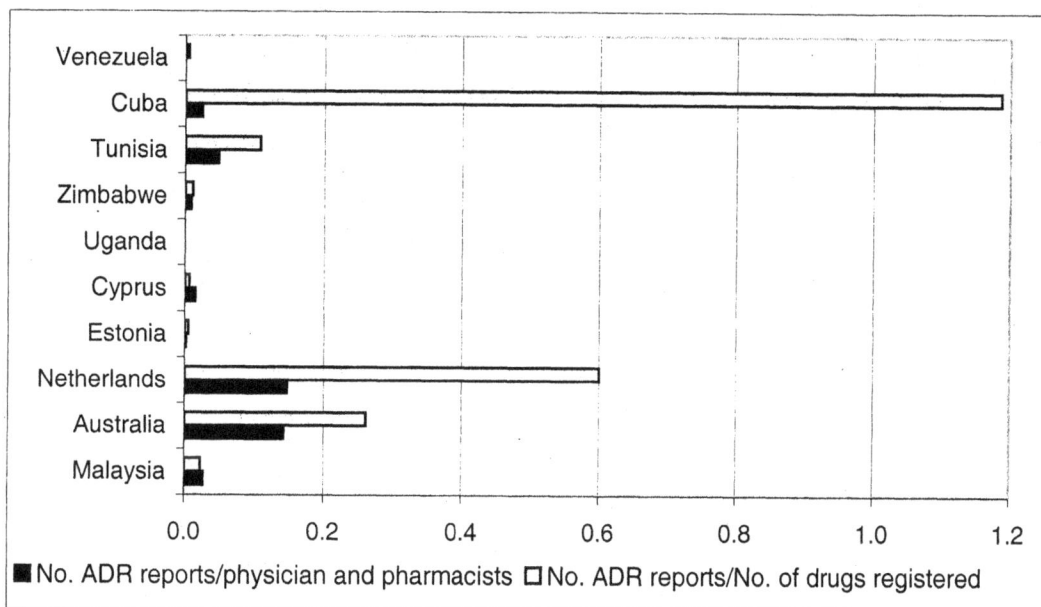

* There is no ADR monitoring in Uganda.

Although there are no set standards for estimating how many reports an ADR centre should receive, it is clear that the more reports the centre receives, the better the information available for evaluation. The large numbers of ADR reports received by centres in Australia, Cuba and the Netherlands certainly enable the experts to perform validation more effectively. But the number of reports received by the Australian Adverse Drug Reactions Advisory Committee, the highest among these countries, is much lower than that received by the MedWatch programme of the United States Food and Drug Administration (FDA), which receives on average more than 250 000 reports per year (25). The first parameter mentioned above — the number of reports per health professional — signifies another aspect of an ADR reporting system, namely the extent of participation by health professionals and other parties. Where this number is low, efforts should be made to increase awareness of and participation in reporting.

8.6 Clinical trials

8.6.1 Clinical trials regulation at work

The conduct of clinical trials is regulated in all the countries, except Cyprus. In Cyprus, the policy of the Ministry of Health is not to permit clinical trials for experimental medical products. Multicountry clinical trials for products licensed in developed countries are undertaken in some institutions and regulated by ethics committees (Table 8.5). In these countries, approval of clinical trials is carried out either by the DRA, as in Estonia, Malaysia, Tunisia, Venezuela and Zimbabwe, or by ethics committees. When the DRA itself is responsible for control, information about the trials is processed centrally. In Tunisia, clinical trials form part of the registration process. Trials are requested, when deemed necessary, by the specialized committee charged with reviewing the new drug. The trial proposal is then evaluated by the technical committee, and forwarded to the Health Minister for final approval. Cuba has a National Centre for the Coordination of Clinical Trials under the Ministry of Health, which performs clinical trials on drugs produced within the country.

Regulation of clinical trials through use of a specialized ethics committee at the trial site constitutes a decentralized approach. This approach is used in the Netherlands, where a local medical ethics committee at the site of the trial is responsible for the evaluation.

In Australia, approval of clinical trials involves both the regulatory authority and an ethics committee. Under the Clinical Trial Exemption (CTX) scheme, a clinical trial proposal must first be evaluated by the TGA, and then approved by an ethics committee on-site. Under the Clinical Trial Notification (CTN) scheme, a trial is evaluated and approved by the local ethics committee, and then notified to the TGA.

Differences in the systems used to regulate clinical trials in Australia and the Netherlands illustrate how the delegation of authority affects the ability of the central agency to monitor the working of the entire system. In Australia, all approved clinical trials must be notified to the TGA. There is no such reporting requirement for the MEB in the Netherlands. Information about the number and details of clinical trials conducted in the Netherlands is therefore not readily available to the MEB.

The majority of these countries have guidelines for evaluating clinical trial proposals. All of them are consistent with the Ethical Principles for Medical Research Involving Human Subjects (the Helsinki Declaration) and also conform to the WHO Guidelines for Good Clinical Practice for trials on pharmaceutical products. This reflects the general trend towards harmonization of standards and norms in technical areas, as well as in drug regulation, as discussed in Chapter 4.

8.6.2 Performance
Quantitative data indicate a general increase in the number of clinical trial applications in Australia, Cuba, Estonia, Malaysia and Venezuela for the period 1994-97. Figure 8.11 shows the four-year average number of clinical trial applications received by the relevant authorities in these countries. During this period, the number of clinical trial applications in Australia far exceeded those received in all the other countries combined. The same is also true when the number of applications is computed against the number of new drug applications (Figure 8.12).

Table 8.5   Control of clinical trials

	Australia	Cuba	Cyprus	Estonia	Malaysia	Netherlands	Tunisia	Uganda	Venezuela	Zimbabwe
Control of clinical trials	●	●	□*	●	●	●	●	●	●	●
Approving body	Local ethics committees**	DRA	N/A	DRA & regional ethics committees	DRA	Local medical ethics committees***	Specialized commission but approved by Min of Health	NDA	INH	As part of MCAZ
Guidelines	●	●	N/A	Yes, procedures of committee of medical ethics for clinical trials	Yes, set up by the Research Committee of the Ministry of Health	●	●	●	Yes, norms and regulation of research in clinical pharmacology	No, applications are sent to external experts for evaluation
Consistency of guidelines with:										
a) Helsinki Declaration[a]	●	●	N/A	●	●	●	●	●	●	-
b) WHO guidelines[b]	●	●	N/A	●	●	●	●	●	●	-

● = Yes   □ = No   - = data or information not available   N/A = Not applicable

* Clinical trials are not allowed in the country.

** All clinical trials must be notified to the Therapeutic Goods Administration.

*** Notification or approval by the drug regulatory authority not required.

[a] Ethical Principles for Medical Research Involving Human Subjects.

[b] WHO Guidelines for Good Clinical Practice for trials on pharmaceutical products.

Figure 8.11   Average number of clinical trials, four-year average*

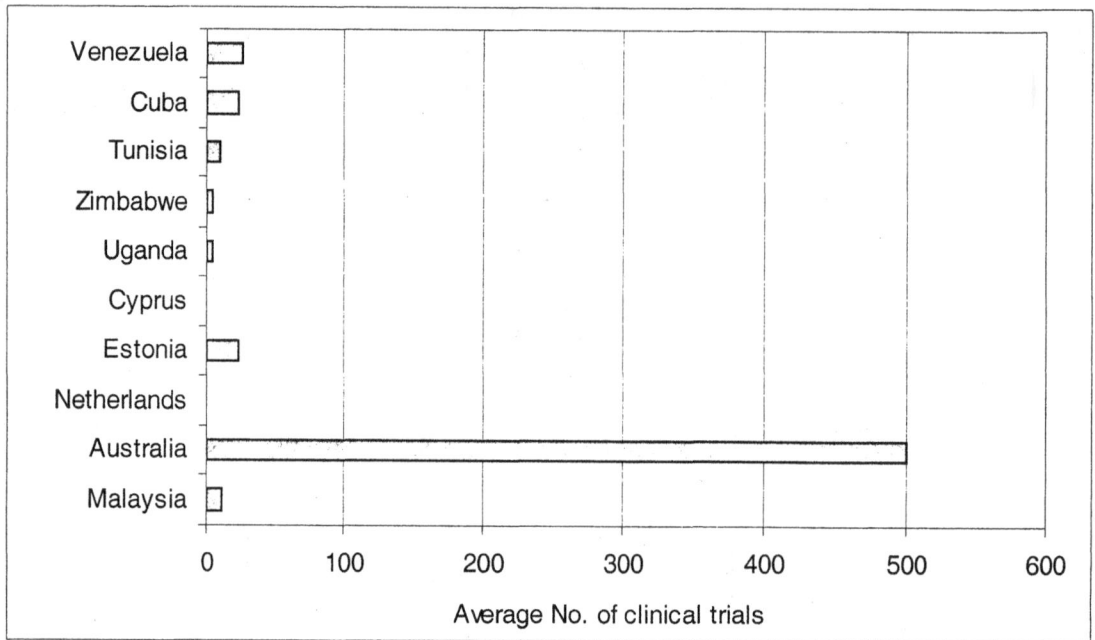

* No data available for Cyprus and the Netherlands.

Figure 8.12   Number of clinical trials requested per new drug application*

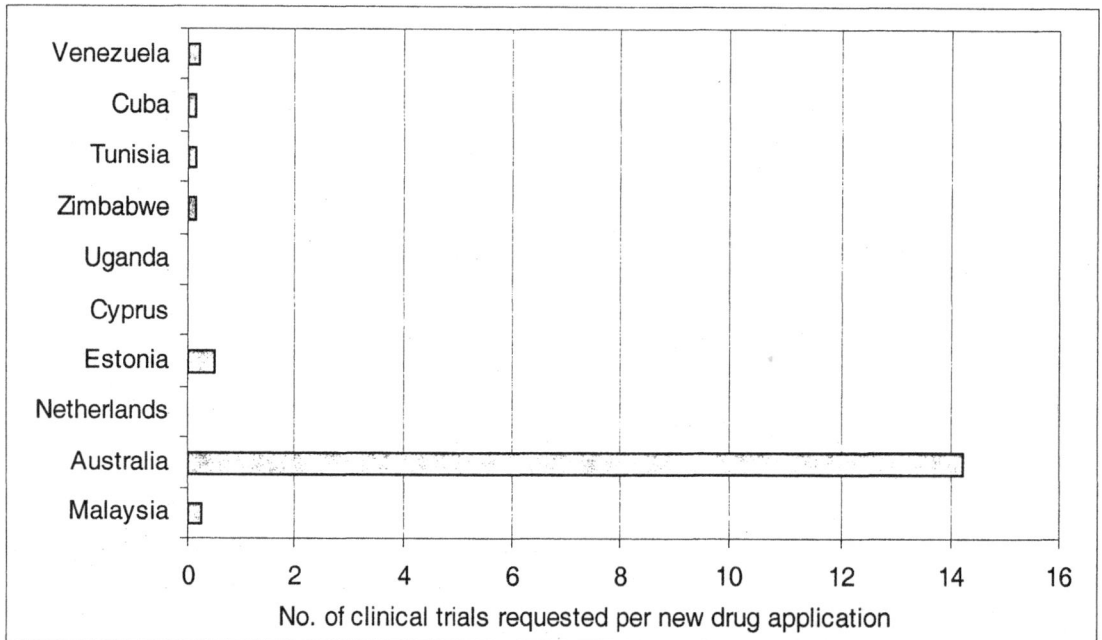

* No data available for Cyprus, the Netherlands or Uganda.

9. Control of drug promotion and advertising

Pharmaceutical manufacturers and suppliers promote and/or advertise their products to health professionals and the general public using a number of methods. These include: advertising in journals or other media; direct mailings; personal selling through sales representatives; provision of gifts and samples; sponsored symposiums and sponsored publication of information materials. Such promotion aims to influence people's attitudes, beliefs and behaviour and encourage them to use a particular brand of product.

Drug information can significantly influence the way drugs are used by consumers and providers of medicines (prescribers and dispensers). Regulation of drug information and promotion is therefore necessary to prevent the dissemination of inaccurate and misleading information. Accordingly, control of drug promotion and advertising is another function of a DRA. Additionally, in some countries, the pharmaceutical industry practises self-regulation, and the DRA and the pharmaceutical industry undertake a degree of co-regulation.

9.1 Power and process: comparing structures and processes

Advertising and promotion of drugs is controlled by law in all the countries.

9.1.1 Scope of control

Cuba stands out as the only country in this group that permits neither drug advertising nor drug promotion. Instead, pharmaceutical products are distributed and product information disseminated within the framework of the centralized State-run management system. Misinformation for commercial purposes is therefore not an issue in Cuba. In all the other survey countries, both the content and the conduct of drug advertising and promotion are regulated. The basis of such controls is found in drug legislation.

Drug legislation exerts various degrees of control over different types of drugs. In nine of the survey countries, prescription drugs can be advertised only to health professionals through professional journals. The only exception is Cyprus, where the Poisons Law permits general advertising of drugs used for certain diseases, provided that the prior approval of the Minister of Health has been obtained. Offences against this law carry a penalty of US$900. The list of drugs is limited to about 10. In Uganda, any prescription drug with indications for treating chronic diseases may not be advertised (Table 9.1).

Table 9.1 *Control of drug promotion and advertising**

	Australia	Cyprus	Estonia	Malaysia	Netherlands	Tunisia	Uganda	Venezuela	Zimbabwe
Legal provision exists	●	●	●	●	●	●	●	●	●
Prescription drugs advertised:									
in professional journals	●	●	●	●	●	●	□	●	●
in the lay press	□	□	□	□	□	□	□	□	□
on radio & television	□	□	□	□	□	□	□	□	□
on billboards	□	□	□	□	□	□	□	□	□
Pre-approval required	●, non-prescription drugs □, prescription drugs	●, restricted products	□	●	●	●	●	●	●
Body issuing pre-approval	PMAA	Pharmaceutical Services	N/A	MAB	KOAG	DPM	NDA	RBPP	MCAZ
Fee for pre-approval	● Non-prescription drugs: US$210 ● TV: US$30 ● Print media: US$100	□	N/A	US$40 per application	Yes, depends on no. of approvals per year	□	●	□	□
Body controlling advertising/ promotion	TGA Trade Practices Commission & APMA Code of Conduct Committee	Pharm. Services & Drug Council	SAM & Consumer Protection Branch	MAB	KOAG	DPM	NDA	RBPP Ministry of Communications	MCAZ
Self-regulation	●	□	●	●	●	□	●	●	●
Association(s) involved in self-regulation	As above	N/A	-	PhAMA MOPI	Nefarma	N/A	Uganda Pharm. Society Uganda Pharm. Dealers Association	CAVEME, LAVE & RBPP norms	Pharm. Manufacturers Association Ethical Drugs Association

● = Yes   □= No   N/A = not applicable   - = data or information not available

* No data for Cuba, since drug promotion is not allowed there.

The DRA in Venezuela allows prescription drugs to be advertised in the press on a one-time basis as an announcement that the drug is now registered in Venezuela. Information presented in the promotion and advertising materials must be based on the product information, as specified in the summary of product characteristics (SPC), approved at the time of registration. In all countries except Australia, patient information leaflets and labels are also subject to approval. In Australia, although approval is not needed, the information must not conflict with the approved product information.

Pre-approval is not required for drug promotion and advertising materials in Estonia, although it is in the other countries. However, the conditions set for pre-approval differ slightly. Australia requires pre-approval of materials for non-prescription drugs only. Since prescription drugs can be advertised only in the professional journals, pre-approval of advertising materials for this class of drugs is not required. For Cyprus, the only pre-approval required is for advertisements for products to treat certain diseases which are defined by law, e.g. epilepsy, diabetes, tuberculosis and cancer. In practice, however, pharmaceutical companies submit most of their advertising materials, even those not required by law, to the DRA for approval before publishing them.

9.1.2 Government regulation, self-regulation and co-regulation

For Cyprus, Estonia, Malaysia, Tunisia, Uganda, Venezuela and Zimbabwe, the government alone has the authority to impose legal controls over drug promotion and advertising. It is therefore the DRA which is responsible for pre-approval of promotion and advertisements. In the Netherlands, the board authorized to oversee drug promotion and advertising is the Inspection Board for Public Advertising of Medicines (KOAG), which includes representatives of the Government, the pharmaceutical industry, health professionals and consumers. In other words, it is a model of co-regulation, dependent on multiple parties. This board must approve all advertisements before they can be used. It also operates a complaints and appeals system.

A co-regulation system is also used in Australia. The TGA, the Trade Practices Commission and the Australian Pharmaceutical Manufacturers Association assume joint responsibility for regulation. The function of pre-approving advertisements, however, is delegated to the Proprietary Medicines Association of Australia on a self-regulation basis. Complaints can be lodged with the committee by companies, professionals or the public. The committee reviews the details of the complaints and decides on sanctions if appropriate, which can range from issuing a corrective advertisement and letters, to fines and expulsion from the Association. Generally, the committee is reactive to complaints rather than proactive in surveying advertisements.

Even in countries where the government assumes the main responsibility for controlling drug promotion and advertising, some forms of self-regulation exist. Trade groups formed within the pharmaceutical industry in Malaysia, Venezuela and Zimbabwe claim to operate a system of self-regulation, with a code of conduct, to control drug promotion by their members. In Cyprus, Estonia and Tunisia, regulation of drug information is entrusted to the DRA only, with no system of self-regulation by the industry (Table 9.1).

9.1.3 Paying for pre-approval of advertising

Fees are charged for pre-approval of promotion and advertising materials only in Australia, Malaysia, the Netherlands and Uganda (Table 9.1). The Australian TGA charges a fee per application, varying according to the type of advertising medium. Malaysia charges a fixed-rate fee for each application. In common with charges for other drug regulatory activities, the fees charged for the review of advertising materials in Australia are much higher than in Malaysia. In the Netherlands, the level of fees charged depends on the number of applications submitted by a pharmaceutical company in the course of a year.

In Cyprus, Tunisia, Venezuela and Zimbabwe, applications for prior approval of advertisements are free. This means that the government, rather than industry, pays for the review of these materials.

9.1.4 Independent drug information

In addition to controlling information used for promotional and advertising purposes, drug regulatory authorities in the majority of the countries also provide independent drug information. This is true of Cyprus, Estonia, Malaysia, the Netherlands, Tunisia, Venezuela and Zimbabwe. Drug information is mainly disseminated via regular bulletins. Other bodies besides the DRA also provide independent information about drugs.

However, the TGA in Australia does not undertake this task. Instead, other units of the Department of Health issue respected and widely distributed publications, such as the *Australian Prescriber* and the *Australian Medicines Handbook*. In Venezuela, a regional publication—*the Pan-American Health Organization (PAHO) Bulletin*—is available for countries in South America. However, the budget for disseminating independent drug information is often very small compared with the budgets for drug advertising and promotion of the pharmaceutical industry. The amount, frequency and reach of independent information are therefore usually no match for the drugs advertising and promotion which the industry can afford. However, the *PAHO Bulletin* is a good example of pooling of resources for sharing and disseminating independent drug information.

9.2 Performance

9.2.1 Monitoring performance

Drug information is probably disseminated over just as wide an area as drug products are distributed, if not further. Moreover, the existence of the power to control does not necessarily guarantee that information reaching the providers and the consumers conforms with the provisions set forth in the legal documents. Monitoring, like inspection, is therefore essential in order to ensure that promotion and advertising comply with the legislation.

How is advertising monitored in the survey countries? Where active means are used, the responsible agencies check whether samples of advertising materials and promotion activities conform with legislation. The drug regulatory authorities of Estonia, Venezuela and Zimbabwe take this approach. For example, samples of promotional materials are checked by the officers at the SAM in Estonia, and television drug advertisements are viewed by staff of the MCAZ. Where passive methods are used, the discovery of violations relies on voluntary reporting, generally by competing companies and consumers filing complaints to the responsible bodies. This approach is the main method used in Australia, Cyprus and others.

Which monitoring approach is more effective? Generally speaking, an active approach allows more systematic and thorough monitoring of advertisements and promotion activities. In practice, its effectiveness depends on how it is done, and what happens after a violation has been identified. If active monitoring is carried out only sporadically, with minimal in-depth examination of drug advertisements and promotion, it is unlikely to be effective. If there are no sanctions, or only small fines are imposed when a violation is discovered, then the deterrent effect is minimal. For example, a pharmaceutical company that violates the law may have to pay nothing more than a small fine. In that case, it may be more cost-effective from the company's point of view, given the large amount it has already spent on advertising, to pay the fine for an extended period of time rather than withdraw the advertisement.

9.2.2 Sanctions
In the survey countries, the types of sanction imposed for a violation range from verbal and written warnings, through fines, prohibition and correction of the advertisement and revocation of registration, to imprisonment. The fines charged for violations in Australia are relatively high. Fines for violations in Estonia (US$4 286 to US$7 143) are much higher than those in either Malaysia (US$780 to US$1 300) or Cyprus (US$900).

The empirical data for assessing the regulation of drug information are highly inadequate. Even records of the number of violations and the percentage of each type of sanction imposed are generally unavailable. So, too, is information on the effectiveness of action to prevent inaccurate and misleading drug information from reaching health care providers and the public. The information obtained through the country reports on the monitoring of promotion and advertising and the sanctions taken against violations is shown in Table 9.2.

Table 9.2   Monitoring mechanisms and sanctions for promotion and advertising

Countries	Monitoring mechanisms	Type and degree of sancitons, if any
Australia	Voluntary monitoring by companies, but anyone can lodge complaints to APMA Code of Conduct Committee	Under Therapeutic Goods Act: possible prosecution/fines (currently US$500-15 000) Under APMA: fines, obligation to correct advertisement or withdraw it, or expulsion from APMA
Cuba	No promotion allowed	None
Cyprus	Competitors can submit complaints	Six months' imprisonment or US$900 penalty, or both
Estonia	Samples of promotional material are checked Complaints by competitors are followed up.	Revocation of registration, issuance of mandatory precepts, fines (US$4 300-7 100)
Malaysia	None, only pre-approval	First offence: US$12 00 and/or one year's imprisonment Subsequent offence: US$2 000 and/or two years' imprisonment
Netherlands	Self-regulation, complaints can be lodged	Advertising is prohibited
Tunisia	N/A	N/A
Uganda	N/A	N/A
Venezuela	Vigilance by regulatory authority Complaints by third parties	Verbal and written warnings, suspensions and prohibitions
Zimbabwe	Officers view television advertisements Consumer reporting	As stipulated in the regulations

N/A = not applicable

10.   Drug quality control laboratory

10.1 Power and process

Controlling the quality of drugs before and after a marketing authorization has been issued is critical for ensuring the quality and safety of drugs. The DRA must therefore have access to a QC laboratory. Indeed, the capacity of a national DRA to undertake quality surveillance is directly related to the operational capability of the QC laboratory. The results of a laboratory assessment of samples of marketed drugs permit the regulatory authority to evaluate the actual quality of products used in the country and to identify problems pertaining to drug quality. In doing so, it minimizes the amount of sub-standard drugs and raw materials in circulation. In general, even a small, simple laboratory may be a sufficient deterrent against unscrupulous or negligent manufacturing and trading practices. It may also encourage improvements in the standard of local manufacture, since manufacturers may be encouraged to upgrade their production sites, for example, by the prospect of an independent assessment of the quality of their products.

This section compares the structures and functions of QC laboratories in the 10 countries.

10.1.1 Quality control capability

The requirement for drug analysis by the government or an independent laboratory is an integral part of the legal provisions of drug regulation in all 10 countries. In each of the countries, the government has established laboratory facilities to perform this function. Most countries have organized a QC laboratory within the DRA. In a few countries, the organizational arrangement is slightly different. Cyprus has two QC laboratories: the General Laboratory is an agency outside the DRA, but which operates under the Ministry of Health, and the Pharmaceutical Laboratory comes under Pharmaceutical Services, which constitutes the DRA. Each of these laboratories performs testing for drug regulation, as well as undertaking analysis for other purposes. The Ugandan NDA, in collaboration with the Department of Pharmacy of Makerere University, uses the laboratory facilities at the university to carry out QC testing, although it has plans to build its own laboratory.

All the laboratories carrying out QC of drugs have the capacity to perform physicochemical testing. Those in Australia, Cuba, Cyprus, the Netherlands and Venezuela are also equipped for testing biological products. In Cyprus, however, the biological products tested are mainly human plasma derivatives and insulin products. Drug regulatory authorities in some countries also make use of external facilities to perform testing for regulation purposes. However, no countries contract out their QC functions to other institutions. Table 10.1 summarizes the key structural features of drug control capacity in these 10 countries.

Table 10.1   Features of the quality control laboratories

	Australia	Cuba	Cyprus	Estonia	Malaysia	Netherlands	Tunisia	Uganda	Venezuela	Zimbabwe
Presence of legal provisions requiring drug analysis	●	●	●	-	●	●	●	●	●	●
Presence of DRA's own quality control lab.	●	●	●	●	●	●	●	●	●	●
Presence of other in-country quality control labs.	□	●	●	●	□	●	●	●	□	□
DRA lab. also serving industry	□	□	□	●	□	□	□	□	□	□
Quality control activity contracted out	□	□	□	□	□	□	□	□	□	□
No. of personnel (technical & admin.) full-time	131.5	14	13	10.5	77	30	32	4	78	18
Job description available	●	●	●	□	●	-	●	□	●	●
Pharmacopoeias available	●	●	●	●	●	●	●	●	●	●
SOPs and guidelines available	●	●	●	●	●	●	●	●	●	●
Reference standards available	●	●	●	●	●	●	●	●	●	●
Preparation of working standards	●	●	●	●	●	●	●	□	●	●
Specific budget for quality control lab.	●	□	□	●	□	●	●	□	□	●
Fees	●	□	●	●	●	-	●	-	●	●
Annual report	●	●	●	●	●	●	●		●	●
Participation in proficiency assessment schemes	●*	□	●**	●***	●****	●	□		●*****	●

● = Yes   □= No   - = data or information not available.

* Official Medicines Control Laboratories (OMCL) survey, collaborative assays on behalf of WHO, International Organization for Standardization (ISO), etc., to set standards.

** General Lab. and Pharma. Lab. participate in proficiency-testing studies and market surveillance studies organised by European Department for Quality of Medicines for Official Medicines Control Laboratories

*** European Network of Official Medicines Control Laboratories

**** ASEAN Regional Training Centre for QCL and WHO Collaborating Centre in the Regulatory Control of Pharmaceuticals.

***** INHRR laboratories are Centres for International Reference on Biological Products, diagnosis kits for Andean area, and are part of the network of quality labs for Pan-American Sanitary Office (OPS) coordinated by the USP. They also participate in OMCL survey.

To be able to perform their tasks effectively, QC facilities must have enough qualified personnel and the necessary equipment and materials, and operate according to established standards.

As indicated in Table 10.1, all the laboratories have access to a variety of pharmacopoeia, and usually the latest editions. The laboratories in the majority of countries follow SOPs and guidelines. Reference standards are available in all the countries, albeit at varying levels. Small laboratories sometimes have difficulty acquiring enough, and the right type, of reference standards to perform the required analysis. With the exception of Estonia and Uganda, laboratories in all the countries prepare their own working standards for drug analysis.

10.1.2 Multiple functions of QC laboratories

Most QC laboratories working for the drug regulatory authorities carry out functions in addition to laboratory analysis (Table 10.2). First and foremost, they all participate in drug analysis for registration purposes. Some of them also analyse samples submitted for post-marketing surveillance. A number of these laboratories also perform tests on other products, such as medical devices, condoms and drinking water. Personnel from the QC laboratories in Australia, Malaysia, Venezuela and Zimbabwe take part in inspecting the QC laboratories of the pharmaceutical industry. This helps to improve the industry's ability to perform QC, eventually leading to better-quality drugs on the market. Most laboratories also conduct research and train analysts. The drug control laboratories of Australia, Malaysia, Tunisia and Zimbabwe provide training for both local and international analysts.

10.1.3 Post-marketing surveillance

In addition to testing for pre-marketing QC, the DRA laboratories in Australia, Cuba, Cyprus, Malaysia, Venezuela and Zimbabwe also collect drug samples for testing as part of post-marketing quality surveillance. Post-marketing surveillance is conducted differently in each country. Planned sampling is carried out in Australia, Cyprus, Estonia, Malaysia and Venezuela. In Australia, sampling is targeted on complementary medicines and non-prescription drugs, while in Malaysia all types of products are sampled. In Cyprus, the emphasis is on products containing sensitive substances, products used for serious diseases and generic products posing interchangeability problems. Quality surveillance in Cuba focuses on samples collected from manufacturers in connection with GMP inspection, rather than on samples collected from the "market", i.e. retailers.

Table 10.2   Functions of QC laboratories

	Australia	Cuba	Cyprus	Estonia	Malaysia	Netherlands	Tunisia	Uganda	Venezuela	Zimbabwe
Testing (non-biological) pharmaceutical products	•	•	•	•	•	•	•	•	•	•
Testing biological products	•	•	•, Pharm. lab.	□	•	•	□	□	•	□
Participation in drug registration activities	•	•	•	•	•	•	•	•	•	•
Inspection of industry QC labs	•	□	□	□	•	□	□	□	•	•
Research	•	•	•	•	•	•	•	□	•	□
Training of analysts	•	•	•	•	•	•	•	□	•	•
Collecting samples for post-marketing surveillance	•	•	•	□	•	□	□	□	•	•
Post-marketing surveillance planned	•	•	•	•	•	N/A	•	□	•	□

• = Yes   □ = No   N/A = not applicable

10.2 Human resources

The number of staff working in these laboratories varies greatly, ranging from as few as four full-time posts (actually two full-time and four part-time staff) in the "mini-lab" in Uganda, to as many as 131.5 full-time posts (actually 129 full-time and five part-time staff) working for the Therapeutic Goods Administration Laboratory (TGAL) in Australia.

Given this difference in personnel numbers, the question arises whether all the QC laboratories have adequate staff to perform the task of drug regulation. If the current number of tests performed by the drug regulatory authorities is taken as the numerator, and the number of staff as the denominator, the workload per person can be calculated, as shown in Table 10.3. These results should be considered as preliminary figures which show the number of drug products submitted per staff member, but do not describe the overall workload. The data used to compute these figures do not take into account the work arrangements of staff, nor the number of tests performed per drug, which may vary according to the type of drug and the purpose of the test, as well as other functions which QC staff perform, such as training, research, inspection of industry QC laboratories, etc.

According to this set of data, the workload in terms of the number of products submitted per person is highest in Cyprus, where the size of the staff team is quite small, followed by Estonia. The lowest workload is in Australia and the Netherlands. The relatively low workload of the Australian TGAL staff is attributable to the large number of personnel, while in the Netherlands the low workload is accounted for by the small number of samples. In Venezuela, the number of samples submitted is eight times that in Australia, which has twice the number of staff. Figure 10.1 shows the workload of QC personnel in the 10 countries.

These figures indicate the current workloads in the countries. However, they do not indicate whether the need to monitor drug quality is being met in each country.

Figure 10.1 Workload of QC personnel — average number of samples submitted over four years, 1994-97

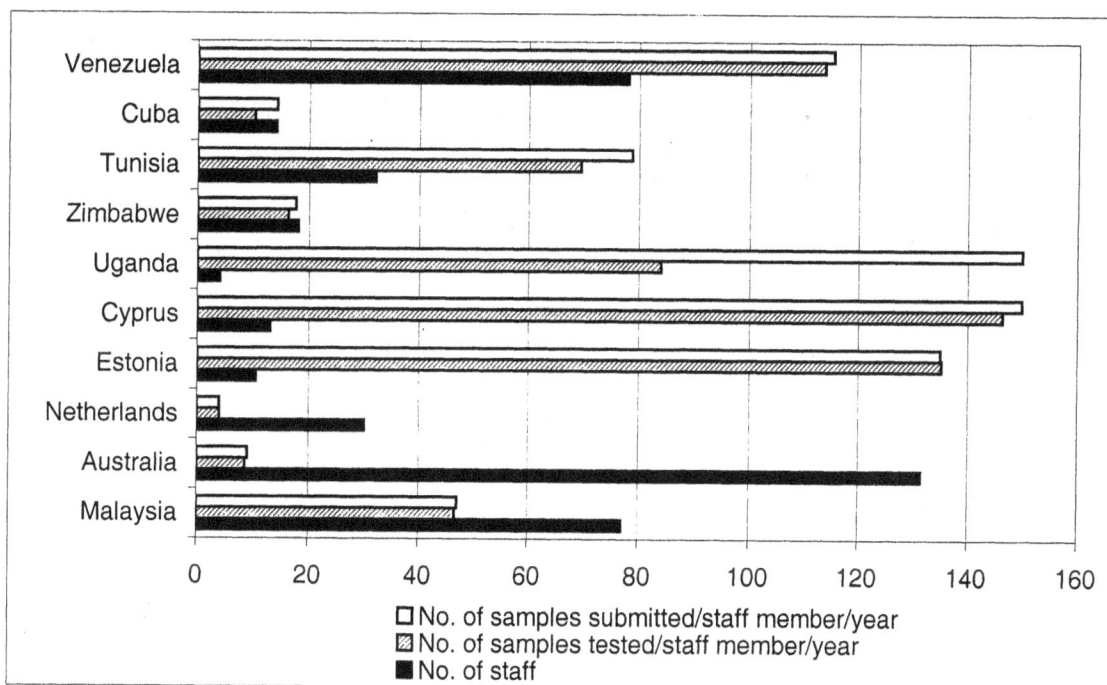

The researchers in Cyprus and Malaysia identified a shortage of personnel for QC. Laboratory staff in Cyprus, in particular, have to allocate time both to regulatory control and to analysing Government-manufactured products. Since priority is often given to conducting analyses for the Medical Stores, delays in carrying out QC for regulatory purposes are common. The TGAL in Australia, on the other hand, has fewer pressures related to staffing problems, compared with other areas of the TGA.

10.3 Paying for quality control

In most countries, the financing of the drug QC laboratory follows the same system as that of the DRA as a whole. Differences in the way budgets are allocated for the QC laboratory, as for other areas of drug regulation, are found in Cyprus, as summarized in Table 10.1. The data are not sufficient to show which method of financing is best for ensuring effective QC.

Fees are charged for all drug analyses performed in the DRA laboratories in Australia, Malaysia and Venezuela. In Cyprus and Estonia, analyses are carried out free of charge for government functions, but a charge is made in the case of private companies and individuals.

Table 10.3   Performance of quality control laboratories, four-year average, 1994-97

	Australia	Cuba	Cyprus	Estonia	Malaysia	Netherlands	Tunisia	Uganda	Venezuela	Zimbabwe
Total samples submitted for testing (average over four years)	1128	198	1940	1420	3589	120	2521	600	8997	317
Samples tested	1128	143	1903	1420	3589	120	2219	336	8868	292
Percentage of samples tested	100	72	98	100	100	100	88	56	98.6	92
No. of samples failing tests	149	6	26	89			405.5	12	1224	21
Percentage of samples failing test	13.2	4.2	1.4	6.3	11.5		18.3	23.8	13.8	7.3
No. of staff	131.5	14	13	10.5	77	30	32	4	78	18
Samples tested /staff member/ year (workload)	9	10	146	135	47	4	69	84	114	16
Samples submitted/ staff member/ year	9	14	150	135	47	4	79	150	115	18
Estimated number of substandard products	prescription drugs<5% complementary, herbals approx. 15-20%*	-	-	5%	5%	-	-	-	7%	12%

- = data or information not available
* High failure rates reflect the fact that high-risk products are targeted.

110

10.4 Performance

10.4.1 Reporting and peer review

A system of annual reporting exists for all the QC laboratories, except the one in Uganda. Another way of assessing the performance of a QC laboratory is to have it reviewed by its peers. Several countries participate in review schemes. The Australian TGAL, the SAM Laboratory in Estonia, and both the General Laboratory and the Pharmaceutical Laboratory in Cyprus participate in the Network of Official Medicines Control Laboratories scheme of the European Directorate for the Quality of Medicines (European Pharmacopoeia). The Drug Analysis Division laboratory in Malaysia is a QC centre for ASEAN and a WHO Collaborating Centre for Regulatory Control of Pharmaceuticals, while the Venezuelan INHRR laboratories are Centres for International Reference on Biological Products.

10.4.2 Ability to meet demand

Table 10.3 presents for each country, for the period 1994-97, the number of drug samples submitted for testing, samples tested and the failure rate in those tests. Data are available from all 10 countries on the total number of samples submitted and the number of samples tested, and these show that seven countries—Australia, Cyprus, Estonia, Malaysia, the Netherlands, Venezuela and Zimbabwe—have been able to meet the demand for testing (92-100%). Uganda has a relatively low test rate of 56% for the submitted samples, followed by Cuba and Tunisia at 72% and 88%, respectively. The lack of certain equipment and materials, such as reference standards and reagents, constrains analysis in Cuba, Cyprus, Uganda and Zimbabwe.

Figure 10.2   *Samples submitted for testing as a percentage of drugs registered**

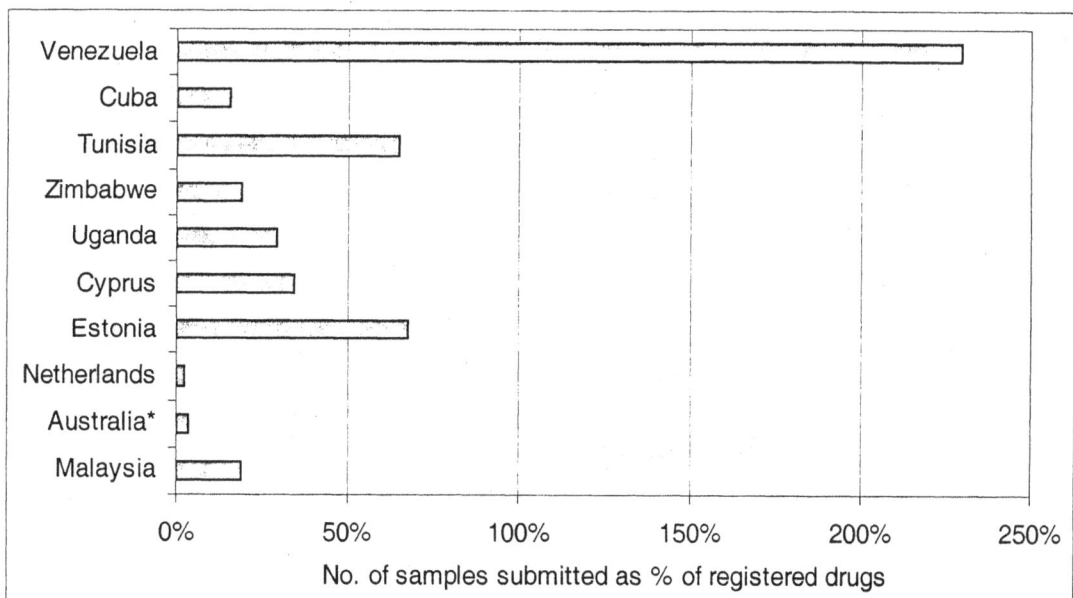

* *Data for registered drugs for Australia only approximate.*

The ratio of samples submitted to samples tested indicates the ability of the QC laboratory to meet demand. As stated earlier, however, these ratios do not indicate whether the current activities of the drug regulatory authorities keep pace with the overall need for pre-marketing and post-marketing drug QC. If the number of drug samples submitted for testing is viewed in terms of the number of drugs registered, the picture looks quite different. Figure 10.2 shows the number of samples submitted for testing as a percentage of drugs registered. Without taking into account the number of drugs submitted for registration, a significantly larger number of samples are submitted for testing in Estonia and Venezuela, as a percentage of drugs in the market, than in other countries.

The adequacy of testing in terms of regulatory needs can also be examined with respect to the kinds of test that the DRA laboratory has the capacity to perform. Laboratories that can perform only physicochemical analyses (see Table 10.2) probably lack the capacity to undertake drug QC.

10.4.3 Quality of drugs tested

The data on drugs tested by the DRA laboratories show that the percentage of drugs failing QC tests ranges from 1.4% in Cyprus to 23.8% in Uganda (Figure 10.3). Because drug regulatory authorities in some countries — Australia and Venezuela, for example — employed a targeted approach to QC testing by collecting samples of drugs which were suspected to have quality problems, test results from these countries are likely to show a higher failure rate than in countries where samples are collected randomly. The interpretation of QC failure rates is probably also affected by the way the terms "pass" and "fail" are defined. With a stricter definition, a larger proportion of samples will fail the tests. In Tunisia, for instance, the National Medicines Monitoring Laboratory considers defective packaging to be a failure to meet standards, and the batch concerned will be recalled.

Figure 10.3   Percentage of drug samples tested and failed during 1994-97*

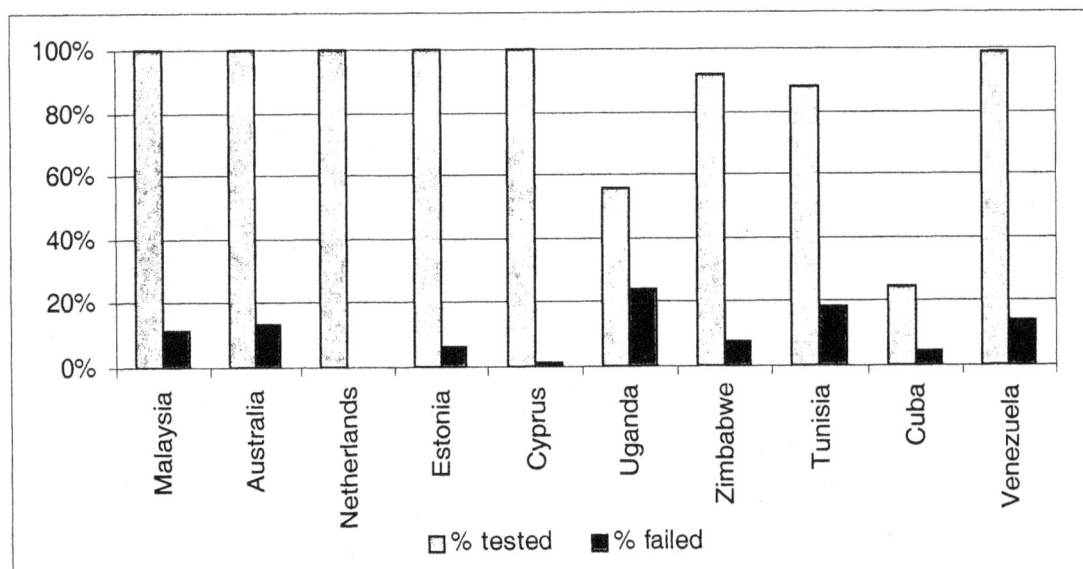

* Data for failed samples not available for the Netherlands.

112

According to information gathered by the principal investigators, the average QC failure rate of drugs ranges from less than 5% to 20%, depending on the country and the type of product. Drug regulatory authorities themselves in Australia, Estonia, Malaysia, Venezuela and Zimbabwe estimate the average QC failure rate of drugs to be: higher than 5% for prescription drugs and 15-20% for complementary drugs in Australia; 5% in Estonia; 5% in Malaysia; 1% in Venezuela and 12% in Zimbabwe (Table 10.3).

The question whether sanctions are imposed—and which sanctions—when a product is found to fail drug QC testing is as important as detection of substandard products itself. The present data sets are, however, inadequate for establishing direct links between the findings of QC analysis and the imposition of regulatory sanctions (area E in Figure 4.1). Certain cases have been documented in Venezuela over the past 10 years. For example, 100 products were prohibited, and a laboratory manufacturing almond oil was closed down.

11.　Assessing regulatory performance

11.1 Assessing government functions: an essential part of policy-making

Drug regulation is a government function serving societal objectives and is thus subject to societal scrutiny. The objectives of drug regulation are the protection and promotion of public health. The question to ask is: are these objectives being effectively achieved?

Effectiveness is not, however, the only value society demands of the DRA. Efficiency, accountability and transparency are also required.

Efficiency means carrying out regulatory responsibilities using as few resources (human, financial and time) as possible. Efficiency is also an issue in relation to the resources which the regulated parties must invest, and the opportunity costs they incur in conforming with regulatory requirements (i.e. in expending resources in that way, which cannot then be used for another purpose).

Accountability and transparency involve conducting the business of government in such a way that it is open to the scrutiny of supervisory bodies and the public. In addition, government procedures and the criteria for decision-making must be clearly defined and available to all.

Governments are responsible for devising measures and mechanisms for assessing their own functions. Government agencies must monitor and evaluate their regulatory activities in order to ensure that they are responsive to society's examination of government functions. Monitoring and evaluating the workings of regulation are essential to enable the responsible agencies to learn about their performance and identify problems and opportunities for improvement.

This chapter explores approaches for monitoring and evaluating the effectiveness, efficiency, accountability and transparency of drug regulatory activities, and examines how the 10 countries perform in these areas. The conceptual spheres of regulation described in Chapter 4 are used as a framework for assessing and analysing country data, where available. Some data are unavailable, but the conceptual foundations laid out for the analysis can still be used to design a system for collecting and analysing data in the future.

11.2 Monitoring and evaluation system

A good monitoring and evaluation system should provide information about an organization's or system's performance of the function(s) which it is perceived to carry out, and show where improvements can be made.

In general, there are four steps in assessing drug regulatory performance:

- identifying regulatory structures;

- deciding whether the regulatory processes are well designed and implemented;

- measuring intermediate outputs at the individual regulatory function level;

- measuring the final outcomes to ascertain whether drug regulation objectives have been met.

Achievement of regulatory goals requires the establishment of the necessary structures and the execution of activities demanded to fulfil the goals. An assessment of the drug regulation that allows evaluating the final performance as well as to identify sources of problems should address not only the outcomes of regulation, but also the structure and process producing such outcomes.

In drug regulation, structures are the inputs that make drug regulation possible, i.e. they are the setting in which drug regulation functions. Structural support for regulatory functions includes, but is not limited to, legal and administrative support.

Legal support involves granting legal authority to organizational and other bodies to perform stated regulatory functions as well as the authority to impose sanctions when violations occur.

Administrative support includes establishing an organization or organizations, supplying them with the necessary personnel, financial and other resources, and instituting standards and procedures for performing the functions (see Figure 2.1). Accordingly, in order to evaluate structural factors we must identify the existence or absence of essential elements in the legal and administrative structures which enable and facilitate implementation of drug regulation. Figure 11.1 highlights the interconnection between the structural and process factors and the regulatory outcomes. These contribute to determining health outcomes, along with other factors such as access and use.

Legal provisions and organizations are essential for attaining regulatory goals, but they are not enough by themselves. A process for putting them into practice effectively is also needed. Monitoring drug regulation thus entails examining both the structures and the type and extent of the actual activities and processes carried out, and relating them to the objectives. An examination of drug regulatory processes will reveal whether appropriate methods and strategies are being applied and activities are being implemented as planned in order to achieve the perceived objectives.

Outcomes, on the other hand, are the final results obtained by carrying out the different regulatory activities and functions.

Ideally, an assessment of drug regulation should begin by studying drug regulatory outcomes to judge overall performance and identify problem areas, which should then be examined in detail. In other words, investigations should proceed by tracing back from the problem to the structural and process factors affecting regulatory outcomes.

As discussed below, outcomes are often not readily measurable. And even if it is possible to develop measures, empirical data may not be available for the assessment, since a long period of time must elapse before relevant outcomes can be seen. The analysis may have to rely on data relating to intermediate outputs.

116

Figure 11.1   Drug regulation: interconnections between structures, processes and outcomes

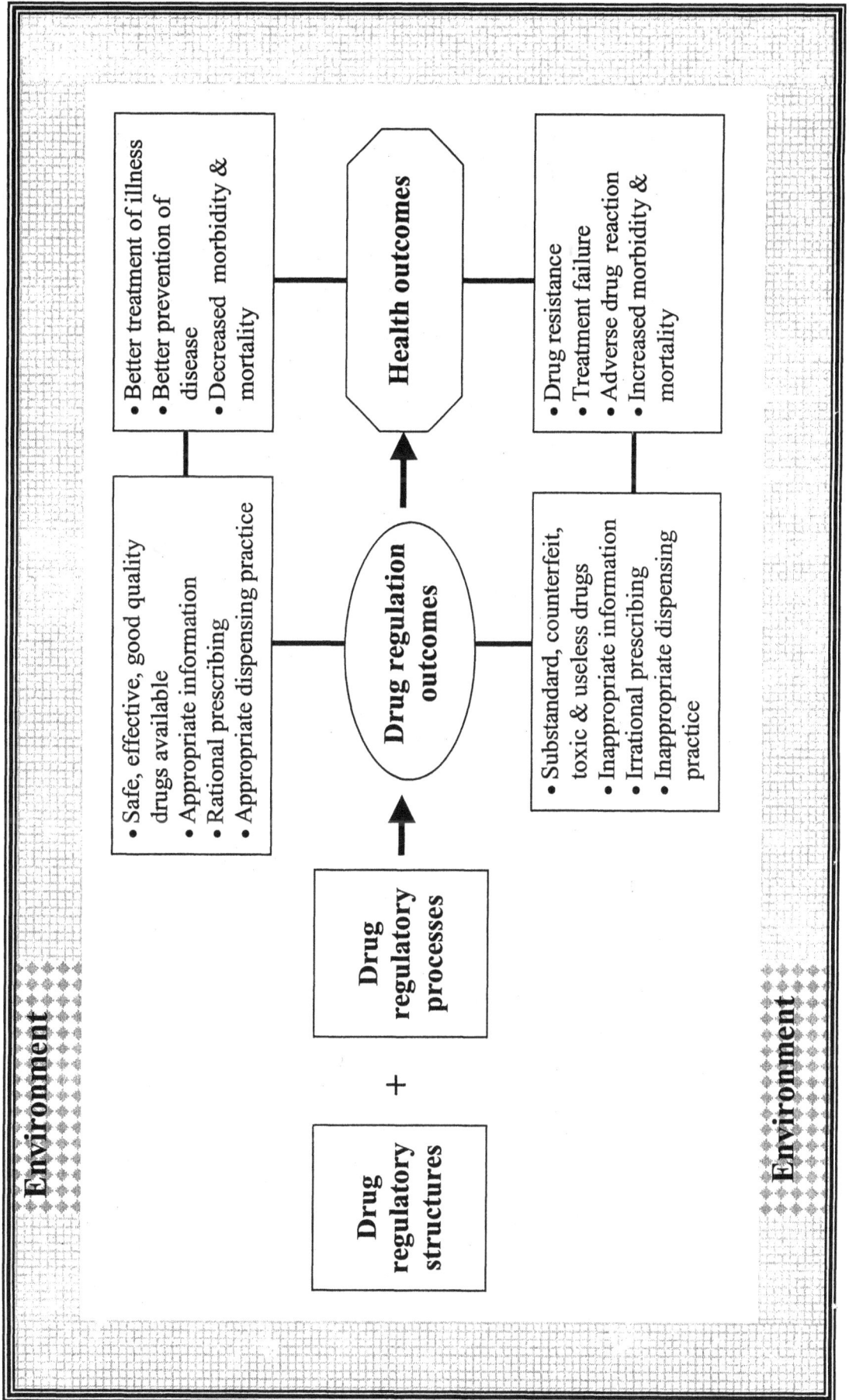

Environment

Drug regulatory structures + Drug regulatory processes → Drug regulation outcomes → Health outcomes

Drug regulation outcomes (positive):
- Safe, effective, good quality drugs available
- Appropriate information
- Rational prescribing
- Appropriate dispensing practice

Health outcomes (positive):
- Better treatment of illness
- Better prevention of disease
- Decreased morbidity & mortality

Drug regulation outcomes (negative):
- Substandard, counterfeit, toxic & useless drugs
- Inappropriate information
- Irrational prescribing
- Inappropriate dispensing practice

Health outcomes (negative):
- Drug resistance
- Treatment failure
- Adverse drug reaction
- Increased morbidity & mortality

Environment

11.3 Monitoring and evaluating the effectiveness of drug regulation

11.3.1 Measures of regulatory effectiveness

How can the effectiveness of drug regulation be measured? Ensuring safety, efficacy and quality of drugs available to the population is the main objective of drug regulation. Effectiveness of drug regulation should, therefore, be judged according to the extent to which such objective is achieved by the drug regulatory functions. One way to measure drug regulation effectiveness is by relating the final outcomes of drug regulation to the various drug regulatory functions, and developing measures to capture the performance of regulation.

The ultimate measures of the effectiveness of drug regulation can be summarized as follows:

- drugs available are efficacious for stated diseases and conditions, and no dubious drugs are distributed on the market (the **efficacy objective**);

- drugs available are adequately safe (the **safety objective**);

- drugs available possess the stated quality characteristics (the **quality objective**);

- drugs are used in accordance with approved claims and methods (the **rational-use objective**).

The first three objectives relate to pharmaceutical products, and the fourth to pharmaceutical usage although, in most countries, promoting rational use of drugs is not part of regulatory activities. In order to achieve the four objectives, the various pharmaceutical activities—manufacturing, importation, exportation, distribution (wholesale and retail), production of product information and promotion and advertising—must be regulated by government. Measures to control these activities are embodied in several regulatory functions (see Figure 2.1):

- licensing and inspection of pharmaceutical establishments;

- product assessment and registration;

- monitoring of drug quality;

- controlling and monitoring promotion and advertising;

- ADR monitoring.

Each of these key drug regulatory functions is designed to accomplish the four interrelated objectives outlined above. Some regulatory functions relate directly to drug regulation objectives, while others play a complementary role in assuring successful implementation of another function. So in evaluating the effectiveness of drug regulatory policy, two concepts must be clear, namely:

- there is a multi-stage causal relationship between policy mechanisms and policy effects;

- policy mechanisms are essential for producing outcomes, but they are not enough by themselves.

118

Relationship between policy mechanisms and policy effects

Policy effects are the results of policy measures, but they are often affected by other issues or areas of activity in a multi-stage causal relationship. Therefore, drug regulation being a policy measure, implementing it may not lead directly to the desired final outcomes: other functions or activities may contribute, positively or negatively. Consider, for example, the policy of providing appropriate information on drug labels and information inserts to promote rational drug use (see Figure 11.2). This policy will be effective in promoting rational use if, and only if:

- the information contained on the label and insert is accurate and complies with regulatory requirements;

- the label and insert are included in the final drug packaging dispensed to the patient (and not discarded by the dispenser during any repackaging which occurs);

- the patient or carer can, and does, read the information;

- the information is clearly understood;

- the patient follows the instructions provided in the information package.

Failure at any one of these stages would break the link between the policy (the provision of information in the label and insert) and the desired outcome (rational use of the medication) (29). The items in bold type in Figure 11.2 indicate those preconditions which may be achieved by means of regulation.

This example shows not only that it is difficult to develop outcome measures, but that measuring outcomes may be rendered more difficult and complicated by other factors. On the one hand, spurious effects may be found, caused by factors other than regulatory functions. On the other hand, even when regulation does work, detection of the desired outcomes and their impact may be difficult.

Figure 11.2   Preconditions for rational drug use

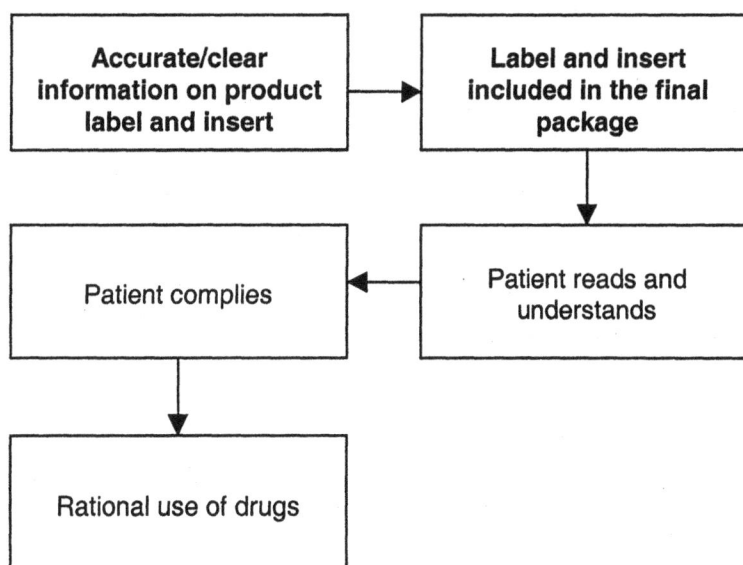

Potential inadequacy of policy mechanisms for producing outcomes

Even though outcome measures may fail to detect the intended effects, this does not automatically mean that regulation is ineffective: it may be that this particular regulatory mechanism, although necessary, is unable to produce the intended outcomes alone. The challenge is to identify factors that will complement the regulatory mechanism in order to achieve the desired outcomes.

The following sections provide examples of how to measure regulatory effectiveness in four important areas of drug regulation (licensing and inspection of pharmaceutical establishments; product assessment and registration, including drug QC and ADR monitoring; control of promotion and advertising; enforcement of drug regulation).

As described above, drug regulation involves a number of interdependent functions and processes:

- licensing of manufacturing, importation and distribution of drugs, as well as of the parties involved in drug promotion and advertising;
- assessment and registration of products (marketing authorization);
- inspection and surveillance of pharmaceutical establishments;
- control of clinical trials;
- control of drug promotion and advertising;
- testing product quality (quality control);
- ADR monitoring.

For regulation to be effective, the necessary structures must be available and should include: enabling legislation and regulations; an organization to implement and enforce the legislation; adequate numbers of qualified staff; sustainable funds and other resources including physical resources (facilities, equipment, supplies, etc.); written guidelines, procedures and standards for implementation of the various functions.

11.3.2 Assessing the effectiveness of licensing and inspection

In almost all countries, drug laws require that establishments engaged in the manufacturing, importation, distribution or sale of pharmaceuticals should be licensed and regularly inspected.

Licensing, authorized by legal mandates, aims to establish appropriate settings for the manufacture, storage and distribution of drugs, and to ensure that manufacturing QC and dispensing activities are carried out under the supervision and guidance of qualified and approved personnel. The purpose of inspection is to confirm that licensing requirements are met and maintained throughout the processes of manufacturing, distribution and dispensing. The ultimate objective of both licensing and inspection is to ensure that drugs reaching the user and/or the consumer are safe and of sufficient quality for their intended use. Therefore, three main steps need to be monitored to ensure the effectiveness of regulation of pharmaceutical establishments:

- compliance with GMP requirements;
- compliance with good storage and distribution practices;
- compliance with dispensing practices.

120

The impact of licensing and inspection on the quality of products is also realized through multi-stage causal links, as shown below (Figure 11.3). Once again, those factors which can be influenced by regulation have been shown in bold type.

Figure 11.3   Relationship between good practice, quality of products and rational drug use

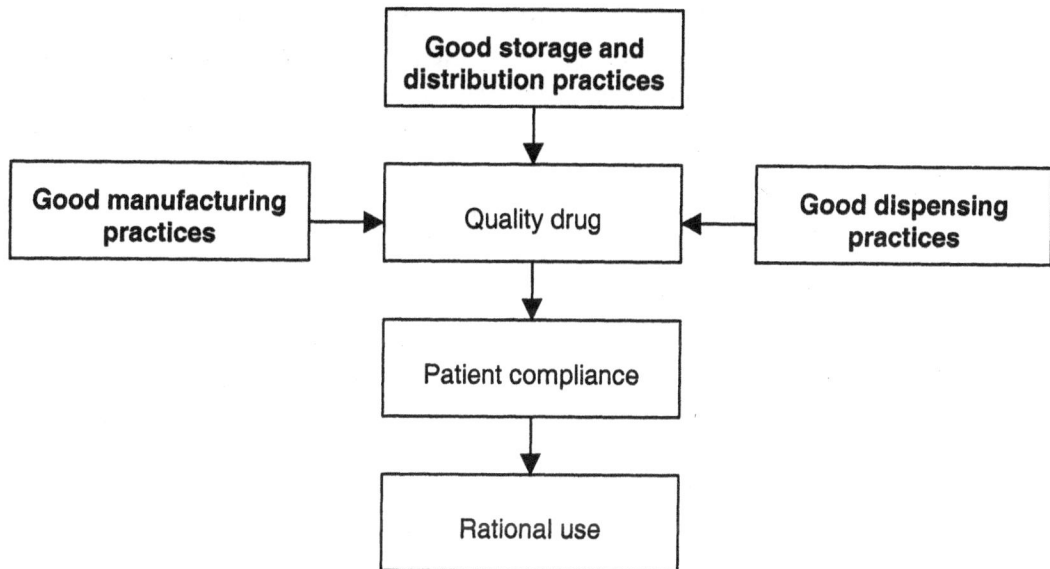

```
                    ┌─────────────────────┐
                    │   Good storage and   │
                    │ distribution practices│
                    └─────────────────────┘
                               │
                               ▼
┌──────────────────┐  ┌─────────────────┐  ┌──────────────────┐
│ Good manufacturing│─▶│   Quality drug   │◀─│  Good dispensing │
│     practices     │  │                  │  │     practices    │
└──────────────────┘  └─────────────────┘  └──────────────────┘
                               │
                               ▼
                    ┌─────────────────┐
                    │ Patient compliance│
                    └─────────────────┘
                               │
                               ▼
                    ┌─────────────────┐
                    │   Rational use   │
                    └─────────────────┘
```

Consequently, measurement of the impact of licensing and inspection on the final outcomes (quality of product and quality of use) is complicated by other factors. The question then becomes: how can we measure the effectiveness of licensing and inspection? Two approaches are possible: a) checking whether the necessary structures for licensing and inspection activities exist or b) using indicators that provide information about the intermediate outcomes of licensing and inspection.

The existence of structures can be determined simply by asking questions that demand a "Yes" or "No" answer. For example, are there:

- legal provisions requiring the licensing of pharmaceutical establishments?
- written guidelines and procedures for the licensing of pharmaceutical establishments?
- written criteria and conditions which must be met to obtain a licence to operate pharmaceutical establishments?
- legal provisions requiring inspection of pharmaceutical establishments?
- legal provisions giving inspectors the power to enter and inspect pharmaceutical premises?
- guidelines on GMP?
- guidelines on GDP?
- checklists and procedures for inspection?

The effectiveness of the licensing and inspection systems can be assessed by using indicators which measure intermediate outcomes at the individual function level. For instance:

- number of licensed pharmaceutical establishments, compared with the total number which should be licensed;
- number of licensed pharmaceutical establishments, compared with the total number of pharmaceutical establishments operating in the country;
- number of licensed pharmaceutical establishments which were inspected before receiving license approval, compared with the total number of licensed drug establishments in the country;
- total number of inspections carried out, compared with the total number of inspections scheduled within a given period of time;
- number of licensed drug manufacturing plants that are currently GMP-compliant, compared with the total number of licensed manufacturing plants in the country.

As well as specifying conditions that pharmaceutical establishments must meet in order to obtain a licence, drug laws forbid unlicensed establishments or individuals to operate. In other words, the existence of pharmaceutical establishments that are not licensed may indicate that the licensing system is ineffective. The significance of knowing of the existence and the approximate number of such establishments is twofold: they are engaged in pharmaceutical business which may harm public health and they are not formal (licensed) pharmaceutical establishments, so they may not be subject to official regulatory activities and may therefore escape inspection. Information about such establishments is thus a necessary component in the assessment of all sources of pharmaceutical products in a country. Generally, information about the estimated number of unlicensed drug establishments is best obtained by conducting a field survey.

Examining the inspectors' workloads will also help to establish reasons for the success or failure of the inspection process. During their inspection of pharmaceutical establishments, inspectors may learn of the presence of unregistered products, counterfeit products, etc. Quantitative information on these and other issues is valuable as an outcome measure.

Performance of the 10 countries

Global and regulatory spheres: The four major types of establishments regulated by the 10 countries are manufacturers, importers, wholesalers and retailers. Each of the countries regulates most or all of these drug sources, although there are some exceptions. For example, importers are not licensed in Cuba or Cyprus, owing to a lack of relevant legal provisions. The question, then, is whether those establishments operating without a licence perform in accordance with the standards necessary for ensuring quality products. In Cuba, the State is responsible for drug imports. Therefore, if the procedures for handling imports also ensure QC, they will compensate for the lack of legal provisions relating to licensing of importers. In Cyprus, although importers are not licensed, drug imports are subject to Pharmaceutical Services monitoring.

The study has shown that most of the countries have licensed their drug establishments in accordance with legislation. There are exceptions in Cuba, where only approximately 50% of the manufacturers are licensed (although all the unlicensed manufacturers are legal), and in Estonia, where only 4% of wholesalers are licensed.

However, it is unclear whether hospital pharmacies, clinics and health centres are regulated in the same manner as private-sector drug outlets.

The study indicates that DRA inspectors in six countries (Australia, Malaysia, the Netherlands, Uganda, Venezuela and Zimbabwe) have at some time detected illegal manufacturing, importing, selling and dispensing of drugs in their countries. Similar illegal activities are likely to exist in the other countries as well. Yet there are no official or reliable estimates of the number of establishments and people engaged in illegal activities related to drugs. The fact that illegal activities have been detected in six of the 10 countries suggests that their inspection systems are effective, since they clearly attempt to cover the informal sector as well.

Monitoring, violation and sanction spheres: Inspection activities are carried out in all countries to monitor the compliance of pharmaceutical establishments with legislation. As discussed in Chapter 7, most inspections in the majority of these countries are reported as being based on inspection plans. However, inspection plans, for both GMP and distribution channels, almost always refer to the formal sector, i.e. licensed establishments. This means that not all pharmaceutical establishments are controlled: illegal, unlicensed establishments are likely to be missed. They are a challenge to drug regulation because they are convenient channels for the distribution of smuggled, substandard and counterfeit drugs. They represent the gap between regulation and monitoring. Yet unless these illegal establishments are regulated, drug regulation cannot be considered effective. Therefore, in order to monitor all pharmaceutical establishments effectively, inspections should cover both licensed and unlicensed establishments.

Inspection plans provide varying degrees of coverage of manufacturers and distribution channels in the various countries. Two points are worth mentioning here. Firstly, the Australian TGA carries out a comparatively large number of GMP inspections per year. A system of targeted inspection is used, combining a risk-management approach with the "GMP history of manufacturers". This enables human resources—the inspectors—to be directed to where inspection is more urgently needed, rather than inspecting all manufacturing establishments at random.

Secondly, structural features in drug regulation in countries operating a federal system of government affect the ability of the DRA to monitor drug distribution throughout the entire country. In Australia, authority over distribution channels is fully delegated to the individual states. As a result, the TGA does not have the authority to assess and control the drug distribution situation for the whole country. In contrast, the Pharmaceutical Services Division in Malaysia appoints a deputy director of health in each of its 13 states with power to issue licences, carry out inspections and submit reports. Under this arrangement, command and control may be exercised and an official channel established for information flow between the federal and state governments.

11.3.3 Assessing product registration

Product assessment and registration serve to ascertain the efficacy, safety and quality of drugs which are to be put on the market. However, the objectives of drug efficacy and safety are, at best, only partially met by the process of product assessment at the registration stage. Only limited research, including clinical trials, is conducted on a drug before it is submitted for registration review. Unknown effects, beneficial or adverse, will therefore probably manifest themselves at a later stage, after the drug has been registered and released for large-scale use. However, a system for monitoring ADRs makes possible the continuous assessment of a drug after it has been registered. Both functions are thus necessary to assure drug safety and efficacy.

Post-marketing surveillance of product quality is carried out by means of a QC system. The quality of products available on the market is therefore an important indication of the effectiveness (or otherwise) of the drug regulatory system.

Two key indicators of the effectiveness of registration are: whether all products on the market with a medicinal claim have been assessed and registered; and whether the efficacy, safety, and quality of products submitted for registration have been fully evaluated. Drug registration is not a bureaucratic formality, but a critical process.

Drug registration can be assessed by examining legal and administrative structures, as well as by measuring intermediate and final outcomes. Examples of indicators that provide qualitative and quantitative information on the effectiveness of drug assessment and registration are:

- existence of legal provisions specifying the types of products which must be assessed before they may be marketed;
- existence of written criteria for approval and registration of products;
- existence of written guidelines on how to assess products;
- existence of written policy on combination products;
- number of registered products, compared with the total number of products requiring registration in the country;
- categories of products by source (government, private, nongovernmental organization) that are currently being registered, compared with the total number of categories of products (by source) required to be registered;
- number of drug products found to be not registered, compared with the total number of samples of products collected and investigated.

However, comparing the number of products registered with the number of products requiring registration is not sufficient to assess the efficacy and safety of products claiming therapeutic effects. The percentage of drug applications rejected (out of the total number of drug applications received) and the number of drugs recalled because of adverse reactions (out of the total number of drugs registered) may also help to show how effectively the registration process functions.

Furthermore, in countries where combination products may not be registered, or where written criteria exist for considering such products, it is possible to measure the effectiveness of the drug assessment process by comparing the number of combination products which have been registered, but do not comply with the relevant guidelines, with the total number of combination products registered in the country.

Performance of the 10 countries
Global and regulatory spheres: Product registration is another area where a clear discrepancy exists between the global sphere and the regulatory sphere. Not all products that make therapeutic claims are subject to product assessment and

registration in all countries. This means that not all drugs have been assessed before they are made available to the public. However, in some countries, the regulatory sphere is expanding. Australia, Malaysia and the Netherlands have recently instituted a system whereby herbal and homeopathic drugs must be registered. Such a system is also in place in Venezuela.

Australia, Cuba, Cyprus and the Netherlands register almost all drugs that are required by law to be registered. However, not all the countries manage to do the same. In Malaysia, for example, the percentage of registered drugs is low, largely because the process for registering herbal drugs is being introduced in stages and is not yet complete. In Uganda, greater efforts will have to be made if all drugs on the market are to be registered.

Monitoring, violation and sanction spheres: For post-marketing surveillance of product safety, ADR monitoring systems exist in all the countries, with the exception of Uganda. But it is difficult to evaluate the effectiveness of these systems in monitoring product safety. Only the Adverse Drug Reactions Advisory Committee in Australia receives a substantial number of ADR reports. For other countries, the numbers of reports are small and may not be sufficient to provide conclusive verification of adverse reactions. To overcome this constraint, the awareness and collaboration of health professionals in reporting should be increased, and information should be pooled by submitting reports to an international ADR centre, thereby increasing the number of ADR reports for evaluation.

Each of the countries operates a quality analysis system for post-marketing control of drug quality, albeit with vast differences in capacity. Data on the outcome measure for drug quality—the number of drug samples that failed quality tests compared with the total number of samples collected—are available in all the countries, except the Netherlands. Failure rates are high in some countries, e.g. Tunisia and Uganda. In Australia, high failure rates are found for herbal and other complementary products, compared with prescription drugs. Empirical data on sanctions applied in such instances are not available.

11.3.4 Assessing control of promotion and advertising

Promotion and advertising affect the way drugs are used. The ultimate aim of regulating drug promotion and advertising (information) is to promote the rational use of drugs. However, as described earlier, the link between drug information and drug use is not a direct one. Because of the nature of regulation, control mechanisms are applied only to ensure that information provided is accurate and not misleading. Assessing the effectiveness of regulation in relation to drug information therefore depends on evaluating whether, and to what extent, advertising and promotion materials and activities targeting consumers and health professionals comply with approved product information.

Performance of the 10 countries

Global and regulatory spheres: Legal provisions for controlling drug information exist in all the countries, with the exception of Cuba, where advertising and promotion of drugs are not permitted. Existing laws invariably apply to the traditional mass media, i.e. publications, radio, television and billboards. Newer information channels, such as the Internet, pose a challenge for information regulation.

Information on drug labels and inserts is controlled through the registration process in all countries. Pre-approval of promotional and advertising materials intended for the public are required in all countries except Estonia.

Monitoring, violation and sanction spheres: Systematic monitoring of drug information is not undertaken in all the countries: a number of countries rely on complaints filed either by competitor companies or by consumers. Self-regulation is also used in most countries, although there are no mechanisms for taking action against those who violate the regulations.

Empirical data which would enable the effectiveness of drug information control to be evaluated are generally unavailable. The lack of outcome data on information regulation is more serious than in other areas of drug regulation.

11.3.5 Assessing enforcement of drug regulation

Law enforcement is indispensable for regulation. Adequate sanctions help to deter future violations and have a significant impact on regulatory effectiveness.

Ideally, separate data for each regulatory function should be used for assessing law enforcement, since this will help to identify and clarify problems. However, the country data collected during this study are inadequate for this purpose. Moreover, where they exist, they are aggregate data for all drug regulatory functions. Data from three countries only are suitable for comparison. Figure 11.4 shows the relative weight of violations and sanctions in terms of overall areas of work of the drug regulatory authorities in Australia, Venezuela and Zimbabwe. The numbers used for this are four-year averages for the period 1994-97.

Figure 11.4   Drug regulatory violations and administrative and judicial sanctions imposed, 1994-97

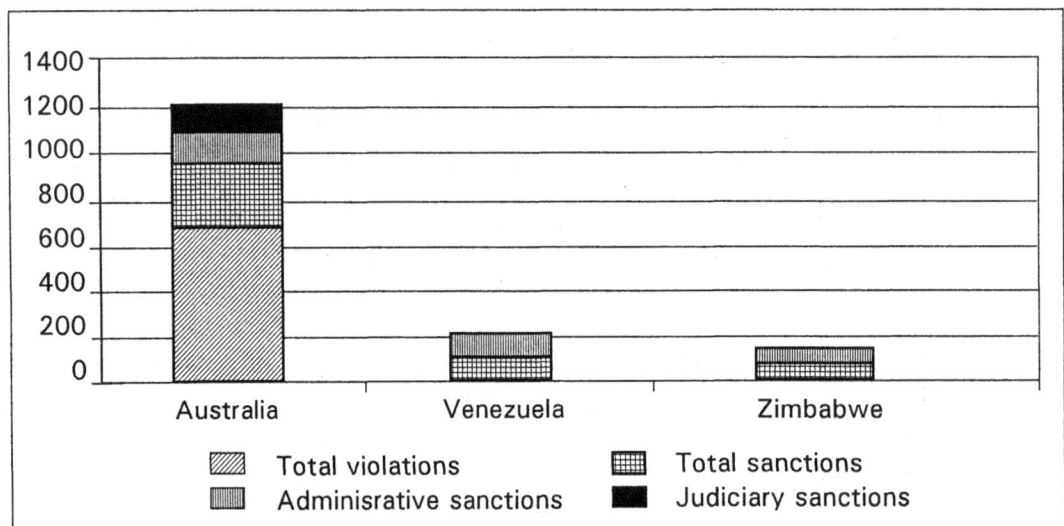

The sanction rates in Australia appear low compared with those for Venezuela and Zimbabwe. Nevertheless, the absolute number of both violations and sanctions are higher in Australia. A higher violation figure may be due to more severe violations, more extensive monitoring, or better-targeted monitoring. In Australia, targeted and extensive monitoring have been employed for products suspected to be of inadequate quality. This is an indirect indication of the effectiveness of the

126

TGA in protecting the public from exposure to hazardous drugs. In Venezuela and Zimbabwe, administrative measures are used much more extensively than judicial measures—indeed, almost exclusively. For 1994-97 judicial measures were used in 6.3-10.7% of cases in Venezuela, and less than 1.6% of cases in Zimbabwe. In Australia, the percentage was much higher— 6.5-31.9%.

11.4 Monitoring and evaluating the efficiency of drug regulation

11.4.1 Measures of regulatory efficiency

Efficiency in drug regulation encompasses all aspects of resource use, whether human, financial or time-related, and concerns all regulatory functions. In this study, however, the speed of drug registration (i.e. efficiency in time) is of the most interest.

Drug registration should strike a balance between protecting public health through an extensive review of existing information on a particular drug — which takes time — and promoting public health by making needed drugs available without undue delay. In other words, public health requires drugs to be assessed both thoroughly and quickly. Given its commercial interests, the pharmaceutical industry also enthusiastically supports measures to speed up the registration process.

The length of registration time can be used to measure the efficiency of assessment and registration. The different categories of products (new products, generic products, etc.) should be differentiated from one another because: a) the type, volume and complexity of work to be performed in each of these categories of drugs differs greatly; b) the number, qualification and competence of personnel involved in assessing and registering these categories of drugs varies from country to country; and c) some countries carry out independent assessments, while others rely partly on information obtained from other countries.

11.4.2 Regulatory efficiency in the 10 countries

Of the 10 countries in the survey, registration of new drugs takes the shortest time (5-6 months) in Cyprus, Malaysia, Uganda and Venezuela, and the longest (12-19 months) in Australia, Cuba, the Netherlands, Tunisia and Zimbabwe (Table 8.1). The highest figure is 3.8 times the lowest. Registration of generic drugs takes 18-19 months in the Netherlands and Zimbabwe, but only 2-6 months in Cuba, Cyprus, Malaysia, Tunisia and Venezuela. The longest registration time in this category is nine times longer than the shortest. Several factors appear to account for such differences. The DRA in Cyprus uses information obtained from "trusted" sources. Malaysia, Uganda and Venezuela ask for the WHO-recommended Certificate of Pharmaceutical Product, in addition to other documents, to assess safety, efficacy and quality of drugs. Australia and the Netherlands carry out independent assessments, while the staff in Zimbabwe are involved in other regulatory activities besides registration. Venezuela employs significant human resources for registration, and the registration workload per staff member is accordingly lower than that of the other drug regulatory authorities.

11.5 Monitoring and evaluating the accountability and transparency of drug regulation

11.5.1 Measures of regulatory accountability and transparency

In general, drug regulatory authorities have powers of independent decision-making, based on technical considerations. Supervision of these authorities is supposed to be less stringent than that of other bureaucratic organizations. Nonetheless, accountability and transparency are key values for all public agencies: even more so in the case of drug regulatory authorities, because of the direct importance of drugs for public health.

Accountability and transparency have several aspects: reporting to and control by supervisory bodies; clarity and openness of procedures; criteria for decision-making and decisions made; and existence of systems for complaint and appeal. Accountability and transparency can be evaluated by examining, in particular: reporting requirements, external reviews of the authority's performance; frequency of publications and content of website (and other means of communication between the DRA, the public and the regulated parties); bodies to which complaints are directed; and appeals procedures. However, the individual details of these elements of regulation make quantitative comparison difficult.

11.5.2 Performance of the 10 countries

Reporting and oversight: Although the drug regulatory authorities in all the countries publish reports, these focus more on the structure and process than on the outcomes of regulation. Self-assessment by the authorities of the effectiveness and the efficiency of their work is generally not the norm. Oversight by external bodies exists only in Australia, where the activities of the TGA are reviewed by the Therapeutic Goods Consultative Committee. In the other countries, no such mechanism exists.

Communication of procedures and decisions: All the countries have an official channel (mostly in the form of an official gazette) through which the drug regulatory authorities communicate with clients and the public concerning regulatory decisions and processes. Some drug regulatory authorities also communicate regulatory information via their website. Nevertheless, access to regulatory information is still perceived as a problem by consumer groups and the pharmaceutical industry alike.

Complaints and appeals: Complaint and appeals systems exist in all the countries. These systems can be classified according to the appeals procedure. In Uganda and Venezuela, appeals can be made only to the body that made the original decision. In Cuba and Tunisia, appeals can be made to the supervisory body, i.e. the Ministry of Health. In a third category, a combination of channels is available for appeal. An appeal may have to be sent first to the DRA or the Minister of Health, and thereafter submitted or forwarded to other channels, e.g. the courts, if the result is not satisfactory. This is the system in Australia, Estonia, the Netherlands and Zimbabwe (see Table 8.3).

Although mechanisms for ensuring accountability and transparency exist in each of the countries, not all of them can be considered adequate and independent.

11.6 Availability of information for assessment

Assessment of performance requires adequate qualitative and quantitative information. The country studies lacked some critical information. In most countries, information on regulatory outcomes is generally scarce. Data regarding the quality of drug products, drug information and distribution channels, especially in the illegal sector, are often unavailable or in short supply. Outcome data are difficult to obtain, and some process data are also unavailable. In most countries, data on violations and sanctions are either lacking or incomplete. This makes monitoring of the actual implementation of drug regulation difficult.

12. Conclusions and recommendations for effective drug regulation

If a drug regulation system is to bring about the ultimate outcome of protecting public health and safety, certain structural and process arrangements must be securely in place.

By comparing and contrasting drug regulation in the 10 countries, conclusions may be drawn about the components of drug regulatory systems which constrain or facilitate the effectiveness of drug regulation. Identification of these components can help in the development of strategies for improving drug regulation. This chapter highlights the lessons about regulatory structures and processes which may be learned from the study.

12.1 Conclusions related to regulatory structures

12.1.1 Regulatory gaps

If the purpose of drug regulation is to promote public health and protect the public from harmful and dubious drugs, it should cover all products for which medicinal claims are made and all activities associated with the manufacture, importation, distribution, dispensing and promotion of drugs.

This study has found that drug regulation does not meet these requirements in all the countries studied. In some countries, legislation omits or exempts certain areas of pharmaceutical activity from the scope of control. In Australia, Malaysia and the Netherlands, legislation requires traditional/herbal medicines to be assessed and registered. But this is not the case in Cyprus, Uganda or Zimbabwe. As a result of such gaps, drug regulation provides only partial protection for consumers.

Since legal structures form the foundation of drug regulation, regulatory gaps should be addressed by modifying or extending existing legislation or introducing new legislation. Drug legislation should be comprehensive, covering all products with a medicinal claim and all relevant pharmaceutical activities, whether carried out by the public or the private sector. It should be updated when necessary in order to meet new challenges. Important factors determining the effectiveness of drug legislation include the extent to which the legislative framework is consistent with national policies and the degree of regulation the government considers it desirable and practicable to exercise. In general, drug legislation must:

- define the categories of medicinal products and activities to be regulated;

- state the missions and goals of drug regulation;

- create the administrative bodies necessary for implementing drug regulation, and define their structural and functional relationships;

- state the roles, responsibilities, rights and functions of all parties involved in drug regulation, including those of the regulators and the regulated;

- define the qualifications and standards required for those handling drugs;

- create mechanisms to ensure that all responsible parties are licensed and inspected and ensure compliance with drug legislation and with the standards and specifications laid down for persons, premises and practices;

- define the norms, standards and specifications necessary for ensuring the safety, efficacy, and quality of drug products, as well as the appropriateness and accuracy of product information;

- state the terms and conditions for suspending, revoking or cancelling licences to import, manufacture, export, distribute, sell, supply or promote drugs;

- establish the administrative measures and legal sanctions that will be applied if drug legislation provisions are violated;

- create mechanisms for ensuring the transparency and accountability of drug regulatory authorities to the government, the public and consumers;

- create mechanisms for ensuring government oversight.

12.1.2 Overall accountability of the DRA

In some countries, all drug regulatory functions fall under the jurisdiction of a single agency, which possesses full authority to command and control these functions, as well as responsibility for ensuring the effectiveness of drug regulation. In other countries, drug regulatory functions are assigned to two or more agencies, at the same or different levels of government. Two phenomena, in particular, which may impede regulatory effectiveness were observed among the 10 countries.

Fragmentation and delegation of responsibilities

In some countries, drug regulatory functions are assigned to more than one agency. For example, in Venezuela, the National Institute of Health and the DDC are each responsible for a number of drug regulatory functions. Similarly, in the Netherlands, the MEB, the Healthcare Inspectorate of the Ministry of Health, the National Institute of Public Health and Environment (RIVM) and the National Registration and Evaluation of Adverse Drug Events (LAREB) are independent agencies, each regulating a different pharmaceutical area. In Tunisia, the National Medicines Control Laboratory, the Pharmaceutical Affairs Department, the Pharmaceutical Inspection Department and the National Pharmacovigilance Centre are independent agencies, each of which is responsible for different areas of drug legislation. When drug regulatory responsibility is dispersed, however, coordination amongst all the agencies is crucial if regulation is to be effective. Yet ensuring such coordination is generally difficult. In the absence of good coordination, lapses in implementation often occur. The risk of duplication of efforts, wastage of resources and even confrontation is increased too. Moreover, no single agency is, or can be, held accountable for overall drug regulatory effectiveness.

Problems relating to delegation of drug regulatory powers generally take one of two forms: a) delegation without authority and accountability; and b) delegation with full authority, but without coordination. The way in which inspections of distribution channels in Uganda are delegated by the NDA to the district assistant drug inspectors is an example of the first type. In this case, the district assistant drug inspectors are given the additional responsibility of inspecting drug distribution channels in their area, but without sufficient authority to enforce the law. Neither are they held accountable for failure to carry out inspections.

While delegation of regulatory authority is found in all types of government, it is most far-reaching in countries with a federal system. Usually, full authority is delegated from the federal or central level to the states. If this is not properly coordinated, there will be problems of accountability. Such arrangements can also affect the national authority's ability to ensure the effectiveness of overall drug regulation. In Australia, the TGA regulates the supply of therapeutic goods by incorporated bodies, and those manufactured and traded across state boundaries. The states and territories have control over drug distribution. The National Coordination Committee for Therapeutic Goods and the National Drugs and Poisons Schedule Committee coordinate the activities of the Commonwealth with those of the states and territories. But it is unclear whether this system enables the TGA to monitor Australia's overall drug situation.

Such a problem is not necessarily inevitable in federal-state delegation of authority. Mechanisms exist in some countries which can provide a link in the line of command and control. In Malaysia, the chief officer of the state regulatory authority is also a member of the federal-level organization. Policy communications between the federal and state levels, such as reporting, thereby become a routine.

It may not be easy to achieve and maintain effective coordination between different regulatory bodies. The missing links resulting from fragmentation and delegation can undermine the overall effectiveness of regulation. Ideally, drug regulatory structures should be designed in such a way that a central coordinating body has overall responsibility and is accountable for all aspects of drug regulation for the entire country. The responsibilities of all agencies involved should be clearly demarcated. However, restructuring of the entire DRA will require a substantial amount of time and effort. There may be a need for intermediate options that allow improvements in the existing divided structure. Another solution is to establish official structures for coordination and information systems within existing organizations in order to overcome their failings. A system with formal channels of coordination and information flow should be created to support drug regulatory decision-making at the national level.

Multiple functions and conflicts of interest

The study has shown that some drug regulatory authorities have been assigned multiple functions and are therefore unable to focus solely on drug regulation. If the authority responsible for drug regulation is also assigned other non-regulatory functions, such as manufacturing, procurement and/or delivery of services, conflicts of interest may occur in respect of mandates and resource allocation. In Cyprus, for example, the Pharmaceutical Services Division is responsible for drug regulation, procurement, supply and dispensing, as well as manufacturing. Distribution of human and other resources to cover all these functions has a significant impact on the adequacy of support for regulatory activities. In Venezuela, the National Institute of Health is not only responsible for assessment, registration and QC of pharmaceuticals, but also manufactures biological products. In Cuba, drug regulation, manufacturing, distribution and sales are all undertaken by the State. Although the DRA is not directly involved in the management of the companies carrying out manufacturing, distribution and sales, implementing drug legislation becomes more difficult.

Regulatory double standards

Not all drug regulatory requirements are applied equally. Exemptions are sometimes made, depending on where the drug comes from, who manufactured or imported it, where the drug is distributed or whether it is sold on domestic or overseas markets. For example, in Cyprus, drugs manufactured or imported by State agencies do not have to be registered, whereas those from private businesses do. Assurance of product quality, efficacy and safety in the case of government-manufactured products rests solely with the agency that manufactured the product, which may not conform to the standards set by the DRA. Such double standards raise questions regarding the DRA's ability to ensure the quality of all drugs distributed.

In Australia, therapeutic goods manufactured for export are not subject to the same standards as those consumed locally. Moreover, therapeutic goods that are manufactured by an unincorporated individual, and goods that are not traded across a state boundary, are exempt goods and not subject to control or registration. Use of double standards in the case of exported products raises questions of fairness in international public health.

Regulatory tools

Drug legislation is the basis of drug regulation, and defines the standards and specifications to be applied. Regulatory tools, such as standards and guidelines, equip drug regulatory authorities with the practical means of implementing this legislation. This study has revealed that not all drug regulatory authorities in the 10 countries make available documented SOPs for registration, and that even fewer countries have documented guidelines and checklists for inspection. When such tools are lacking, application of the legislation may become erratic and even lead to questions about the transparency of law enforcement.

Standards and guidelines should be established in written form for all drug regulatory functions. These tools should then be used to guide regulation practice, as well as being made publicly available in order to ensure the transparency of the drug regulatory process.

Resources

Human and financial resources are critical for successful drug regulation.

Governments should employ people with the specialized knowledge and skills required to ensure effective drug regulation. Employees must be individuals of integrity and should be well remunerated, particularly since drug regulation involves various stakeholders with commercial interests who may try to exert pressure on the authority in order to secure decisions favourable to themselves. Adequate and sustainable financing mechanisms are clearly crucial.

The study has shown that shortage of qualified personnel is the main problem faced by drug regulatory authorities. This is partly due to the lower salaries offered to DRA employees, which makes attracting and retaining staff difficult. The limited pool of pharmaceutical professionals in some countries owing to a shortage of institutions for pharmaceutical education may be another factor.

With regard to the financing of drug regulatory authorities, the study showed that the government budget is the main means of financing for eight out of the 10 countries. In each of the 10 countries, the drug regulatory authorities charge fees for their services. Countries vary both in the type of service for which fees are charged and in the level of the fee. Only two drug regulatory authorities in the group are entirely self-financed from fees. Fees collected by government-financed authorities are transferred to the government treasury. The fees charged by these authorities are almost always much lower than the actual cost of performing the regulatory function. Fees charged by the drug regulatory authorities of Australia and the Netherlands are much higher than fees charged by the developing countries.

Clearly, government resources alone are not sufficient to promote effective drug regulation in most of the countries. The drug regulatory authorities in these countries should set fees at a level that reflects the real cost of drug regulatory services, and should be allowed to retain the fees. The fee system should cover all services provided, including licensing, of establishments registration of products, inspection, QC and control of promotion and advertising. That said, the DRA should not be entirely dependent upon the fees charged for its services. The government should be fully committed to ensuring the sustainability of drug regulation. Financing for the authority should therefore be structured so that a balance is struck between a sufficiently high fee to cover the cost of services and provision of government support. Also, the salaries of DRA employees and the remuneration of expert committee members performing reviews should not be directly linked to specific fees or to the agency's overall earnings. This will help to ensure that regulatory decisions are not influenced by payment of fees.

Other ways of overcoming human resources problems include the following.

- Coordination may be established, where appropriate, between the DRA and the country's educational institutions, to provide the number and types of pharmaceutical competency which are needed. The aim is not merely to increase the number of professionals, but also to develop skills through short training courses. A coherent, module-based educational package may be developed by collaboration between countries. The individual modules may be "housed" in institutions with the relevant expertise. The DRA may then choose where to send its personnel for the training they most require.

- The information and knowledge needed for the regulation of a specific area or a specific drug product are usually available in countries where more advanced technologies can be acquired more easily. This information could be made available more widely to developing countries, and the resulting pooling of information resources may help to reduce the regulatory workload. Networks of information sources and users may be built up to facilitate the transfer of information and technologies.

- Drug regulatory authorities in various countries, WHO and other international bodies may collaborate to identify QC laboratories with sufficient capacity which adhere strictly to good laboratory practice. Standards may be set for accreditation of these laboratories. Drug regulatory authorities and other organizations in countries with fewer resources may then send products to them for testing. Pooled resources and division of labour among countries may also be applied to the production of secondary reference substances.

- Where salary rates are low, some way of increasing them, or providing other incentives such as transport or housing allowances and health insurance, must be sought. Good salaries and benefits not only help to attract and retain employees, they also help to minimize corruption.

- To reduce its workload while not compromising on quality, a DRA may identify countries with strong drug regulation and waive some procedures for products imported from those countries. Alternatively, it may decide to consider functions certified in those countries as legally valid in its own country. In Cyprus, foreign manufacturers exporting pharmaceuticals to Cyprus must normally submit documents certifying that GMP standards have been met, but manufacturers in Australia, Canada, the European Union, Japan and the USA are exempted from this requirement. In addition, a number of "reputable" authorities have been identified, and documents certified by these authorities are recognized under the Cypriot regulations. For example, inspections of a foreign manufacturer conducted by the United Kingdom Medicines Control Agency or the United States FDA are considered as equivalent to those made by Cypriot inspectors.

  The assumption underlying this approach is that the same high standards apply to all products and all drug regulatory functions. But for countries where **double standards** are applied to regulatory requirements, and different sets of standards are applied to pharmaceutical products depending on whether they are marketed within the country or exported, this approach may mean that products of lower standard are accepted. The "trusted authority" system may also give some legal leeway for manufacturers exporting pharmaceutical products not registered in the country. In other words, the burden of drug evaluation is shifted to the importing country.

- Prioritization and streamlining of work processes are used by the Australian TGA to enhance efficiency. Using this method, each product or facility is classified according to its "risk". High-risk products or facilities receive a more intensive review. Thus prescription drugs are higher-risk than non-prescription drugs, and facilities for manufacturing sterile products are higher-risk than packaging facilities. Under this scheme, products and facilities classified as low-risk receive less intense scrutiny, freeing up human resources for high-risk targets.

- Job enlargement and job enrichment methods may also be employed. The multi-skilling approach used in Zimbabwe is one such strategy. The MCAZ streamlines its procedures and uses teamwork in the performance of drug regulatory functions. Staff are trained to handle multiple functions.

12.2 Conclusions related to regulatory processes

12.1.1 Formal and informal sectors

As stated in Chapter 11, drugs distributed through the informal sector receive little attention compared with those distributed through the formal sector. Counterfeit products, products of dubious quality and faulty information — especially exaggerated claims of efficacy — are often widespread in the informal sector. Monitoring of pharmaceutical activities should cover both sectors.

12.1.2 Balance of priorities

Each drug regulatory function helps to ensure the efficacy, safety and quality of pharmaceutical products and their rational use. Drug regulation should therefore be carried out in such a way that each function receives sufficient attention and resources. Yet experiences in the countries studied indicate that the different drug regulatory functions receive varying degrees of emphasis. The disparities are found in three key areas.

Pre-marketing versus post-marketing product assessment: Drug legislation in all the countries assigns two types of power to drug regulatory authorities: the authority to assess pharmaceutical products and determine whether they should be registered, and the authority to monitor and change the information and registration status of a drug after it has been marketed. However, much more time is assigned to pre-marketing assessment than to post-marketing review. Only a small number of ADR reports, which are the main mechanism for post-marketing surveillance, are received in most countries. Few countries use them systematically in regulatory decision-making. Registered products are rarely re-evaluated routinely. Yet even if pre-marketing assessment has been thoroughly conducted, it may not be sufficient to guarantee the efficacy and, especially, the safety of drugs. Emphasis should also be placed on post-marketing surveillance.

Product registration versus regulation of distribution: The study showed that product registration is considered a major responsibility by all the drug regulatory authorities. In contrast, regulation of drug distribution and information does not seem to enjoy the same level of attention. This is particularly so in countries where licensing and inspection of distribution channels are assigned or delegated to another agency or another level of government. Yet the regulatory objective of ensuring public health and safety in the use of pharmaceuticals can be achieved only when every pharmaceutical activity operates properly, from the source to the user. All regulatory functions should therefore be given due attention.

GMP versus distribution-channel inspection: In many countries, GMP inspection receives more attention and resources than inspection of distribution channels. It is true that GMP ensures the quality of a product from the start. But it is not in the interests of the consumer if a product that has been produced according to GMP is later stored and distributed under adverse conditions. Inspection of distribution channels should therefore be given equal emphasis, particularly in countries where the drug distribution system has several intermediate levels and the climate is unfavourable.

12.2.3 Implementation

Besides structural constraints, e.g. human and financial resources, the way in which DRA employees perceive their jobs and how they perform are key factors in drug regulation performance. A clear sense of mission on the part of employees is important if regulatory processes are to be pursued consistently.

Regulatory processes should be systematically monitored in order to identify problems and determine whether the actual activities match the intended actions.

12.2.4 Assessment of DRA performance

Several approaches can be employed to assess a DRA's performance.

Self-assessment: Self-assessment can help an organization to learn about its own strengths and weaknesses. Transforming a DRA into a learning organization which routinely conducts self-assessment and continuous quality improvement can be a powerful approach to enhancing drug regulatory performance.

Review by supervisory body: Drug regulatory legislation normally specifies the official chain of command and the supervisory body to which the DRA must report. Administrative and legislative supervision is an important means of accountability if properly applied. However, supervision should not be used as a means of political influence over legitimate regulatory decisions.

Peer review: This involves setting up mechanisms for mutual review of drug regulation systems. It serves as a means of external auditing, whereby the performance of one agency can be compared with that of others. Systems for international peer comparison of QC laboratories are one example. Proficiency tests are performed by the participating laboratories in such a way that each laboratory learns how well it is performing in comparison with the others.

The above approaches are not mutually exclusive: they may complement one another in appraising performance, as well as helping to identify areas for improvement.

The key to all the review approaches is that performance should be systematically and regularly assessed. Systematic evaluation allows an objective and comprehensive appraisal of performance and identification of strengths, weaknesses and measures for improvement. Regular evaluation enables a DRA to learn continually about the quality of its performance, and to develop awareness of any positive or negative changes in that performance. It also helps the authority to understand whether improvement strategies are working and, if so, to what extent.

12.2.5 Communication with clients and consumers

The task of the DRA is to serve the public. Its operations must therefore be transparent to both clients (e.g. drug manufacturers) and consumers. Communication with clients should be a routine activity throughout the regulatory process. Information regarding its functions and the results of decisions should also be communicated regularly to the public.

12.2.6 Consumer empowerment

Drug regulation is a societal function intended to protect the public. Traditionally it has been considered as a process involving two actors, the DRA and the regulated firms. But policies that foster such arrangements run the risk of encouraging corruption. In order to promote effective drug regulation, arrangements that foster the participation of independent third parties should therefore be considered.

Since consumers are the end-users of drugs, all drug regulatory efforts should lead, ultimately, to protection of the consumer. Consumer groups or public interest groups can contribute to these efforts by participating both in the development of regulatory policies and in regulatory activities. They can act as independent attorney generals and protect the public from undue pressure from industry or politicians. Because of the highly technical nature of drug products and information, however, support from the DRA and other organizations is needed to empower consumers so that they can make an appropriate contribution.

Educating consumers about the efficacy, safety, quality and rational use of drugs can also enhance the achievement of regulatory objectives.

12.3 Recommendations for effective drug regulation

- A clear sense of the mission of the regulatory authority is important in motivating DRA staff to pursue regulatory processes in order to achieve drug regulation. Governments should state clearly the mission and objectives of drug regulation, so that the attainment of the intended objectives can be easily assessed.

- Drug laws should be sufficiently comprehensive, covering all activities involving drug products and information, and updated regularly.

- One central agency should be accountable for the overall effectiveness of drug regulation.

- Personnel engaged in drug regulation should be individuals of integrity and appropriately trained and qualified. Human resources development programmes should be made available to help staff to improve their knowledge and skills and to enable them to cope with developments in pharmaceutical science and technology. They should also have access to the latest scientific and technological information to facilitate their work.

- Appropriate standards and guidelines should be developed and used as tools for the application of all regulatory processes. They should be freely available to all stakeholders, including the public, in order to increase the transparency of the DRA's operations. The same standard of regulation should be applied to all drugs, whether they are imported and/or manufactured by the public or the private sector, and destined for domestic consumption or for export.

- Sustainable financing is essential to promote effective drug regulation. Drug regulatory authority financing should strike a balance between fees covering the full cost of services and government support. Fees should provide increased revenue to the authority so that it can perform effectively, and serve to discourage clients from "flooding" the system with applications that do not meet official requirements.

- Every regulatory function contributes to ensuring the safety quality and efficacy of drugs. The action taken by the authority should cover all drug regulatory functions in a balanced fashion. Support for drug regulation should not be compromised by other non-regulatory tasks with which the DRA may also be charged.

- The regulatory process should be systematically monitored in order to identify problems and determine whether actual activities match the intended actions. Moreover, the DRA should become a learning organization which routinely conducts self-assessment and continuous quality improvement. There should be administrative and legislative supervision in order to guarantee accountability. Peer review by drug regulatory authorities in other countries can serve as a means of external auditing, whereby the performance of one agency can be compared with that of its peers.

- Any inefficiency in the regulatory process delays decision-making and may lead to shortages of critically needed drugs, thus endangering human lives. Drug regulatory authorities should employ various strategies to increase efficiency of resource use, e.g. prioritization and streamlining of the work process; job enlargement and job enrichment for regulatory staff; pooling of international information resources; and sharing and pooling of international QC resources.

- Drug regulatory authorities should communicate regularly with their clients. They should also acknowledge the right of citizens to be provided with accurate and appropriate information on drugs marketed in their country. Educating citizens about the efficacy, safety, quality and rational use of drugs will ultimately enhance the achievement of regulatory objectives.

References

1   World Health Organization. *Global comparative pharmaceutical expenditures: with related reference information* (Health Economics and Drugs EDM Series No. 3). Geneva, 2000 (Document EDM/PAR/2000.2).

2   Geiling E, Cannon P. Pathogenic effects of elixir of sulfanilamide (diethylene glycol) poisoning. A clinical and experimental correlation. Final report. *Journal of the American Medical Association,* 1938, 111:919-926.

3   Dukes G. *The effects of drug regulation: a survey based on the European studies of drug regulation.* Lancaster, MTP Press Ltd., 1985.

4   O'Brien KL et al. Epidemic of pediatric deaths from acute renal failure caused by diethylene glycol poisoning. *Journal of the American Medical Association,* 1998, 279(15):1175-78.

5   Singh J et al. Diethylene glycol poisoning in Gurgaon, India, 1998. *Bulletin of the World Health Organization,* 2001, 79(2):88-95.

6   Fake meningitis vaccine in Niger (editorial). *Scrip,* 23 August 1996, 2157:12.

7   Howells S. World Health Organization: international workshop on counterfeit drugs, Geneva, 26-28 November 1997 (abstract). (Document WHO/DRS/CFD/98.1).

8   Csillag C. Epidemic of counterfeit drugs causes concern in Brazil. *Lancet,* 15 August 1998, 352:55.

9   Italian police seize counterfeit medicines (editorial). *Scrip,* 14 July 2000, 2557:6.

10   Aiken J. *Panel criticizes FDA inspections of imported drugs.* (CNN Online report, 9 June 2000.) http://www.cnn.com/2000/HEALTH/06/09/tainted.drugs/index.html.

11   Adams C. FDA launches probe of drugs from overseas. *Wall Street journal,* 12 September 2000.

12   Thompson FJ. The enduring challenges of health policy implementation. In: Litman TJ, Robins LS, eds. *Health politics and policy,* 2nd ed. New York, Delmar Publishers Inc., 1991.

13   Peters BG. *The politics of bureaucracy,* 3rd ed. White Plain, NY, Longman, 1989.

14   Wilson JQ. Introduction. In: Wilson JQ, ed. *The politics of regulation.* New York, Basic Books, 1980:vii-xi.

15   World Health Organization. *Effective drug regulation: what can countries do?* (discussion paper). Geneva, WHO Essential Drugs and Medicines Programme, 1999 (Document WHO/HTP/EDM/MAC(11)/99.6).

16   Heidenheimer AJ, Heclo H, Adams CT. *Comparative public policy: the politics of social choice in America, Europe and Japan,* 3rd ed. New York, St. Martin's Press, 1990.

17   Association of South-East Asian Nations (ASEAN) and World Health Organization. *ASEAN technical cooperation in pharmaceuticals: a success story.* 1997.

18.   Mazmanian DA, Sabatier PA. *Implementation and public policy.* Glenview, IL, Scott, Foresman and Co., 1983.

19.   Goggin ML. *Policy design and the politics of implementation: the case of child health care in the American States.* Knoxville, TN, University of Tennessee Press, 1987.

20.   Goggin ML et al. *Implementation theory and practice: toward a third generation.* Glenview, IL, Scott, Foresman and Co., 1990.

21.   Walt G. *Health policy: an introduction to process and power.* London, Zed Books, 1994.

22.   Rosenbloom DH. *Public administration: understanding management, politics, and law in the public sector,* 3rd ed. New York, McGraw-Hill, 1993.

23.   Baume P. *A question of balance.* Canberra, Australian Government Publishing Service, 1991.

24.   Vaughan G. The Australian drug regulatory system. *Australian prescriber,* 1995, 18(3):69-71.

25. Good manufacturing practices for pharmaceutical products. In: *WHO Expert Committee on Specifications for Pharmaceutical Preparations. Thirty-second report.* Geneva, World Health Organization, 1992 (WHO Technical Report Series, No. 823, Annex 1).

26. *ASEAN good manufacturing practices guidelines*, 2nd ed. Jakarta, Association of South East Asian Nations, 1988.

27. *Good manufacturing practice for medicinal products in the European Community.* Brussels, Commission of the European Communities, 1992.

28. Friedman MA et al. The safety of newly approved medicines: do recent market removals mean there is a problem? *Journal of the American Medical Association*, 12 May 1999, 218(18):1728-34.

29 Ratanawijitrasin S. Soumerai S, Weerasuriya K. Do national drug policies and essential drug programs improve drug use?: a review of experiences in developing countries. *Social science and medicine* (in press).

Annex 1

GUIDE FOR DATA COLLECTION TO ASSESS DRUG REGULATORY PERFORMANCE

Contents

1. BACKGROUND INFORMATION

Country information

BG1:   Country: _____

BG2:   Area of country (square km): _____

BG3:   Type of government (federal or centralized/unitary): _____

BG4:   Administrative divisions of country (number of provinces, states, districts):

   _____

   _____

Demographic and social and economic data

Demographic data	Figure:	Year:
BG5: Total population		
BG6: Average annual growth rate of population		
BG7: Urban population (%)		
BG8: Life expectancy (a) male (b) female	(a) (b)	
BG9: Literacy rate (a) male (b) Female	(a) (b)	
Economic data		
BG10: Gross national product (GNP)		
BG11: Gross domestic product (GDP)		
BG12: GNP per capita		
BG13: Annual rate of inflation		

Health information

Health status data	Figure:	Year:
BG14: Infant mortality rate (per 1000 live births)		
BG15: Maternal mortality rate (per 100,000)		

Health system data

	Figure:	Year:
BG16: Total government health expenditure (million US$)		
BG17: Total government sector health expenditure as % of GNP		
BG18: Total value of international aid for health sector (million US$)		
BG19: Total national health expenditure (million US$)		
BG20: Total number of: (a) government hospitals (b) private for-profit hospitals (c) private not-for profit hospitals (d) other types of health care facilities (specify):	(a) (b) (c) (d)	

Pharmaceutical sector information

	Figure:	Year:
BG21: Total government pharmaceutical expenditure (million US$)		
BG22: Total national drug expenditure (government +household + international aid, etc.) (million US$)		
BG23: Per capita drug expenditure (million US$)		
BG24: Total value of domestic pharmaceutical production (million US$)		
BG25: Total value of imports of finished pharmaceutical products (million US$)		
BG26: Total value of imports of pharmaceutical active ingredients (million US$)		
BG27: Total value of exports of finished pharmaceutical products (million US$)		
BG28: Total value of exports of pharmaceutical active ingredients (million US$)		

Health and pharmaceutical human resources

	Figure:	Year:
BG29: Type and number of health professional training schools: (a) medical school (b) pharmacy school (c) other relevant schools (specify):	(a) (b) (c)	
BG30: Type and number of drug prescribers in the country: (a) physicians (b) dentists (c) others	(a) (b) (c)	
BG31: Total number of pharmacists (degree)		
BG32: Total number of pharmacy technicians (diploma)		

Pharmaceutical production status

	Figure:	Year:
BG33: Pharmaceutical manufacturing plants: (a) Total number of pharmaceutical manufacturing plants in the country (b) Number of pharmaceutical manufacturing plants producing pharmaceutical active ingredients only (c) Number of pharmaceutical manufacturing plants producing finished pharmaceutical dosage forms (d) Number of pharmaceutical manufacturing plants packaging finished pharmaceutical dosage forms only	(a) (b) (c) (d)	
BG34: Total number of research-based pharmaceutical industries		
BG35: Total number of generic pharmaceutical products (including branded generics) manufacturers		
BG36: Total number of nationally owned pharmaceutical industries (government and private)		

4

Distribution

	Figure:	Year:
BG37: Total number of pharmaceutical:		
(a) importers	(a)	
(b) wholesalers	(b)	
BG38: Total number of:		
(a) government hospital pharmacies	(a)	
(b) private for-profit pharmacies	(b)	
(c) private not-for-profit pharmacies	(c)	
(d) other drug dispensing outlets e.g. dispensing doctors clinics	(d)	

Pharmaceutical products

	Figure:	Year:
BG39: Total number of pharmaceutical products registered in the country[1]		
BG40: Generic products, including branded generics, registered (as % of the total number of pharmaceutical products registered in the country)		

---

[1] In this guide the term "pharmaceutical product" is understood to include the finished pharmaceutical product, the device for administration where it is an essential part of the product, and the product information.

2. DRUG REGULATION: OVERVIEW

History of evolution of drug regulation

DR1: When was drug regulation first introduced in the country (year)?

_____

DR2: Title and date of enactment of the first drug law/act/regulations of the country:

_____

DR3: Mission/objective(s) of drug regulation at that time, if a written document/statement is available. Indicate the title and date of publication:

_____

_____

DR4: Important milestones in the development of drug regulation and/or drug legislation/regulations (What happened? When?):

Description	Date

Present drug regulation mission and drug legislation/regulations

DR5: What is the mission of national drug regulation at present? If there is a written document, indicate the title and date of publication.

_____

DR6: Indicate below the title(s) and date(s) of enactment of the different drug legislation/regulations currently used to regulate drugs in the country, including international/regional conventions, schemes, etc. to which the country is signatory.

Description/title	Date of enactment

DR7: Is there a written National Drug Policy (NDP) of the type recommended by WHO?

Yes
No
Draft only

DR7.1: If yes, indicate the title and date of adoption of the policy document.

_____

DR7.2: Does the NDP mention that it is the government's responsibility to regulate drugs and to ensure the safety, quality and efficacy of drugs?

Yes
No

Organization

DR8: What body is responsible for the following regulatory functions?

Function	Name and address of authority/organization	Personnel (full-time employees)	
		Technical/ Professional	Administrative
Licensing of pharmaceutical manufacture			
Licensing of pharmaceutical imports			
Licensing of pharmaceutical wholesale trade			
Licensing of drug retail/ dispensing outlets			
Product assessment and registration/marketing authorization			
Good manufacturing practice (GMP) inspection			
Inspection of distribution channels			
Control of drug promotion and advertising			
Performing drug quality tests/ quality control laboratory			
Price regulation/control			
Regulating generic substitution			
Control of prescribing			
Adverse drug reaction (ADR) monitoring			
Clinical trial control			
Provision of drug information to professionals and the consumer			
Others (specify):			

DR9: What body coordinates drug regulation centrally at national level?

_____

DR10: Is there an organizational chart for drug regulation?

Yes
No

DR10.1: If yes, collect a copy; if no, make a drawing to show the linkage between the different bodies responsible for regulatory functions based on the information collected.

DR11: Does the drug regulation system use the support of external experts/committees?

Yes
No

DR11.1: If yes, list below the committees/external expert groups (not individuals) that participate in regulatory functions and indicate their role:

Name of committee/expert group	Function/role

DR11.2: Is there a written and accepted code of conduct for external committees/experts and staff with regard to conflict of interest?

Yes
No

DR11.3: If yes, indicate the title and date of publication of the code of conduct:

_____

DR12: Does the government run any of the functions mentioned below?

Function	Yes/no	If yes, give the name of the organization(s) or attach a list
Pharmaceutical manufacturing?		
Pharmaceutical import and distribution?		
Retail pharmacy?		

DR12.1: Is the drug regulatory authority (DRA) also responsible for managing any of the functions mentioned under DR12?

Yes
No

DR12.2: If yes, indicate which function(s) is/are managed by the DRA:

_____

DR13: What kinds of regulatory function(s) is/are carried out at the different government administrative (state, province, etc.) levels?

Administrative level	Functions
Central/federal level	
Province/state level	
District level	
Others (specify):	

DR13.1: Are there any written materials describing the roles, responsibilities, functions, and powers of the regulatory bodies at the different government levels?

Yes

No

DR13.2: If yes, obtain copies.

DR14: Is there a system of reporting or information exchange between the regulatory authorities at the different levels?

Yes

No

DR14.1: If yes, obtain copies of the latest report.

DR15: Is there written material showing the regulatory and enforcement strategies applied in drug regulation?

Yes

No

DR15.1: If yes, obtain a copy of the material.

Human resources

DR16: What is the total number of staff working in drug regulation throughout the country?
a) technical staff _____
b) administrative staff _____

DR17: Do all the staff working in drug regulation have job descriptions?

All have   Some have   Needs to be developed

DR18: Do the regulatory authorities have the power to hire or dismiss employees?

Yes

No

DR18.1: If yes, give reference to the document that gives such power:

_____

DR19: Is there a human resources/staff development plan (training, career structure, etc.)?

Yes

No

DR19.1: If yes, give reference to the document.

_____

DR19.2: How many people have been trained in the last five years (please indicate correct year) in the areas mentioned below?

Area of training	Year:		Year:		Year:		Year:		Year:	
	Planned	Trained	Planned	Trained	Planned	Trained	Planned	Trained	Planned	Trained
Quality assurance of drugs										
GMP inspection										
Distribution channel inspection										
Product assessment and registration										
Quality control of drugs										
Control of promotion and advertising										
Drug regulation authority (DRA) administration and management										
Others (specify):										

DR20: How does the salary of the technical staff working in drug regulation compare to the salaries of people with the same qualifications/functions but working in the private sector?

Similar   Higher   Lower

DR21: Is there a staff shortage?

Yes
No

DR21.1: If yes, indicate the main reasons?

_____

DR22: Is there a high turnover of DRA staff (continuity problem)?

Yes
No

DR22.1: If yes, how many people have left their jobs in the last five years?

	Year:	Year:	Year:	Year:	Year:
Number of staff who left the DRA					

DR22.2: If yes, what are the reasons for the staff leaving their jobs?

_____

Financing

DR23: Is the government committed to drug regulation?

Yes
No

DR23.1: If yes, is there a specific budget allocated by the government for drug regulation?

Yes
No

DR23.2: If yes, what was the budget of drug regulation in each of the last five years (in US$)?

Budget section	Year:	Year:	Year:	Year:	Year:
Capital budget					
Salaries					
Miscellaneous					
Total					

DR23.3: What was the source of the budget in the last five years (answer yes/no) ?

Source	Year:	Year:	Year :	Year:	Year:
Government contribution					
Grant/aid					
Fees					
Others (specify):					

DR23.4: If there is no specific budget for drug regulation, what was the estimated expenditure of the country for drug regulation in the last five years?

Estimated expenditure	Year:	Year:	Year:	Year:	Year:
US$					
Local currency					

DR24: Is there a fee system for the regulatory services provided?

Yes
No

DR24.1: If the DRA has a fee system, indicate below the main services for which fees have been levied as well as the amount of fees charged:

Type of service provided	Fee charged (US$)

DR25: Is the authority allowed to use the fees collected?

Yes
No

DR25.1: If yes, give reference to the document that gives the DRA power to use the fees collected?

_____

DR25.2: What were the total fees collected during each of the last five years?

Fees collected	Year:	Year:	Year:	Year:	Year:
US$					
Local currency					

DR26: Is there a problem of financial sustainability?

Yes
No

DR27: Is there a financial audit system?

Yes
No

DR27.1: If yes, is it internal, external or both?

External
Internal
Both

Monitoring and evaluation

DR28: Is there a working system of self-assessment of regulatory activities within the DRA?

Yes
No

DR28.1: If yes, describe the system:

_____

DR29: Are drug regulatory activities carried out on the basis of a work plan?

Yes
No

DR29.1: If yes, give reference to the last work plan developed and used:

_____

DR30: Is monitoring/evaluation carried out to assess the implementation/performance of drug regulation?

Yes
No

DR30.1: If yes, give reference to the last monitoring/evaluation report:

_____

DR30.2: Is the monitoring/evaluation done internally or externally?

_____

DR30.3: What are the main weaknesses, problems and strengths mentioned in the last monitoring/evaluation report (indicate year of monitoring and evaluation)?

Weaknesses/problems	Strengths

DR31 Is the submission of a performance report to the supervisory body a requirement?

Yes
No

DR31.1: If yes, what are the main weaknesses or strengths indicated in the performance report and the reasons given for them?

Weaknesses/strengths	Reasons

DR32: Is there legal provision for pharmaceutical product liability for drug-related death, disability or other harm to consumers (e.g. as in thalidomide)?

Yes
No

DR32.1: If yes, give reference to the title, date of enactment and article number of the legislation:

_____

DR32.2: How many product liability cases have been recorded in the last 10 years? Indicate also the products reported.

_____

Accountability and transparency

DR33: Are contacts between the DRA and the firms it regulates formalized?

Yes
No

DR34: Does the DRA have a system of accountability?

Yes
No

DR34.1: If yes, to whom is it accountable?

_____

DR34.2: If yes, how is the accountability organized in relation to the following?

	Method of accountability
The government	
The public	
The regulated firms	
Individual consumers	

DR35: Is the DRA transparent in its decision-making?

Yes
No

DR35.1: If yes, how is transparency achieved with respect to the following:

	Means of achieving transparency
The regulated firms/industry?	
The public?	

DR36: Does political pressure have an influence on regulatory decisions in the country?

Yes
No

DR36.1: If yes, in which area and in what manner? Explain:

_____

DR37: Mention below the main constraints faced in carrying out the different regulatory functions:

Regulatory function	Main constraints
Licensing of persons, premises and practices	
Product assessment and registration	
Inspection (manufacturing and distribution channels)	
Quality control	
Control of promotion and advertising	
ADR monitoring	
Clinical trial control	
Others (specify):	

Enforcement

DR38: Does the drug law provide for sanctions against offences?

Yes
No

DR38.1: If yes, what are the different types and ranges of sanctions provided?

Type of offence	Range of sanctions

DR 39: How many violations were registered and administrative measures and judiciary sanctions applied in the last five years?

	Year:	Year:	Year:	Year:	Year:
Total number of violations registered					
Number of administrative measures implemented by the regulatory authority					
Number of legal sanctions implemented by a judicial body/court					

Indicators

1. Number of violations against which administrative measures have been taken in each of the last five years by the regulatory authority, out of the total number of violations registered in each year.
2. Number of violations against which penal sanctions have been applied by the judiciary in each of the last five years, out of the total number of violations submitted to court in each year.

If there is any specific and important information that is not covered by the above questions, please provide additional information as appropriate.

3. REGULATORY FUNCTIONS

3.1 Licensing: persons, premises and practices

Legal provisions

LI1: What is the title and date of enactment of the drug legislation/regulations and the article number of the provision giving power to issue licences:

_____

Organization

LI2: Give below the different types of licences issued and the names of the issuing authorities:

Type of licence issued	Issuing authority

LI2.1: Are the conditions for issuing the different licences published and known by the applicants?

Yes
No

LI3 Is the submission of an inspection report one of the requirements for issuing a licence to engage in pharmaceutical business?

Yes
No

LI3.1 Is such an inspection report also a requirement for renewal of licences?

Yes
No

Human resources

LI4: What is the number and level of qualification of the staff working in the licensing unit?

	Number	Qualifications
Technical/professional staff		
Administrative staff		

Financing

LI5: Is there a specific budget for the licensing unit/body?

Yes
No

LI5.1: If yes, what was the budget of the licensing unit/body during each of the last five years (US$):

Budget section	Year:	Year:	Year:	Year:	Year:
Capital budget					
Salaries					
Miscellaneous					
Total					

LI5.2: If yes, what was the source of the budget in the last five years (answer yes/no)?

Source	Year:	Year:	Year:	Year:	Year:
Government					
Fees					
Others (specify):					

LI5.3: If the answer to LI5 is no, indicate the estimated expenditure of the licensing authority in each of the last five years:

Estimated expenditure	Year:	Year:	Year:	Year:	Year:
US$					
Local currency					

LI6: If fees are collected, indicate the different fees charged for the various licensing services:

Type of licence issued	Fee charged (US$)

Activities

LI7: How many licences have been issued, renewed, suspended or revoked in the last five years?

Action	Year:	Year:	Year:	Year:	Year:
New licences issued					
Renewed					
Suspended					
Revoked					
Other (specify):					
Total					

LI8: Indicate, in the table below the total number of licensed drug establishments in the country. If a licence is not required by law, indicate the type of drug establishments that are not required to be licensed by law.

Type of pharmaceutical establishment	Government/ public	Private-for-profit	Private-not-for profit	Others
Manufacturers of pharmaceutical products				
Manufacturers of traditional medicines				
Pharmaceutical importers				
Pharmaceutical wholesalers				
Retail pharmacies				
Hospital pharmacies (all)				
Other health care facility drug outlets, e.g. clinics (all)				
Pharmaceutical product exporting companies				
Dispensing physicians				
Other (specify):				
Total				

LI9: Are there unlicensed/illegal establishments engaged in the manufacture of pharmaceutical products?

Yes
No

LI9.1: If yes, what is their estimated number?

_____

LI10: Are there unlicensed/illegal establishments engaged in the importation of drugs?

Yes
No

LI10.1: If yes, what is their estimated number?

_____

LI11: Are there unlicensed wholesalers of pharmaceutical products?

Yes
No

LI11.1: If yes, what is their estimated number?

_____

LI12: Are there unlicensed drug outlets dispensing or selling pharmaceutical products?

Yes
No

LI12.1: If yes, what is their estimated number?

_____

LI13: Are there persons engaged in dispensing/selling pharmaceutical products outside licensed premises (peddlers/hawkers)?

Yes
No

LI13.1: If yes, what is their estimated number?

_____

LI14: What is the legally required professional qualification to obtain a licence to engage in or operate the following activities/establishments?

Activity/establishment	Professional requirement
Manufacturing	
Importation	
Wholesale distribution	
Retail pharmacy	
Hospital pharmacy	
Other health care facility drug outlet	

LI15: Are lists of licensed premises/establishments and persons published and distributed to interested parties?

Yes
No

LI15.1: If yes, collect copies of the lists.

LI16: Is an import permit required to bring consignments of the following types of drug products into the country?

Type of consignment	Yes/No
Registered product	
Unregistered product	
Investigational product	
Unregistered product for individual patient	

LI17: Can one company import a product registered by another company into the country?

Yes
No

LI17.1: If yes, which is responsible for the recall of defective products?

_____

LI18: What mechanisms does the country use to prevent illegal importation/smuggling of pharmaceutical products into the country? Explain.

_____

LI19: Are export licences issued for exported pharmaceutical products?

Yes
No

LI19.1: If yes, do they differ from licences issued for imported products?

Yes
No

Monitoring and evaluation

LI20: Is there a process for the monitoring and evaluation of the licensing system?

Yes
No

LI20.1: If yes, collect a copy of the latest report.

LI20.2: If yes, what are the main constraints, weaknesses or problems and the strengths of the licensing system?

Constraints/weaknesses/problems	Strengths

Indicators

1. Number of licensed pharmaceutical manufacturing plants, out of the total number of pharmaceutical manufacturing plants in the country (indicate year).
2. Number of licensed pharmaceutical importers, out of the total number of pharmaceutical importers in the country (indicate year).
3. Number of licensed pharmaceutical wholesalers, out of the total number of pharmaceutical wholesalers in the country (indicate year).
4. Number of licensed dispensing/selling outlets with established premises, out of the total number of pharmaceutical dispensing/selling outlets with established premises operating in the country (indicate year).
5. Estimated number of unlicensed:
    (a) Pharmaceutical manufacturers (including cottage/backyard producers) in the country;
    (b) Pharmaceutical importers in the country;
    (c) Pharmaceutical wholesalers in the country;
    (d) Pharmaceutical dispensers/sellers in the country;
    (e) Persons selling drugs outside premises (peddlers/hawkers) in the country.

If there is any specific and important information that is not covered by the above questions, please provide additional information as appropriate.

3.2   Inspection and surveillance

3.2.1   GMP inspection

Legal provisions

GIN1: What is the title and date of enactment of the drug legislation/regulations and the article number of the provision requiring GMP inspections?

_____

GIN2: Are there provisions in the drug law/regulations that define the powers and status of GMP inspectors?

Yes
No

GIN2.1: If yes, what are the powers of GMP inspectors?

_____

Organization

GIN3: Is there an GMP inspectorate?

Yes
No

GIN3.1: If yes, to whom does it report?

_____

GIN4: What is the relationship of the GMP inspectorate to the:
    (a) Manufacturers' licensing unit? _____
    (b) Product registration unit? _____

GIN5: Are there written national GMP guidelines?

Yes
No

GIN5.1: If yes, give reference to the title and date of publication of the guidelines:

_____

GIN5.2: Have the GMP guidelines been enacted as a law/regulations?

Yes
No

GIN6: Are there manuals or a standard operating procedure (SOP) for GMP inspectors?

Yes
No

GIN6.1: If yes, give reference to the date of publication of the SOP:

_____

GIN7: Are there procedures for the consideration of appeals against enforcement measures taken by the GMP inspectorate?

Yes
No

GIN7.1: If yes, to whom are appeals referred and what is the procedure for handling appeals?

_____

GIN8: Is there a job description pertaining to the duties and responsibilities of GMP inspectors?

Yes
No

GIN9: Is a GMP certificate issued to manufacturers of pharmaceutical products?

Yes
No

GIN9.1: If yes, is the certificate issued on a product basis or is it a general certificate? Explain.

_____

GIN10: How many pharmaceutical manufacturers have GMP certificates for export?

_____

Human resources

GIN11: How many GMP inspectors are there in the country (indicate if the inspectors also serve as inspectors of the distribution chain)?

       (a) full-time employees   _____
       (b) part-time   _____

GIN11.1: If there are no GMP inspectors, who inspects manufacturing plants? Is the work contracted out? Explain.

_____

GIN12: Do the GMP inspectors receive training in GMP inspection/auditing?

                                         Yes
                                         No

GIN12.1: If yes, provide information on their qualifications, the type of training offered and their experience (number of years) as GMP inspectors:

Qualification of inspectors	Type of training offered	Experience (number of years)

GIN13: What is the average net salary of a GMP inspector compared to other categories indicated in the table?

Categories	Salary (US$)
GMP inspector	
Pharmacist working in a private retail pharmacy	
Head of production in a private pharmaceutical plant	
Person responsible for the release of batches of finished products in a manufacturing plant	

Financing of GMP inspection

GIN14: Is there a specific budget for the GMP inspectorate?

                                         Yes
                                       No

GIN14.1: If yes, what was the budget of the GMP inspectorate during each of the last five years (US$)?

Budget section	Year:	Year:	Year:	Year:	Year:
Capital budget					
Salaries					
Miscellaneous					
Total					

GIN14.2: What was the source of budget in the last five years (answer yes/no)?

	Year:	Year:	Year:	Year:	Year:
Government					
Fees					
Other (specify):					

GIN14.3: If the answer to GIN14 is no, what was the estimated expenditure of the GMP inspectorate in the last five years?

Estimated expenditure	Year:	Year:	Year:	Year:	Year:
US$					
Local currency					

GIN15: Does the inspectorate charge fees?

Yes

No

GIN15.1: If yes, what fees are charged for the various inspection services?

Type of GMP inspection on which fees are levied	Fees charged (US$)

GIN15.1: Is the inspectorate allowed to use the fees collected?

Yes

No

GIN15.2: If yes, what are the total fees collected in the last five years?

Fees collected	Year:	Year:	Year:	Year:	Year:
US$					
Local currency					

Activities

GIN16: Is there planned GMP inspection?

Yes

No

GIN16.1: If yes, what are the criteria for planned inspections? Obtain a copy of the criteria used if there is a written document; otherwise, collect the information.

_____

GIN17: What is the frequency of planned inspections?

_____

GIN18: Give below information on GMP inspections carried out in the last five years:

Number of plants and type of inspection	Year:	Year:	Year:	Year:	Year:
Total number of manufacturing plants in the country					
Total number of plants subjected to inspection					
Plants inspected for issue of new licence					
Plants inspected for renewal of licence					
Plants inspected because of complaints					
Plants inspected as follow-up					
Other (specify):					

GIN19: What is the number of planned GMP inspections conducted in the last five years, out of total number of planned inspections targeted to be carried out in those years?

Planned inspections	Year:	Year:	Year:	Year:	Year:
Planned inspections targeted					
Planned inspections carried out					

GIN20: Indicate below the number of manufacturing plants holding a GMP certificate (or complying with GMP), out of the total number of manufacturing plants in the country, in each of the last five years:*

Number of manufacturing plants	Year:	Year:	Year:	Year:	Year:
Total number of manufacturing plants in the country					
Total number of licensed manufacturing plants in the country					
Manufacturing plants having GMP certificate					
Manufacturing plants complying with GMP					

*In some countries, GMP certificates are awarded on the basis of production categories or dosage forms (for example, capsule, injection) instead of a general certificate to manufacture. Please make a note if this is the case for this country.

GIN20.1: What are the major problems found/reported when pharmaceutical manufacturing plants do not comply with GMP?

GIN21: Indicate in the table below the number of enforcement measures taken against manufacturing plants in each of the last five years for noncompliance with GMP requirements. (Please also describe any other strategies used for improving the level of GMP compliance in the country.)

Enforcement measures	Year:	Year:	Year:	Year:	Year:
Written warning					
Fines					
Imprisonment					
Licence suspended					
Licence revoked					
Production suspended					
Permanently closed					
Others (specify):					
Total					

GIN22: Are samples collected during GMP inspection of manufacturing plants and then tested? (Describe also any other strategies applied for checking the quality of products from local manufacturers.)

Yes
No

GIN22.1: If yes, indicate the number of drug products collected and tested during each of the last two years:

Samples collected and tested in connection with:	No. of samples collected		Passed		Failed	
	Year:	Year:	Year:	Year:	Year:	Year:
Planned inspections						
Follow-up inspections						
Complaints						
Others (specify):						
Total						

GIN23: Are there sanctions for products that fail laboratory tests?

Yes
No

GIN23.1: If yes, who is empowered to take action on the basis of the results of laboratory tests?

_____

GIN23.2: What actions/sanctions have been taken against products that failed laboratory tests in the last two years?

_____

GIN24: Is there a product recall system?

Yes
No

GIN24.1: If yes, indicate the number of recalls made per year in the last five years:

	Year:	Year:	Year:	Year:	Year:
Number of recalls made					
Number of products affected by the recall					

Monitoring and evaluation

GIN25: Is there an audit and/or review system to examine the performance of inspectors and the inspectorate?

Yes

No

GIN25.1: If yes, indicate whether this is external, internal or both:

_____

GIN25.2: Indicate below the actions that have been taken as a result of audits or reviews in the last five years:

Year:	Year:	Year:	Year:	Year:

GIN25.3: What are the main constraints, weaknesses or problems and the strengths of GMP inspection in the country?

Constraints/weaknesses/problems	Strengths

Indicators

1. Number of planned pharmaceutical plant inspections conducted, out of the total number of planned inspections carried out (indicate year):
   a) locally (within the country)?
   b) outside the country?

2. Number of pharmaceutical manufacturing plants inspected, out of the total number of licensed pharmaceutical manufacturing plants in the country (indicate year).

3. Number of pharmaceutical manufacturing plants in violation of the regulations, out of the total number of licensed manufacturing plants inspected (indicate year).

4. Number of pharmaceutical manufacturing plants holding a GMP certificate, out of the total number of licensed pharmaceutical manufacturing plants in the country (indicate year).

5. Number of GMP compliant pharmaceutical manufacturing plants, out of the total number of pharmaceutical manufacturing plants in the country (indicate year).

If there is any specific and important information that is not covered by the above questions, please provide additional information as appropriate.

3.2.2 Inspection of distribution channels

Legal provisions

DIN1: What is title and date of enactment of the drug law/regulations and the article number of the provision requiring inspection of distribution channels?

_____

DIN2: Are there provisions in the drug law/regulations that define the powers and status of the inspectors?

Yes
No

DIN2.1: If yes, what are the powers of distribution channel inspectors?

_____

Organization

DIN3: Is there a distribution channel inspectorate?

Yes
No

DIN3.1: If yes, to whom does it report?

_____

DIN4: What is the relationship of the inspectorate with other bodies involved in drug regulation, particularly with the licensing unit?

_____

DIN5: Are there written guidelines for Good Distribution Practices (GDP)?

Yes
No

DIN5.1: If yes, give reference to title and date of publication of the guidelines:

_____

DIN6: Is there a job description pertaining to the duties and responsibilities of distribution channel inspectors?

Yes
No

DIN7: Are there inspection guidelines or SOP for inspectors of distribution channels?

Yes
No

DIN7.1: If yes, give reference to the date of publication of the guidelines or SOP:

_____

Human resources

DIN8: How many distribution channel inspectors are there in the whole country?

    (a)   Full-time ————————————

    (b)   Part-time ————————————

DIN9: Do inspectors of distribution channels receive training in distribution channel inspection?

Yes
No

DIN9.1: If yes, collect information on the qualifications, training and experience of the inspectors.

Qualification	Training offered	Experience

DIN10: What is the average net monthly salary of a distribution channel inspector compared to other categories indicated in the table?

Categories of staff	Salary (US$)
Inspector of distribution channels	
Pharmacist working in a private retail pharmacy	
Pharmacist working in a private hospital pharmacy	
Pharmacist working in an import/wholesale distribution channel	

Financing of distribution channel inspection

DIN11: Is there a specific budget for the distribution channel inspectorate?

Yes
No

DIN11.1: If yes, what was the budget of the distribution channel inspectorate during each of the last five years (US$):

Budget section	Year:	Year:	Year:	Year:	Year:
Capital budget					
Salaries					
Miscellaneous					
Total					

DIN11.2: What was the source of the budget in the last five years (answer yes/no)?

Source	Year:	Year:	Year:	Year:	Year:
Government					
Fees					
Other (specify):					

DIN11.3: If the answer to DIN11 is no, what was the estimated expenditure of the distribution channel inspectorate in the last five years?

Estimated expenditure	Year:	Year:	Year:	Year:	Year:
US$					
Local currency					

DIN12: If fees are collected for inspection services, collect information on the types of inspection services on which fees have been levied and the amount of the fees charged.

Type of inspection services on which fees are levied	Fees charged (US$)

Activities

DIN13: Is responsibility for inspecting distribution channels decentralized?

Yes
No

DIN13.1: If yes, which body conducts inspections at the following levels?

Level of inspection	Inspecting body
Capital city (central)	
Provincial/state/regional level	
District level	
Peripheral level	
Customs warehouse or ports of entry	

DIN14: What is the structural and functional relationship between the various inspection levels? Is there a reporting mechanism? Explain.

_____

DIN15: Are there planned inspections of distribution channels at the different levels?

Yes
No

DIN15.1: If yes, what is the number of planned inspections conducted, out of the total number of planned inspections targeted in each of the last five years? (If possible, give information about each level.)

Planned inspections	Year:	Year:	Year:	Year:	Year:
Planned inspections targeted					
Planned inspections carried out					

DIN16: What are the different enforcement measures (administrative or legal sanctions) taken against those who do not comply with the drug laws/regulations? Explain.

Administrative measures	Legal sanctions

DIN17: Give information below on the total number of violations registered and the number of the different enforcement measures taken in each of the last five years. (If other enforcement strategies are used, describe them.)

Violations and enforcement measures taken	Year:	Year:	Year:	Year:	Year:
Total number of violations					
Warning letters issued					
Fines					
Imprisonment					
Suspension of licence					
Revocation of licence					
Others (specify):					

DIN18: Do the inspectors collect samples from distribution channels as part of planned quality surveillance activities?

Yes
No

DIN18.1: If yes, provide the following information for each of the last two years:

Samples collected in connection with:	Number of samples collected		Passed lab. test		Failed lab. test	
	Year:	Year:	Year:	Year:	Year:	Year:
Planned quality surveillance						
Follow-up of complaints						
Target testing/risk assessment						
Others (specify):						
Total						

DIN18.2: If the testing is targeted against a limited list of products, what are the products and what criteria are used for selecting them? If there is a written sampling procedure for inspectors provide information:

_____

DIN19: What actions/sanctions have been taken against products that failed laboratory test in each of the last two years?

Year:	Actions taken

DIN20 If inspectors of distribution channels have found any of the following in their planned inspection activities in the last two years, provide information below:

Inspection finding	Number of cases found	
	Year:	Year:
Unlicensed pharmaceutical premises, (manufacturing, import, wholesale and retail)		
Premises operated by nonprofessionals (not in accordance with the law)		
Unrenewed/expired licences		
Counterfeit products		
Illegally imported products		

Sale of expired products		
Unregistered products		
Products stored under improper conditions		
Products not authorized to be sold in the establishment		
Other (specify):		

DIN21: Are quality requirements for drug products for export purposes the same as for those products for use within the country? Explain:

Monitoring and evaluation

DIN22: Is there an audit and/or review system to examine the performance of inspectors and the inspectorate?

Yes
No

DIN22.1: If yes, indicate whether this is external, internal or both:

DIN23: What actions have been taken as a result of the audits or reviews in the last five years?

	Year:	Year:	Year:	Year:	Year:
Actions taken					

DIN24: What are the main constraints, weaknesses or problems and the strengths of distribution channel inspection in the country?

Constraints/weaknesses/problems	Strengths

Indicators

1. Number of pharmaceutical distribution channels (importers, wholesalers, dispensing outlets) inspected, out of the total number of licensed pharmaceutical distribution channels (importers, wholesalers, dispensing outlets) in the country (indicate year).

2. Number of planned distribution channel inspections carried out, out of the total number of planned distribution channel inspections (indicate year).

3. Number of pharmaceutical distribution channels in violation of the regulations, out of the total number of licensed pharmaceutical distribution channels inspected (indicate year).

4. Number of samples collected, out of the total number of samples planned to be collected (indicate year).

5. Number of drug products beyond the expiry date, out of the total number of drug products collected from pharmaceutical distribution channels (indicate year).

If other strategies are used to prevent mistakes or improve compliance with the requirements of good distribution practice, describe them.

If there is any specific and important information that is not covered by the above questions, please provide additional information as appropriate.

3.3 Product assessment and registration

Legal provisions

RE1: What is the title and date of enactment of the drug law/regulations and the article number of the provision requiring the assessment and registration (marketing authorization) of pharmaceutical products?

_____

Organization

RE2: Is there an operational product assessment and registration system?

Yes

No

RE2.1: If yes, when did it commence?

_____

RE3: Is there a written standard application form or guideline for the submission of dossiers for the registration of drug products?

Yes

No

RE3.1: If yes, collect a copy of the application form/guidelines:

RE4: Who can apply for the registration of a pharmaceutical product?

_____

RE4.1: What prerequisites should be met by a company/individual to apply for the registration of a pharmaceutical product? Explain:

_____

RE5: Is there a fast-track registration system?

Yes

No

RE5.1: If yes, what are the conditions for a product to be eligible for fast-track registration?

_____

RE6: Does the process of drug assessment and registration apply to all pharmaceutical products for human use?

Yes

No

RE6.1: If yes, does it cover the following?

Category of products required to be registered	Yes/No	Not applicable
Locally manufactured by private for-profit sector		
Locally manufactured by government/public sector		
Locally manufactured by private not-for-profit sector		
Imported by private for-profit sector		
Imported by government purchasing agency		
Imported by private not-for-profit organizations		
Donations/aid		
Other (specify):		

RE6.2: For products in the categories listed in RE6.1 where the answer is no, is there a system for ensuring quality, efficacy and safety?

Yes
No

RE7: Which classes of medicinal products are currently assessed and registered?

Class of pharmaceutical products	Yes/No
Well-established interchangeable multi-source (generic) pharmaceutical products	
Products containing new active pharmaceutical ingredients/substances	
Biological products	
Herbal medicines	
Veterinary drug products	
Other (specify):	

RE8: Indicate the information and evidence that are required to be submitted with applications for registration of:

Type of product	Information and evidence required for registration
Multi-source (generic) pharmaceutical products	
Products containing new active pharmaceutical ingredients	
Fast-track drugs	
Other (specify):	

RE8.1: What information and evidence are required to be submitted for renewal of the registration of a product? Indicate any differences between product categories.

Type of product	Information and evidence required for renewal
Multi-source (generic) pharmaceutical products	
New active pharmaceutical ingredients	
Fast-track drugs	
Other (specify):	

RE8.2: Do variations have to be approved?

Yes
No

RE8.3: Can the registration authority initiate a change in the registration status of a product?

Yes
No

RE9: Is a WHO-type Certificate of Pharmaceutical Product a requirement for the registration of imported drugs?

Yes
No

RE9.1: If no, what kind of certificate is requested? Explain:

_____

RE10: Are there written standard operating procedures (SOPs) for drug assessment and registration staff?

Yes
No

RE10.1: If yes, collect a copy of the SOPs.

RE11: If there is a flow chart showing the process of drug assessment and registration collect a copy. If not, either make a chart or describe the process:

_____

RE12: Are criteria for drug assessment and registration (reasons for approving or rejecting applications for registration) written down?

Yes
No

RE12.1: If yes, get a copy of the criteria and indicate how applicants are made aware of them:

_____

RE12.2: Is there a written policy or criteria for the registration of combination products?

Yes
No

RE12.3: If yes, what is the policy or criteria? Explain:

_____

RE13: Does the assessment and registration authority have committees to support its activities?

Yes
No

RE13.1: If yes, indicate the titles of the committees (not names of individuals), their respective functions, their powers, and members' terms of office:

Title of committee	Functions	Powers	Members' term of office

RE14: Are any of the activities of drug assessment and registration contracted out?

Yes
No

RE14.1: If yes, indicate which function(s) is/are contracted out and the conditions for contracting out:

Function contracted out	Conditions

RE15: Who makes the final decision regarding the registration of a product?

_____

RE15.1: What types of documents are issued following approval for registration? Explain:

_____

RE16: For how long is the registration of a product valid?

_____

RE16.1: If there is no registration expiry, is there a system of product re-evaluation?

Yes
No

RE16.2: If yes, describe the system or get a copy of a written document on the system:

_____

RE17: Indicate the average time taken to evaluate and register:

Class of product	Average time taken (in days)
Generic products	
Products containing a new active pharmaceutical ingredient	
Fast-track products	

RE18: Is there a maximum time-limit for the registration authority to process applications for registration?

Yes
No

RE18.1: If yes, indicate the time limit below:

Class of product	Maximum time limit allowed (in days)
Generic products	
Products containing a new active pharmaceutical ingredient	
Fast-track products	

RE18.2: What happens if the limit is not met by the registration authority? Explain:

_____

RE19: Is there an appellate body?

Yes
No

RE19.1: If yes, indicate the name of the appellate body and its powers:

_____

RE19.2: Is the appellate body independent?

Yes
No

RE20: Is drug registration process computerized?

Yes
No
Partly

RE20.1: If yes, what system/software is used and when did computerized registration begin?

_____

RE21: Does the authority issue and update the list of registered drugs regularly?

Yes
No

RE21.1: If yes, to whom is the list of registered products distributed and how?

_____

RE22: Do pharmaceutical industries/manufacturers have access to decisions made by the regulatory authority in drug registration?

Yes
No

RE22.1: If yes, what are the mechanisms? Explain:

_____

RE22.2: Do interested parties have access to decisions of the DRA on drug registration?

Yes
No

RE22.3: If yes, what are the mechanisms by which decisions of the DRA on drug registration are made accessible to the interested parties? Explain:

_____

RE23: Are certificates issued for exported products?

Yes
No

RE23.1: If yes, collect samples of the certificates issued.

RE24: Does the assessment and registration authority have its own internal organigram?

Yes
No

RE24.1: If yes, collect a copy. If no, indicate the different sections of the unit and their relationship below:

_____

Human resources

RE25: Provide information below on the type and number of regular and part-time staff working for the registration unit (do not include committees):

Position	Full-time	Part-time
Administration/management staff		
Staff engaged in evaluation and registration activities:		
Physicians all types		
Pharmacists		
Chemists		
Microbiologists		
Pharmacologists/clinical pharmacologists		
Toxicologists		
Others (specify):		
Total		

Financing

RE26: Is there a specific budget for the registration unit?

Yes
No

RE26.1: If yes, what was the budget of the unit during each of the last five years (US$)

Budget section	Year:	Year:	Year:	Year:	Year:
Capital budget					
Salaries					
Miscellaneous					
Total					

RE26.2 What was the source of the budget in the last five years (answer yes/no)?

Source	Year:	Year:	Year:	Year:	Year:
Government					
Fees					
Other (specify):					

RE26.3: If the answer to RE26 is no, what was the estimated expenditure of the unit in the last five years?

Estimated expenditure	Year:	Year:	Year:	Year:	Year:
US$					
Local currency					

RE27: If fees are collected for registration, provide information on the types of registration services on which fees are levied and the amount charged:

Types of registration services on which fees are levied	Fees charged (US$)

Activities

RE28: How many applications have been received in the last five years?

No. of applications received	Year:	Year:	Year:	Year:	Year:
New applications for registration of products containing new active pharmaceutical ingredients					
New applications for registration of generic/well-established multi-source products					
New applications for registration by fast-track procedure					
Applications for variation of data					
Applications for renewal					
Applications for export certificate					
Other (specify):					
Total					

RE28.1: How many applications have been processed in the last five years?

No. of applications processed	Year:	Year:	Year:	Year:	Year:
New applications assessed and marketing authorization issued					
New applications assessed and marketing authorization refused					
New applications assessed, application withdrawn before decision					
Applications for variation of data assessed and approved					
Applications for variation of data assessed and refused					
Export certificates issued					
Applications for export certificates refused					
Other (specify):					
Total					

RE28.2: How many appeals were made against decisions made by the DRA in the last five years?

No. of appeals	Year:	Year:	Year:	Year:	Year:
Number of decisions appealed					
Number of appeals where decisions were reversed					
Number of appeals where decisions were confirmed					

Monitoring and evaluation

RE29: Is there a monitoring and evaluation system for drug assessment and registration?

Yes
No

RE29.1: If yes, obtain a copy of the most recent report.

RE30: What are the main constraints, weaknesses or problems and the strengths of the drug assessment and registration system?

Constraints/weaknesses/problems	Strengths

Categories by type - allopathic, homeopathic, veterinary, etc. Categories by source - locally manufactured or imported by government, private for-profit sector, private not-for-profit sector, donations, etc.

If there is any specific and important information that is not covered by the above questions, please provide additional information as appropriate.

3.4   Adverse drug reaction monitoring

ADR1: Is there an adverse drug reaction (ADR) monitoring system?

Yes
No

ADR1.1: If yes, collect information on when it started and how the system operates (who submits reports and whether the reporting is obligatory or voluntary):

_____

ADR2: How many ADRs have been recorded per year in the last five years?

	Year:	Year:	Year:	Year:	Year:
Number of ADRs reported					

ADR3: What is done with the reports received? Explain how and to whom they are disseminated locally and internationally?

_____

ADR4: Are decisions made on the basis of ADR monitoring?

Yes
No

ADR4.1: If yes, describe how:

_____

ADR5: Are manufacturers/importers required to monitor and report ADRs in respect of their products?

Yes
No

ADR6: What are the main constraints, weaknesses or problems and the strengths of the ADR monitoring system?

Constraints/weaknesses/problems	Strengths

Indicators

1. Number of ADR reports assessed for causality, out of the total number of ADR reports recorded through the monitoring system (indicate year).
2. Number of products recalled based on ADR reports, out of the total number of ADR reports recorded and confirmed for causality (indicate year)
3. Number of regulatory decisions taken on the basis of ADR reports, out of the total number of ADR reports confirmed for causality (indicate year).

3.5   Clinical trials

CT1: Are there legal provisions requiring the control of clinical trials on drugs?

Yes
No

CT2: Is the drug regulatory authority responsible for controlling clinical trials of pharmaceutical products carried out in the country?

Yes
No

CT2.1: If yes, what is the number of clinical trial applications received and approved per year in the last five years?

No. of clinical trial applications	Year:	Year:	Year:	Year:	Year:
Applications received					
Applications approved					

CT2.2 If no, what body is responsible for controlling clinical trials?

_____

CT3: Are there guidelines for clinical trials?

Yes
No

CT3.1 If yes, indicate whether they are consistent with :

	Yes/No
The Helsinki Declaration?	
The WHO Good Clinical Practice (GCP) guidelines?	

CT4: What are the main constraints, weaknesses or problems and the strengths of the clinical trial control system?

Constraints/weaknesses/problems	Strengths

If there is any specific and important information that is not covered by the above questions, please provide additional information as appropriate.

3.6 Control of drug promotion and advertising

PA1: Is there legal provision for the control of drug promotion and advertising?

Yes
No

PA1.1: If yes, indicate the title, date of enactment and article number of the legislation/regulations:

_____

PA2: State any restrictions specified in the law on drug promotion and advertising:

_____

PA3: Are prescription drugs advertised:

	Yes/No
In the lay press?	
In health professional journals?	
On radio and television?	
On billboards?	

PA4: Which body controls drug advertising/promotion?

_____

PA5: Is pre-approval required for promotional and advertising materials?

Yes
No

PA5.1: If yes, what body issues the pre-approval?

_____

PA5.2: Is there a fee for pre-approval?

Yes
No

PA5.3: If no, how is drug advertising/promotion monitored?

_____

PA6: Is a product information sheet/summary of product characteristics approved at the time of registration?

Yes
No

PA6.1: Are patient information leaflets and labels subject to approval?

Yes
No

PA7: Are there sanctions for violations of laws on product information and promotion?

Yes
No

PA7.1: How many violations have been registered and administrative measures and legal sanctions taken in the last five years?

Violations and enforcement measures taken	Year:	Year:	Year:	Year:	Year:
Number of violations of drug promotion law/regulations registered					
Number of judicial sanctions implemented					
Number of administrative measures taken					

PA7.2: Are sanctions effective?

Yes
No

PI8: Is/are there association(s) of pharmaceutical manufacturers/companies that practise self-regulation?

Yes
No

PI8.1: If yes, indicate the name(s) of the association(s), obtain copies of the code of practice, and provide information on the extent to which they are effective:

_____

PA9: Does the drug regulatory authority provide independent drug information to prescribers, dispensers and the public?

Yes
No

PA9.1: If yes, obtain a copy the latest publication.

PA9.2: If no, does any other body provide information independent of the industry?

Yes
No

PA9.3: If yes, indicate the name (s) of such bodies:

_____

PA10: How are the public and prescribers informed about newly registered drugs? Explain:

_____

PA11: Is there a mechanism whereby false medical claims in advertisements are controlled? If yes, explain.

Yes
No

PA12: What are the main constraints, weaknesses or problems and the strengths of control of drug promotion/advertising?

Constraints/weaknesses/problems	Strengths

Indicators

1. Number of advertisements/promotions found to be in violation of the law, out of the total number of promotions/advertisements monitored (indicate year).
2. Number of labels/inserts found to be inconsistent with what was approved during registration, out of the total number of labels and inserts assessed (indicate year).
3. Number of product information documents found to be in inappropriate language, out of the total number of product information documents assessed (indicate year).

If there is any specific and important information that is not covered by the above questions, please provide additional information as appropriate.

3.7 Drug quality control laboratory

Legal provisions

QC1: Does the country have a legal provision requiring analysis of drugs by government or other independent laboratories?

Yes
No

QC1.1: If yes, indicate the title and date of enactment and the article number of the provision:

_____

Organization

QC2: Does the DRA have its own quality control laboratory ?

Yes
No

QC2.1: If yes, give the name, address and date of establishment of the laboratory:

_____

QC3: If no, does the DRA use other in-country or external drug quality control laboratories?

Yes
No

QC3.1 If yes, provide the names and addresses of other quality control laboratories used by the DRA:

Laboratories used by the DRA	Main functions

QC3.2: If yes, do such laboratories also work for the private pharmaceutical industry'?

Yes
No

QC3.3: If yes, are contracts issued on the basis of a written agreement?

Yes
No

QC3.4: If yes, collect a copy of the agreement used?

Yes
No

QC5: Does the DRA's quality control laboratory have the necessary facilities, materials and resources to carry out its functions?

Yes
No

QC5.1: If no, what are the main problems in terms of lack of equipment, human resources, supplies, funding, etc.?

_____

QC6: Does the DRA laboratory prepare its own working standards?

Yes
No

QC7: Do the functions of the DRA laboratory include the following?

Functions	Yes/No
Testing of pharmaceuticals (non-biological products)	
Testing of biological products such as vaccines	
Participation in drug registration activities	
Inspection of industry quality control laboratories	
Research	
Training of analysts	
Other (specify):	

Human resources

QC8: What is the number of staff working in the DRA laboratory(ies)?

Type of staff	Full-time	Part-time
Administration / management staff		
Technical staff BSc and above		
Technicians and assistants (all categories)		
Total		

QC8.1: Do the staff of the DRA laboratory have job descriptions?

Yes
No
Some have

Financing

QC9: Is there a specific budget for the DRA's quality control laboratory?

Yes
No

QC9.1: If yes, what was the budget for the last five years (US$)?

Budget section	Year:	Year:	Year:	Year:	Year:
Capital budget					
Salaries					
Miscellaneous					
Total					

QC9.2: What was the source of the budget in the last five years (answer yes/no)?

Source	Year:	Year:	Year:	Year:	Year:
Government					
Fees					
Other (specify):					

QC9.3: If the answer to QC9 is no, what is the estimated expenditure of the DRA quality control laboratory in the last five years?

Estimated expenditure	Year:	Year:	Year:	Year:	Year:
US$					
Local currency					

QC10: If the DRA laboratory charges fees, indicate the fees charged for the various services provided:

Type of quality control services provided	Fees charged (US$)

Activities

QC11: Indicate below the number of drug samples submitted to the DRA laboratory for testing in the last five years, for each of the various sources of test requests listed:

Requested by	Year:	Year:	Year:	Year:	Year:
Government drug inspectors					
Drug registration authority					
Manufacturers					
Private importers/wholesalers					
Public sector procurement agencies					
Hospitals, clinics					
Individuals					
Others (specify):					
Total					

QC12: Does the DRA laboratory also collect samples for testing?

Yes

No

QC12.1: If yes, indicate if it does so as part of planned quality surveillance and what kinds of products are targeted.

QC13: Indicate below the activities of the DRA laboratory in the last five years:

Activities	Year:	Year:	Year:	Year:	Year:
Total number of drug products submitted for quality control (QC)					
Total number of drug products on which QC was performed					
Total number of drug products that failed QC					
Total number of products that passed the tests					
Total number of samples on which QC could not be performed (because of lack of reagents, reference standards, procedures, expertise, equipment, etc.)					

QC14: Is the general level of substandard products known (e.g. from testing of random samples)?

Yes
No

QC 14.1: If yes, what is the general level of failure of samples tested for quality in the country?

QC15: Indicate below the tests/assays methods performed by the DRA laboratory?

Test/assay method performed	Yes/No	Remarks (if any)
All types of chemical tests and assays		
Identification by infra-red spectrophotometer		
Identification by thin layer chromatography (TLC)		
UV-visible spectrophotometer		
Polarimetry		
High-performance liquid chromatography		
Atomic absorption spectrophotometer		
Disintegration test		
Dissolution test		
Microbial limit test		
Pyrogen test , LAL or rabbit method		
Sterility test		
Toxicity		
Other (specify):		

Monitoring and evaluation

QC16: Are the activities of the DRA laboratory based on a work plan?

Yes
No

QC16.1: If yes, obtain a copy of the most recent plan and provide information on the implementation rate:

_____

QC17: Is the DRA laboratory required to submit an annual report?

                                                                Yes
                                                                No

QC17.1: If yes, get a copy of the last report and/or information on the main findings of the report.

QC18: Does the DRA laboratory participate in schemes that show its level of performance compared to other laboratories (proficiency test)?

                                                                Yes
                                                                No

QC18.1: If yes, give details of the scheme (s) in which the laboratory participates:

_____

QC19: What are the main constraints, weaknesses or problems and the strengths of the DRA laboratory?

Constraints/weaknesses/problems	Strengths

Indicators

1. Number of drug products tested, out of the total number of drug products submitted/collected (indicate year).

2. Number of drug products that failed quality test, out of the total number of drug products tested (indicate year).

3. Number of drug products that could not be tested due to lack of (reagents, equipment, reference standard, etc), out of the total number of samples submitted (indicate year).

If there is any specific and important information that is not covered by the above questions, please provide additional information as appropriate.